Robin Neillands is a journalist and military historian, a regular contributor to national and regional newspapers and magazines, and the author of more than thirty books. A former Royal Marines Commando, he read Modern History at Oxford and Reading Universities, and has been a full-time writer since 1968. He leads battlefield tours in France, North Africa and the USA. He is a Fellow of the Royal Historical Society, the Royal Geographical Society, and he was the first Chairman of the Confraternity of Saint James, the pan-European pilgrim association. He was Chairman of the British Guild of Travel Writers from 1991–3 and is a member of the British Commission for Military History. He and his wife divide their time between Wiltshire and France, and are regular visitors to the USA. His latest book, *The Military Campaigns of Field Marshal Montgomery*, is due to be published in 2007.

By Robin Neillands

In the Combat Zone: Special Forces since 1945
D-Day 1944: Voices from Normandy (*with Roderick de Normann*)
The Conquest of the Reich, D-Day to VE Day
The Desert Rats: 7th Armoured Division 1940–1945
By Sea and Land: The Royal Marines Commandos, 1942–1982
The Raiders: The Army Commandos, 1940–1945
A Fighting Retreat: Military Campaigns in the British Empire,
1947–1997
The Great War Generals on the Western Front 1914–1918
Wellington and Napoleon: Clash of Arms
The Dervish Wars: Kitchener and Gordon in the Sudan
The Hundred Years War
The Wars of the Roses
True Stories of the SAS
True Stories of the SBS
True Stories of the French Foreign Legion
True Stories of the Paras
The Bomber War: Arthur Harris and the Allied Bomber Offensive
1939–1945
Attrition: The War on the Western Front 1916
The Battle of Normandy – 1944
Eighth Army: From the Western Desert to the Alps, 1939–1945
The Old Contemptibles: The British Expeditionary Force 1914
The Battle for the Rhine 1944
The Dieppe Raid 1942
The Death of Glory: The Western Front 1915

The Wars
of the Roses

ROBIN NEILLANDS

PHOENIX

A PHOENIX PAPERBACK

First published in Great Britain in 1992
by Cassell plc
This edition published in 1999 by
Brockhampton Press,
a member of Hodder Headline PLC Group
This paperback edition published in 2006
by Phoenix,
an imprint of Orion Books Ltd,
Orion House, 5 Upper St Martin's Lane,
London WC2H 9EA

1 3 5 7 9 10 8 6 4 2

Copyright © 1992 Robin Neillands

A CIP catalogue record for this book
is available from the British Library.

ISBN-13: 978-0-30-436316-2
ISBN-10: 0-30-436316-2

Printed and bound in Great Britain
by Mackays of Chatham, kent plc

The Orion Publishing Group's policy is to use papers that
are natural, renewable and recyclable products and
made from wood grown in sustainable forests. The logging
and manufacturing processes are expected to conform to
the environmental regulations of the country of origin.

www.orionbooks.co.uk

DEDICATION

This one is for
Geoffrey Hodges
with my grateful thanks

ACKNOWLEDGEMENTS

This book could not have been completed without the help and advice of Geoffrey Hodges, a scholar of the Wars of the Roses, who gave me constant support and whose suggestions I have not hesitated to adopt. Thanks go to the staff at the London Library and the Buckinghamshire County Library for tracking down obscure works of reference, and to the staff of the Bosworth Battlefield Centre and Middleham Castle for showing me over the ground. The last and most constant supporter was Estelle Huxley, who read my writing, corrected my spelling and typed all the drafts.

CONTENTS

INTRODUCTION

This is the second book I have written about the medieval world. It takes up the tale related in *The Hundred Years War* and continues until the last Plantagenet King of England rode to his death on Bosworth Field in August 1485, and so ushered in the Age of the Tudors.

Most historians, and certainly those who write popular history, are motivated partly because they enjoy their subject and partly to learn about and perhaps understand a period that interests them. These are certainly part of my motivation, but there is another reason: it is my belief that the study of history is important, because history teaches, as no other subject can, the sad fact that acts have consequences.

As to what acts lead to which consequences, there is considerable scope for debate. My aim is to be accurate – and to this end I must acknowledge the invaluable help of Geoffrey Hodges, whose knowledge of the Wars of the Roses is encyclopaedic – but also to *entertain*, for if history is not presented in an entertaining fashion, few but the devotees will bother to read it.

The Wars of the Roses is a subject that has enjoyed a revival in recent years. Books with this title abound, and scarcely a year, and never a decade, passes without another one being added to the already extensive canon of work on that complex and confusing period of English history. The reason for adding this book to the rest is to offer an entertaining guide to a complex subject and, perhaps, to encourage those whose interest has been aroused to pursue their studies with the help of the bibliography, for the story of the Wars of the Roses is nothing if not complex.

Even the beginning is uncertain. Did the trouble start when Henry Bolingbroke usurped the throne of Richard II, or when Henry V died in 1422 with his conquests incomplete, with the power struggle between Cardinal Beaufort and Humphrey, Duke of Gloucester, or when Henry VI concluded decades of incompetent rule with his bout of insanity in 1453? The brief answer to this catalogue is 'Yes'; all these situations and many more besides had their part to play in the Wars of York and Lancaster, and therefore feature in this book.

I have chosen to begin this book where *The Hundred Years War* ended, with the English defeat at Castillon, because it is my belief that this was the final straw in the strained relations between Henry VI and his subjects, and between the Dukes of York and Somerset; the point at which the cracks in the body politic of England could no longer be papered over. There is no single cause or event which triggered off that 30-year period of civil strife which we now call the Wars of the Roses. In the fifteenth century, England itself was so confused and lawless, so disturbed by disputing magnates, so poorly governed, that civil strife was almost inevitable.

The complexity of the period does not end after the civil war finally broke out at St Albans in 1455, and continues until Bosworth. To this day there are disputes as to where the Battle of Bosworth Field was actually fought, and on the formation adopted by King Richard's army . . . not to mention that most memorable of medieval mysteries, the deaths of Edward, Prince of Wales, and Richard, Duke of York, the Princes in the Tower.

Taken all in all then, this period of history proves almost irresistible to popular historians. It has knights and ladies, great battles, intrigue, secret romances and more secret murders, and a great mystery and final tragedy to round the period off, with the death of the Princes in the Tower and the final extirpation of the Plantagenet dynasty. Those who enjoy fascinating, complex tales from England's colourful past will find this period both entertaining and frustrating. Those in search of further enlightenment are directed to the bibliography.

Robin Neillands

CHAPTER ONE

THE CAUSES OF THE WAR (1399–1422)

O, if you raise this house against this house,
It will the woefullest division prove
That ever fell upon this cursed earth,
Prevent it, resist it, let it not be so,
Lest child, child's children, cry against you 'woe'.

THE BISHOP OF CARLISLE, *RICHARD II*

In the dreary autumn months of 1453 a defeated army returned to England. From small coasting craft and great, deep-hulled trading nefs, in empty vessels taken up from the wine trade, from anything that would float and could brave the gales of Biscay, the soldiers streamed ashore at a dozen southern ports from Winchelsea to Bristol, a host so downcast and bedraggled that it was difficult to imagine that it had ever been an army.

A few weeks before, on 17 July 1453, the last field army of King Henry VI, a great force commanded by his most experienced and formidable general, John Talbot, Earl of Shrewsbury, 'great Marshal to our Lord, King Henry VI, for all his wars within the realm of the French', had gone down to death and defeat before the entrenched infantry and cannon of Charles VII of France. English armies had known such defeat before, at Bouvines in 1214, and more recently in 1451, when Gascony first fell to the French, but this defeat at Castillon spelt the end of everything. On the banks of the River Dordogne, south-east of Bordeaux, three centuries of Plantagenet dominion had ended, and of all their French territories, only Calais remained.

Sick and starving, many half-clad, weaponless and nursing untreated wounds, the disillusioned survivors of this host scattered far and wide across England, the final act of an English tragedy that had been playing since the English armies had been driven from Normandy in 1450.

Harried out of town by the sheriff's officers whenever they stopped to rest, given scant subsistence by the townspeople and the monasteries, squatting exhausted beside the muddy roads, these ramshackle survivors of Castillon spread the word of their King's final defeat across the realm. In the next few weeks and months, many soldiers died of neglect and starvation, the lucky ones drifting into the uncertain security of some great lord's retinue, to gather strength for the fresh conflict that was coming.

That long dynastic struggle between Plantagenet and Valois, which later generations were to call the Hundred Years War, was finally over. The English kings no longer had the men or the money, the means or the will to maintain their dominion over France. Five English monarchs had tried in their turn, but now, 116 years after it all began, the French war was finally over. Now there was time for quarrels at home.

*   *   *

History does not come in convenient segments or small, contained packages, sealed at both ends. Each period or event is a result of what went before and contributes, to a greater or lesser extent, to what follows. The seeds of the Hundred Years War were sown when William the Bastard crossed the Channel in 1066 and killed Harold the Saxon on Senlac Hill. The seeds were fertilized when Henry II of England married Eleanor of Aquitaine in 1152 and so created a power which exceeded that of his feudal overlord, the King of France. The quarrel finally burst into flower in 1337 when, for his own good reasons, Edward III claimed the throne of France by right of descent through his mother, Isabelle, daughter of Philipe IV. In its turn, in the same implacable fashion, the Hundred Years War and a long series of apparently unconnected incidents, dynastic murders and casual slaughters, from 1399 to 1455, lead to the start of that 30-year period of civil war in England which has come down to posterity as the Wars of the Roses.

It should not be thought, however, that the civil wars which decimated the English nobility between 1450 and 1485 were prompted by England's defeat in France; that was the catalyst, but the fuel for that conflagration had been laid down long before – by Henry Bolingbroke's usurpation of 1399, when the heir of Lancaster seized the throne of Richard II. That dynastic cause was cited later in the struggle between York and Lancaster (and it will be discussed shortly), but the conflict has other causes too. The troubles began because Henry VI could not rule his kingdom, and rival factions therefore competed to control his Councils, his lands, and the King himself. The dynastic part of the so-called Wars of the Roses – a term only invented by Sir Walter Scott in the nineteenth century – did not begin until 1460. The seeds of conflict, however, were laid down decades before that particular year.

Shakespeare traced the roots of this conflict to 1399, when Henry Bolingbroke, heir to the Duchy of Lancaster, rebelled against his King and cousin, Richard II, and came to the throne of England as Henry IV, the first sovereign of the House of Lancaster. It was another half-century before that act recoiled upon his House, and another ten years before more direct descendants of Richard II put forward their own claim to that dangerous inheritance.

The final defeat of Plantagenet ambitions at Castillon was simply the spark which set alight many long-smouldering quarrels in England, but it is generally conceded that had Shrewsbury triumphed at Castillon and the ambitions of Charles VII received a check, then the long slide to chaos and civil war in England might have been halted. As it was, and as always happens after a defeat, those in power on the defeated side looked about for someone to blame. In the England of 1453 there was no lack of suitable candidates, but the chief of these was the unhappy King of this unsettled realm, Henry of Windsor, the sixth of that name.

King Henry VI had been born at Windsor Castle on 6 December 1421, the son of Henry V, victor of Agincourt, and his wife, Catherine of Valois, daughter of Charles VI of France. The young Prince Henry arrived at a most fortunate hour and with the best of prospects. That rare relic, the foreskin of Our Lord, was brought over from the Halidom of St Louis at the Sacré Coeur in Paris to aid in his birth, and he seems to have been a healthy baby. He was also the living symbol of the success of his father, the great King Harry, who in the six years since Agincourt had concluded an alliance with the powerful Duke of Burgundy, regained the old Plantagenet Duchy of Normandy and captured most of France north of the Loire.

Military triumphs, economic pressure and skilful diplomacy had succeeded in forcing the often deranged Charles VI to come to terms with England at the Treaty of Troyes, which was signed on 14 June 1420. This treaty gained for King Henry both the succession to the French throne for himself and his heirs – the treaty having declared the Dauphin Charles of France a bastard – and the hand of Princess Catherine, whom the King had married the same afternoon in Troyes Cathedral.

In the months between that happy day in 1420 and the birth of the young Henry VI in December 1421, there had been a series of setbacks.

The Dauphin Charles had defeated an English army at Baugé in March 1421, killing Henry V's brother, the Duke of Clarence, and capturing, among others, John Beaufort, the first Duke of Somerset, who was to remain in captivity for the next 17 years. By 1421, in spite of six years of constant campaigning since Agincourt, the English had still not rooted out French resistance to their rule; but, on the whole, matters were going to plan. All Henry V had to do was to have a son by his new Queen and so secure the succession to both kingdoms.

Queen Catherine was already pregnant when the King departed again for the wars in June 1421. In October, his army sat down to besiege Meaux. King Harry was still besieging the town in December when his son was born. He was still there nine months later, in early August 1422, when he fell ill. On 31 August, the warrior king died of dysentery at his castle of Vincennes, on the outskirts of Paris, leaving as his heir Prince Henry of Windsor, who was just eight months old. Then, two months later, the mad King of France, Charles VI, also went to his grave, and the infant Henry of Windsor became the heir to two contending kingdoms.

The English knew one thing about the rule of an infant king: it was dangerous. Henry V also realized this. As we shall see, he left clear instructions for the management of his realm during his son's minority and his councillors tried, with some success, to carry out his wishes. However, not even King Harry could rule from beyond the grave. Young princes had to have councillors and were very prone to the influence of their advisers. Those advisers might not only usurp the Royal authority and use it for their personal advantage, but they might also be reluctant to give up their powers when the time came for the king to rule as well as reign.

Besides, while all men accepted the rule of a king, the rule of an imperious peer, a fellow lord, was quite another matter. Minority rule meant a council of ministers, drawn from the magnates of the realm, and that meant argument, faction, unrest and defiance of the rule of law. Sensible men in 1421 viewed the long years that must elapse before the king could rule as well as reign with considerable trepidation. This worry aside, there were other problems for the young heir of Lancaster, a baby still gurgling in the cradle, for his very succession was open to question. To explain that, we must go back to the end of the previous century.

The House of Lancaster was descended from one of the great noble families of England. Edmund Crouchback, Earl of Lancaster, a son of Henry III, had been one of the mighty pillars of the state in his time, and his grandson, Henry of Grosmont, Earl of Derby and eventually Duke of

Lancaster, had been a fine soldier in the long wars of Edward III's reign. Duke Henry had campaigned for his King in Aquitaine and on the march of Normandy, served at the siege of Calais in 1346, as well as giving the monarch much wise counsel. These successes gained Henry of Grosmont many rewards from his master, including the marriage of John of Gaunt, the King's third son, to the Duke's younger daughter, Blanche.

After the death of her elder sister and then of Duke Henry himself in 1362, the titles and a vast fortune of the House of Lancaster went with the Duchess Blanche to her husband, John of Gaunt. The House of Lancaster became second only to that of the Royal House itself and by Gaunt's royal connection, the Lancastrians nosed ahead of the other great magnates of the realm, the Percies, the Nevilles, the de Veres, the Beauchamps, the Montacutes and the Mowbrays, traditional props of the throne and Royal authority.

John of Gaunt, Duke of Lancaster, was a marrying man. His first wife, Blanche, died soon after the birth of her only son, Henry of Bolingbroke. John of Gaunt then had ambitions in Spain, so he married Constanza of Castile, daughter of Pedro the Cruel, by whom he had a daughter. On her death, he married his long-time mistress, Katherine Swynford, by whom he already had three sons. These children were eventually legitimized by the Parliament of 1397, taking the family name of Beaufort. This legitimacy was later confirmed by Richard II, and again, though with certain reservations concerning their right of succession to the throne, by their half-brother, Bolingbroke, when he overthrew Richard II and came to the throne of England as Henry IV. Gaunt, however, was only the third surviving son of Edward III. Others stood closer to the line of succession than the heirs of Lancaster.

Edward III's eldest son, Edward of Woodstock, the Black Prince, predeceased his father, dying of dysentery in 1377 and leaving as heir his young son, Richard of Bordeaux, who came to the throne as Richard II at the age of 10, in 1377. John of Gaunt was nominally in charge of the kingdom during the King's minority, but he proved a less than competent guardian. Faction ruled; there was rebellion and civil unrest, and on commencing his personal rule at the then late age of 20 in 1387, Richard II proved himself a wilful and reckless monarch. In 1398, unable to handle his turbulent lords or the pressing economic problems of his kingdom, he took advantage of a quarrel between Gaunt's heir, Henry Bolingbroke and Thomas Mowbray, Duke of Norfolk – who accused each other of treason – to banish both peers from the realm; Mowbray for life,

Bolingbroke for ten years. A few months later, in February 1399, old John of Gaunt, 'time honour'd Lancaster', went to his grave.

Richard II then made a fatal mistake. Ignoring all custom and justice, he seized all the wealth of the House of Lancaster. Richard II needed the money but this was an act which struck at every man's inheritance. Within months Henry Bolingbroke, the Earl of Derby, came home to claim his rights as Duke of Lancaster. Many lords flocked to his banner and when matters escalated, Bolingbroke's claim changed from a simple demand for his father's dukedom to a struggle for the crown. Within a few weeks, Richard II was in the Tower and Bolingbroke sat on the throne of England. Less than a year later, Richard II was dead, most probably murdered in Pontefract Castle.

Henry's usurpation was more than an act of personal power and will: it struck at the very foundations of kingship. Although the doctrine of the Divine Right of Kings had not yet been formulated, the king was at least God's deputy on earth. His coronation was a sacrament; his coronation oaths and those acts of homage made to him, were solemn compacts, given before God. To overthrow an anointed king was a dreadful thing, and there were those who said that no good could come of it. Fifty years later, the wars of York and Lancaster were seen as a form of divine retribution, for did not the Bible say that the sins of the father would be visited on the children, 'unto the third and fourth generation'?

Henry's usurpation also created a new situation and put forward a novel idea: that the king was simply *primus inter pares* – first among equals. This meant that the divinity of kingship could be aspired to by other, more competent, members of the Royal family, the princes of the Blood Royal. This theory may have comforted Henry IV, who was never entirely happy about overthrowing King Richard, even to the point of claiming that his ancestor, Edmund Crouchback, had been the eldest son of Henry III, but there was a snag to it. The Blood Royal flowed through other veins, and some of the princes of the blood stood closer to the line of succession than Henry IV and his heirs. However, for the moment, the House of Lancaster ruled competently in England and the axe and block could cut short the voices of any who disputed its right to do so.

The reigns of Henry IV (1399–1413) and his son Henry V (1413–22) were not untroubled by rebellion, but they were both successful monarchs. They were able to win battles if not wars, and contained both rebellion and treason by successful campaigns and the periodic recourse to the axe and the block. Nevertheless, their reigns were a foretaste of what was to follow. Henry IV faced rebellion from his original supporters, the Percies of Northumberland, and attack from the Welsh lord, Owen Glendower. Henry V had to deal with a plot even on the eve of his departure for France in 1415, which he terminated with the execution of his cousin, Richard, Earl of Cambridge, son of Edmund, Duke of York, third surviving son of Edward III. Cambridge left an heir, another Richard, whose wardship was given to that Earl of Westmorland, Ralph Neville, Henry V's 'My cousin Westmorland', who fought with the King at Agincourt and wished for the support of 'but one ten thousand of those men in England that do no work today'.

Henry Bolingbroke's reason for overthrowing his King was that Richard II was unfit to rule. Even so, there were other contenders with claims to the throne just as strong as those of Henry Bolingbroke. What it came down to after 1399 was that any prince of the blood who had the money to raise an army and cause for dissatisfaction with the king could become a contender for the throne. When moral justification combines with righteous self-interest, no throne in the world is safe.

At this point, it would be advisable to study the genealogical table charting the extended family of Edward III on pages 18 and 19, for this will help to explain the links between York and Lancaster. Edward had 13 children, three of whom died in infancy. The crucial members were his five sons who lived to be adults. The eldest, Edward of Woodstock, the Black Prince, father of Richard II, died in 1377. Interest now concentrates on the second surviving son, Lionel, Duke of Clarence. He had a daughter, Philippa, who married Edmund Mortimer, third Earl of March. Philippa and Edmund Mortimer's eldest son, Roger, fourth Earl of March, had three children. The eldest, another Edmund, died in 1425 without issue, and the other son, another Roger, died young. The wealth and claims of his House then descended to Richard, the son of his dead sister Anne Mortimer, who married Richard, Earl of Cambridge, a grandson of Edward III, nephew to the second Duke of York.

This Richard of Cambridge was the one attainted and executed by Henry V in 1415 for attempting to put his brother-in-law, Edmund Mortimer, on the throne, and it was Edmund who betrayed him to the King. Cambridge had a son, another Richard, to whom, for the sake of clarity, we shall now give the name which he later adopted, Richard Plantagenet. Richard Plantagenet inherited the Duchy of York when his uncle, Edward, the second Duke, died fighting for Henry V at Agincourt, and the Mortimer Earldom of March when Edmund Mortimer died in

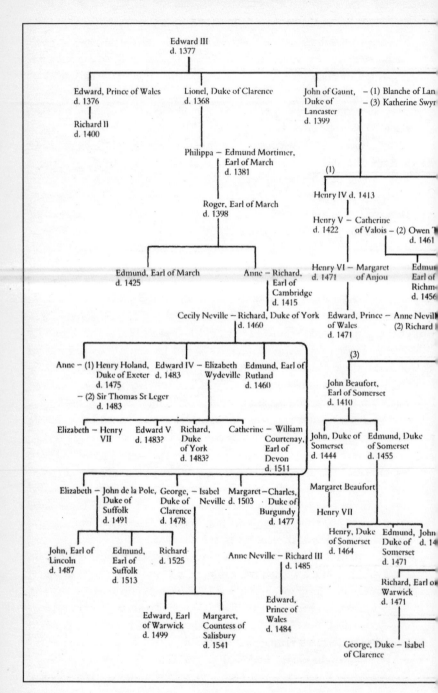

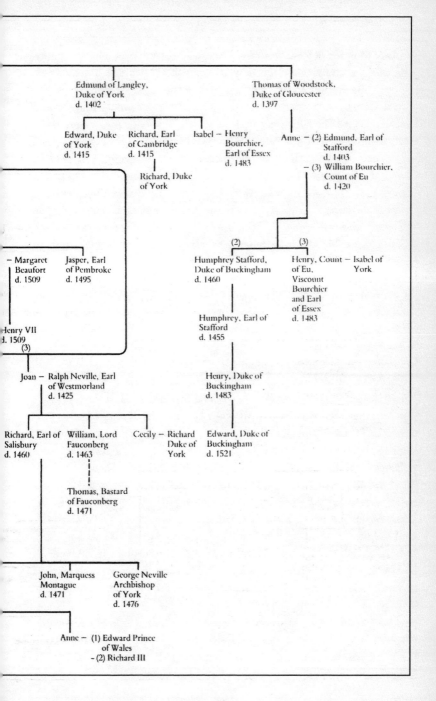

1425. It is this Richard Plantagenet who founded the House of York and began the wars of York and Lancaster. Although Richard Plantagenet initially took his descent from his grandfather of York, and bore his arms and title, he could also claim descent from the closer line of Mortimer, through his mother, Anne, a descendant of the Duke of Clarence.

The House of Lancaster was well aware of the potential dangers posed to their rule by the Mortimer Earls of March. The Mortimer claim to the throne was drawn from Lionel, Duke of Clarence, the *second* surviving son of Edward III, while the Lancastrian claim was from Gaunt, Edward III's *third* surviving son. The caveat that Richard Plantagenet's claim was through the female line via Anne Mortimer has no validity, not least because the current English claims to the throne of France were also made through the female line, Edward III being the grandson of the French King Philipe IV by his mother, Isabella, the notorious 'She-wolf of France'. So, as Shakespeare puts it in the second part of Henry VI, 'if the issue of the elder son succeed before the younger', the issue of Mortimer in the person of Richard Plantagenet should, by right of descent, be King of England. It is necessary to add at this point that until the 1450s, when he was already 39, Richard Plantagenet, Duke of York, was a loyal Lancastrian and a good servant of the King. Had he been well treated and trusted, he might have remained so.

Apart from the Houses of York and Lancaster, two other great English families need some explanation now. The first are the Beauforts, Gaunt's children by Katherine Swynford, who became the Dukes of Somerset. The elder brother, John, Earl of Somerset, died in 1410. The second son, Henry Beaufort, became Bishop of Winchester, a Cardinal and Chancellor to Henry VI. The younger brother, Thomas, Duke of Exeter, died in 1426. Earl John had five children and numerous grandchildren, who were to play a prominent part fighting for the Lancastrians in the Wars of the Roses. Earl John's eldest son, Henry, died childless in 1418, and the title went to his brother, another John, later Duke of Somerset, who as already related, had been captured and imprisoned at the battle of Baugé in 1421. It is this John's daughter, Margaret Beaufort, who married Edmund Tudor, and Edmund's heir, Henry Tudor, eventually became Henry VII of England, the first Tudor monarch.

Duke John, a remarkably incompetent soldier, died in 1444 and the title went to his brother, Edmund, Marquis of Dorset, who became the second Duke of Somerset, a supporter of King Henry VI's Queen, Margaret of Anjou, and the deadly enemy of Richard Plantagenet, Duke of York. This

Edmund married Eleanor Beauchamp, daughter of Henry VI's tutor, Richard Beauchamp, Earl of Warwick, and their son was to take up the quarrel of York and Lancaster when his time came.

The other House which should be introduced here, and which played a part at the start of the wars, is that of the de la Poles, the Earls, Marquis and later Dukes of Suffolk. The de la Poles were not of noble stock but came from the rising merchant class of England. The family had made their fortune in the wool trade, and were successful merchants from Kingston-on-Hull, rich enough to lend money to Edward III. However, by the time William de la Pole was born in 1396, the family had been ennobled for three generations and William became the fourth Earl and later the first Duke. The de la Poles were still regarded as upstarts by the old nobility and for support naturally leaned towards the new House of Lancaster. Suffolk married Alice Chaucer, granddaughter of the poet, who had married a sister of Gaunt's wife and former mistress, Katherine Swynford. Duchess Alice's magnificent tomb, bearing the blazonry of Chaucer and Suffolk, can still be viewed in the church at Ewelme in Oxfordshire.

William de la Pole, Duke of Suffolk, who features in this story, was more of a courtier and a politician than a soldier, though he served at the famous siege of Orléans in 1428 and was captured by Joan of Arc at Jargeau. He later became custodian and a close friend of Charles, Duke of Orléans, a prisoner in England since his capture at Agincourt in 1415. William de la Pole continued to thrive during the early years of Henry VI's rule, becoming Chamberlain of England and Ambassador of England to the Council of Tours, even standing in for the King at his betrothal ceremony to Margaret of Anjou at Tours in May 1444.

All these people will have their parts to play in the story which follows, but it is important to fix them in place at the start, for the story of the wars of York and Lancaster is nothing if not complicated. As we shall see, the greatest complication of all is the people involved.

It should also be noted that since Richard II was childless, the succession was open to question even before Bolingbroke usurped the throne. The actual position in the 1390s was that Bolingbroke was the heir-male, while Edmund Mortimer was heir-general. Edmund's father had been, in practice, heir-presumptive to Richard II, but Richard II had never acknowledged this fact. The early Lancastrian fears of the Mortimer line were largely unfounded, and had Henry VI ruled well, or been able to rule competently, their claim may never have been pressed.

We run ahead of ourselves, but this background and the introduction of some of the later protagonists does serve to make the underlying situation clear and spells out, briefly, some underlying causes of the Wars of the Roses. The House of Lancaster, represented by the three Henrys, IV, V and VI, was not the legitimate heir *by right of descent* of either Richard II or Edward III. They held the throne by right of conquest and because their conquest had been first supported by a majority of magnates of the realm and later confirmed by Parliament, which later settled the crown on the heirs of Lancaster by an Act in 1406.

Most of all though, the first two Lancastrian kings retained power because they were successful. In medieval times a king did not merely reign, he ruled: he was in charge of the kingdom and responsible for its success, in war and in commerce. He was also expected to give good justice and enforce the Common Law. Henry IV and Henry V reigned because they had the essential ability to rule and wise men obeyed and supported them. If, or when, a weak king were to come to the throne, then the always doubtful Lancastrian claim might be contested. In medieval times a king had to be strong and successful in many spheres; in diplomacy, in finance, in the handling of his fractious people and ambitious lords, but success in one activity was paramount. A king must be successful in war.

CHAPTER TWO

ḢENRY VI AND THE WAR IN FRANCE (1422–53)

Each man may have a glass to see things past
whereby he may judge justly of things present, and
wisely of things to come.

GRAFTON'S CHRONICLE (1569)

The infant King, Henry VI, inherited the French war in his cradle. Before Henry V died at Vincennes, he left clear instructions as to how his conquests were to be maintained, his realm secured and his son's interests protected. In these ambitions the dying King had two great assets and one great problem. The assets were his brother John, Duke of Bedford, and a body of loyal and competent councillors. The problem was his youngest brother, Humphrey, Duke of Gloucester. The Royal brothers had this much in common: both were competent, warlike and faithful to the aims and memory of their elder brother, the late King. They were both anxious to do their best for their nephew, the young King, and maintain the conquests of his father. The difference was a matter of temperament. Duke John was quiet, mature, steady, a diplomat as well as a soldier. Duke Humphrey was volatile, artistic, short-tempered, intolerant and fractious.

On his deathbed in 1422, Henry V decreed that Bedford was to take charge in France, as Regent. He was to pursue the war against the Dauphin Charles, hang on to Normandy at all costs and maintain the alliance with that slippery prince, Philip the Good, Duke of Burgundy. He must also keep a watchful eye on England, where the situation was more complicated.

The young King Henry VI had many relatives, uncles and great-uncles, brothers or half-brothers of the late King. Among them was the second son of John of Gaunt by Katherine Swynford, now a rich and powerful cleric, Henry Beaufort, Bishop of Winchester.

The Beaufort family was to play a prominent part in England's affairs during the first half of the fifteenth century, but the main protagonist of the family during the King's minority was the Cardinal-Bishop, Henry Beaufort. Henry V had always kept an eye on his ambitious uncle. Bishop Henry had asked for and obtained a cardinal's red hat from Pope Martin V, but King Henry ordered him to return it, citing the request as an offence under the Statute of Praemunire, which forbade English clerics to appeal over the King's head to the Vatican. Henry Beaufort received his long-awaited promotion to the cardinalate in 1427, after King Harry was dead, but he was quarrelling with Duke Humphrey long before that. By 1422 Henry Beaufort was Chancellor of the realm and in charge of the King's private fortune – the lands and revenues of the Duchy of Lancaster. He also enjoyed the revenues of several wealthy sees, and was one of the richest men in England.

Henry V was well aware of the characters of all his relatives. On his deathbed he declined to appoint the volatile Duke Humphrey as his Regent in England, as John of Bedford was in France. Instead, he made Humphrey Protector of the Realm, but only while Bedford was out of England. The guardianship of the young Prince of Wales went to another Beaufort, the Duke of Exeter. The day-to-day conduct of affairs was entrusted to a council of ministers, which included Duke Humphrey, as well as the Archbishop of Canterbury, the Bishops of London, Norwich, Winchester and Worcester, the Duke of Exeter, and five earls, including Mortimer and March, but where the balance of power rested with the Beauforts and their adherents. King Henry V was therefore hardly in his grave before his son's ministers began to quarrel.

By the time Henry V died, England had changed a great deal from the England that had begun the French wars under Edward III. The country was now wholly English, and had completely absorbed the old Anglo-French nobility. A knowledge of French was now rare enough to be remarked on, and Henry V's laws and proclamations were now promulgated in English. Society, though still sharply divided by class, had become more egalitarian; nobles indulged in trade and married their daughters to rich merchants, who could and did aspire to the knightly class.

In the latter half of the fifteenth century, England was not a happy, prosperous or united country. The ransoms and plunder from France which had flowed in so copiously in the past had now stopped. The wool trade still flourished but the wars and the disputes with Burgundy had not permitted any expansion. Trade in general was not helped by lawlessness at home and piracy abroad.

Much of the blame for this lay with the Royal Council, and the all-powerful magnates and clerics who composed it. Parliament was called when and where the King required it, and Parliament, though growing in influence, only had control over matters of taxation and war. The day-to-day running of the realm was left to the Council, which farmed the realm and its revenues to its own advantage.

All that apart, the realm was changing. The middle classes, the merchants, lawyers, rich yeomen, were growing in wealth and therefore in power, and even the lords were not above marrying into their ranks, for the wealth of trade was not to be despised. The lower classes were also on their way up. The peasants were still grindingly poor but the small population, estimated at between 2 and 2.5 million, meant that there was a permanent labour shortage. Wages were relatively high and in spite of statutes to prevent them, more and more peasants left the land for the better pay and easier life in the cities.

The peasants were also getting control of the land they worked, and their old customs and rights were gradually being confirmed in law. In 1467, Chief Justice Danly confirmed this trend by declaring 'If the lord ousts his tenant, he does him wrong, for the tenant is as entitled to inherit the land for himself and his heirs according to the custom of the manor as any man is at common law'. One of the great dynamics of change was the spread of education: literacy was growing and not just, as in former times, among those destined for the Church. The new trade and businesses needed literate men to run their affairs, so grammar schools sprang up and flourished among the children of the wealthier laymen, even if the actual education was still in the hands of the clergy.

As for the Church, it felt itself under siege. The translation of the Bible into English, coupled with the spread of literacy, had removed that great clerical prerogative of signposting the path to Heaven. The wealth of the Church and the ostentation and greed of the clergy also made a poor impression among an increasingly critical population. There were still more than 800 monasteries in England, owning about a third of the cultivated land, controlling much of the wool trade and the wealth that went with it; but in spite of their economic power the spiritual influence of the Church was in decline.

Given good government, law and order, and a stable currency, England in the latter half of the fifteenth century should have been a happy and prosperous country, progressing smoothly from the dark days of feudalism into the bright sunshine of the Renaissance. As it was, and as this story will reveal, faction ruled in the higher councils of the state, and poor government became one of the main causes of the wars between York and Lancaster.

The dark side of all this was that the English, irrespective of class, were notoriously difficult to rule. By the 1440s the rule of law was largely ignored and breaking down everywhere. Robbery, murder, riot and disorder were common; juries were intimidated, sheriffs and judges corrupt. The common law was, in effect, the king's law, and the king was the fount of justice; but as the common law fell into disuse or was ignored, men sought the protection of local lords and powerful magnates, who could protect them from others and condone their crimes, giving them 'good lordship'. In this lay the beginnings of that so-called 'bastard feudalism' which was another feature of English life in the fifteenth century.

Law and order at home, however, took second place to pursuing the war in France. This had not gone well since Joan of Arc appeared on the scene in 1429, and there was continual division in the Council over how the war should be pursued, or even if it should be pursued at all. If Henry VI came to the throne and was half the man his father was, all might be well, but for the moment wise men kept their heads down and their mouths shut and hoped in their hearts for better times.

Meanwhile, the young Prince stayed with his mother, Queen Catherine, and his realms of France and England were ruled by his uncles. Under their direction England continued to prosecute the war with the Dauphin Charles, who had claimed the French throne after the death of Charles VI on 22 October 1422.

* * *

King Henry VI's childhood was conventional, the normal upbringing for a medieval prince. His involvement in state affairs began early, in November 1423, when he was taken to the House of Commons at Westminster to inaugurate the second Parliament of his reign. The King was not yet 2 years old but he sat still enough during the Speaker's loyal address and returned to spend Christmas with his mother at Hertford Castle. This early introduction to his Parliament and people was not entirely unconnected with the fact that a scion of the House of Mortimer, Sir John Mortimer, cousin of the Earl of March, who had been interned in the Tower by Henry V for plotting against the throne, had been caught attempting to escape. The infant King's appearance reminded the realm, and in particular the Commons, where their true loyalties must lie. The Royal Council then drove home the message by having Sir John Mortimer hanged, drawn and quartered on Tower Hill at the end of February 1424.

Over the next few years, Henry went to lessons, learned his letters and the duties of a young gentleman and played with his small group of chosen companions. The king was shown to his subjects at frequent intervals, and though he must have sensed the conflict between his uncles of Gloucester and Beaufort, he was still far too young to play more than a ceremonial part in state affairs. The most significant change in his life came at the age of 6, in May 1428, when he was given into the charge of the 'Good Master', selected by the Royal Council, Richard Beauchamp, Earl of Warwick, who was made responsible for the King's further education. Warwick was an ideal choice for this post. A long-time adherent of the House of Lancaster, he was a noted linguist and fluent in French, a facility which was now becoming rare among the English nobility. A good soldier and a kindly and patient tutor, he was also extremely rich.

Warwick's duties were to instruct the King in skill-at-arms and courtesy, to teach him discipline, self-control and self-reliance; in short, to show him by instruction and example all that was needed and required in a Christian prince. The young Prince of Wales seems to have been a lively boy, and the time arose when the Earl found it necessary to apply to the Council for permission to give his charge a good thrashing. There was no sign in Henry's boyhood of the affliction that would trouble him later on.

The King gave himself over quite willingly to this instruction and two years later, in November 1429, when he was 8 years old, Henry was crowned King at Westminster Abbey. He was still too young to rule, so his ministers continued in office, the Council striving to control the creaking affairs in the two kingdoms of France and England and soothe the quarrels between the cardinal and Duke Humphrey. Their differences had escalated to the point where at the Leicester Parliament of 1426, all those summoned had been forbidden to carry arms. The Members, therefore, arrived carrying cudgels and clubs, for which reason this session came to be called 'The Parliament of Bats'. This dissension among the nobility did nothing to check the spread of lawlessness in the country at large.

By the terms of the Treaty of Troyes, Henry of Windsor was heir to the kingdoms of France and England. However, by November 1429, when he put on the crown of England, the throne of his maternal grandfather, Charles VI of France, was no longer empty. In 1428, according to the letters of Duke John of Bedford, 'a certain witch of France', called Joan the Maid, or Jeanne d'Arc, had 'succeeded by enchantments' in defeating an English army before Orléans and then taken the bastard Dauphin Charles to his coronation at Rheims in July 1429. Seven years after the death of Henry V, the realm of France had a king again, and this Charles VII was to prove himself a most formidable opponent. The English and their Burgundian allies might refer to Charles VII as 'the King of Bourges', but he was more than a match for them in politics and the field and more Frenchmen flocked to his standard each day.

Therefore, on St George's Day 1430, Henry VI of England landed at Calais on his way to be crowned in Paris. He waited there and in Rouen for more than a year while his captains attempted to secure the way to Paris. Accompanied by a large army, Henry finally entered Paris, where he was crowned King of France at Notre-Dame on Sunday, 2 December 1431, a few days before his tenth birthday. This coronation completely failed to impress the French. A King of France must be crowned at Reims, and anointed with the holy oil of St Rémy. The French saw Henry's Paris coronation as a political manoeuvre and nothing more. More and more aid flowed to King Charles VII, who continued to thrive, and with the Burgundian alliance faltering, the English began to fall back.

The first ten years of King Henry's life had seen an almost total reversal of English fortunes in France. After Henry V's death, matters at first went very well. The Anglo-Burgundian armies totally defeated the Dauphinist forces at Cravant in 1423 and again at Verneuil, in Normandy, in 1424 when Duke John of Bedford destroyed a Franco-Scots army under the Earl of Douglas.

However, periodic victories could not conceal the underlying economic political weakness of the English position. Unable to support the war from their own resources, the English had come to depend on the help of the Valois Dukes of Burgundy. The first Valois Duke, Philip the Bold, or le Hardi, had taken over the reins of power in France when Charles VI went mad, but he had quarrelled with the other dukes on the French Council. In 1407, his son, John the Fearless, the second Valois duke, had murdered their rival, the Duke of Orléans, igniting the quarrels between Burgundy and Armagnac which divided France from 1407 to 1419. These escalated further when Duke John was murdered on the bridge at Montereau in 1419 during a parley with the Dauphin Charles.

It was this murder of his father by the Dauphin's adherents, rather than any love for the Plantagenets, which threw the third Valois duke, Philip the Good, into the arms of the English. This alliance was motivated solely by self-interest and proved very fragile. Duke Philip could never forget he was a French prince and by 1424 he was making overtures to the Dauphin. Duke Philip gave little practical or military help to his English allies and charged them a stiff price for doing virtually nothing. His demands for subsidy were another steady drain on English funds, and when he quarrelled with Duke Humphrey in 1425, the whole Burgundian alliance looked set to fall apart. The Dauphin Charles was still at large south of the Loire and he was recognized as the rightful King of France by the majority of the French population. Slowly and steadily the French drove the English back, and after his coronation as Charles VII in 1429, the Treaty of Troyes was a dead letter. The Hundred Years War had begun again, and would now be fought to the finish.

* * *

If matters were deteriorating steadily in France, the state of affairs was little better in England. Disputes between the Beauforts and Gloucester were always acrimonious around the Council table and sometimes descended to street violence. As early as October 1425 the Cardinal brought armed men and archers from Lancashire and Cheshire into London to confront the Duke's supporters, where they were met by armed apprentices and 300 men of the city militia under the lord mayor. A pitched battle in the streets was only avoided by the hurried intervention of the Archbishop of Canterbury. This constant bickering placed an additional burden on the Duke of Bedford, who had to shuttle between England and France to pursue the war abroad as well as keep the peace at home.

The situation which had developed between the Beauforts and Duke Humphrey was a foretaste of what was to follow when Henry VI began to rule, for the argument boiled down to who should control the policy and direction of the King's Council.

John, Duke of Bedford, was a sorely tried man. His chief charge was to hang on to his brother Henry's conquests and hand them on to his nephew. To do this, he had fought the French for years, won the great battle at Vermeuil, and endured the torment of handling the slippery Duke of Burgundy, even to the point of marrying first the Duke's sister, and on her death, the Lady Jacqueline, sister of Burgundy's ally, the Count of St Pol. He might have felt, with good reason, that he had more than enough to do without the recurrent problems of England.

His brother, Duke Humphrey, had other reasons for feeling aggrieved. He had expected the position in England that Bedford had in France – and together what deeds they might have done! Instead, he was saddled with the Beauforts, whose policies ran contrary to the late King Harry's wishes and were not even successful. How much better life would be if only he could find more men like his protégé, young Richard Plantagenet, the Duke of York, who knew that the best way to deal with a Frenchman was to hit him with your battle-axe?

The Beaufort's faction, the Cardinal, his brother and nephews of Somerset, John and Edmund, and their ally, the Duke of Suffolk, were not deliberately setting out to undo King Harry's work, ruin the kingdom or betray the young King – far from it: they were simply acting in the King's best interests as they saw them. They thought that Gloucester was wrong.

With the Dukes of Somerset and Suffolk though, there was perhaps a second reason. They had something to prove. Both Somerset and Suffolk were 'new men', the first descended from a mistress of Gaunt, the second from a line of Humberside merchants. They had both come a long way in a short time and had no intention of becoming subservient to the wishes of any of the old nobility. That apart, most of the nobility, 'new' or 'old', had a personal axe to grind, positions to maintain, offices to aspire to. The King they all claimed to serve was not merely their sovereign lord and the son of their revered King Harry, he was the fount of honour and, more important, a source of profit.

*   *   *

As time passed, the animosity between the Beauforts and Duke Humphrey had settled into a difference over policy. The Beauforts had decided that the war in France could not be won. They, therefore, believed that they should settle and end the war on the best terms they could get. Duke Humphrey, on the other hand, thinking of his dead brother, King Harry, believed the war should be fought with the full resources of the realm. He refused to admit even the possibility of defeat and accused the Cardinal, Somerset and Suffolk of failing to prosecute the war with either enthusiasm or competence.

Hindsight may tell us that the Beaufort party was right, for peace is always more appealing than war, but Duke Humphrey of Gloucester did not see it like that. Two of his brothers, King Harry and the Duke of Clarence, had died fighting to win the land of France, and his last brother, Duke John, was still in arms and dying from his exertions. What else could Duke Humphrey do but support them; but somewhere, somehow, there must be an honourable end to this endless, debilitating war.

Once King Henry was crowned in France and England there would be an opportunity for a negotiated peace, for clearly the King must marry and beget an heir. If he could marry a princess of France, as his father and many of his ancestors had done, surely there were possibilities here for both peace and advantage? Some sort of accommodation was certainly becoming necessary, for in 1433 the Royal Council had the unhappy task of telling the King and his uncles that they could neither see an end to the war nor the means to finance further campaigns. A truce, or better still, a peace, was imperative, not least because the much-needed Burgundian alliance was visibly crumbling.

There was, inevitably, a dispute over whom the King should marry. The Beauforts, hoping for a peaceful outcome, favoured a match with a Valois princess as the basis for a settlement of Plantagenet affairs in France and in this bid for peace they had the support of the King. Duke Humphrey and his supporters favoured an alliance with one of the Gascon families, which would bind these warlike nobles to the English cause, and help protect the Plantagenet holdings in Aquitaine.

The snag in finding a French princess to seal an alliance between the kingdoms was that there were now two Kings of France, Henry of Lancaster and Charles of Valois. Both were crowned kings, which left little room for compromise. The deadlock was finally broken in 1434 by Philip the Good, who called for a meeting between all the parties at Arras in July 1435. Duke Philip then appointed himself as arbiter between the kingdoms, although he had long been the ally of England, and had recognized the Plantagenets as Kings of France since the Treaty of Troyes in 1422.

Sensing a trap, the English stalled. Cardinal Beaufort again proposed that the matter be resolved by marriage between a daughter of Charles VII and the 13-year-old King Henry. This Charles rejected. Bedford then suggested a compromise. Henry VI should be recognized as King of France while Charles kept his half of the kingdom, but as Henry's vassal. The French did not even consider this suggestion worthy of reply.

Attended by interested observers from the princely houses of Europe, the Congress of Arras duly began in July 1435. As a first step, the French demanded that Henry drop his claim and title to the throne of France. As this was the basis for all their wars in France, the English delegation promptly walked out. The long-suffering and patient Duke of Bedford died on 14 September 1435, and on 25 September the Duke of Burgundy broke his oath to the English king and returned to his French allegiance, an act King Henry VI neither forgot nor forgave: 'for he broke all his promises to me, made in my youth, when I had never done him any harm.' Six months later the French army entered Paris and with their alliance with Burgundy at an end, the English position was hopeless.

By the end of 1435, when King Henry was 14, all the triumphs of his late father lay in ruins. During 1436 the French continued to make advances. The following year another link with a more glorious past snapped when the King's mother, King Harry's widow, Catherine of Valois, died. There is little evidence that Queen Catherine ever spent much time with her first-born and her death revealed the surprising news that for some years she had been married to a Welsh squire, Owen Tudor, who had drawn himself to the Queen's attention by collapsing on to her lap when drunk.

Not only was the Queen married, but she had four children by Owen Tudor, two of whom, Edmund and Jasper, were to play a significant part in the later history of York and Lancaster. Edmund, later Earl of Richmond, was the father of Henry Tudor, later Henry VII; while Jasper became Earl of Pembroke and a stout supporter of both the Lancastrians and his nephew in the warlike years ahead.

It was curious that a queen of England could remarry and have several children without the world being aware of it, a fact which was 'Unwitting to the common people till she dyed' according to the *Great Chronicle of London*. King Henry appears to have been pleased to discover he had half-brothers, though he was less pleased with his ne'er-do-well stepfather, Owen Tudor, who was summoned before the Council to explain his conduct. Tudor was arrested, released and then re-arrested, but he was eventually allowed to retire to his estates in Wales, where he lived peacefully until 1461. To prevent another such occurrence, the Parliament of 1427–28 passed an Act forbidding any man to marry a Queen-dowager without the permission of the King or his Council; an Act later extended to embrace all the immediate members of the Royal family, which still applies today.

Concerning the war in France, the English still had, or at least thought they had, another unrealized asset, in the person of the Duke of Orléans, a prisoner in England since his capture at Agincourt in 1415. Orléans had been kept in the household of the Duke of Suffolk and the two men were now friends. Orléans maintained that if he were set at liberty, he could negotiate a peace. In July 1440 terms for his release were agreed, though when he swore to them in Westminster Abbey, Duke Humphrey stalked out in disgust. In return for a down payment of 20,000 marks towards his ransom and his promise to work towards a peace, Orléans was set free, and in November 1440 he sailed for Burgundy. He did try to stop the war, but the French were winning and they knew it. Charles VII paid over the balance of his ransom and Orléans never returned to captivity, but the war went on. The last card left to play was a marriage.

Gloucester favoured a daughter of Jean IV, Count of Armagnac, a Gascon noble whose aid was needed to uphold the English position in Aquitaine. The King seemed pleased with this idea, and negotiations went on throughout the summer of 1442 until, with a French army at his frontiers, Count Jean abruptly broke off negotiations and ordered the English envoys home. Failure for this breach was laid on William de la Pole, Earl of Suffolk, and eyes again turned to France.

From 1436, Charles's army, now a mixture of trained professional infantry, the *gens d'ordonnance*, and field artillery, began to sweep all before it, campaigning successfully first in the Seine valley and then in Aquitaine. By 1444 the then English lieutenant in France, Richard Plantagenet, now restored to his estates as the Duke of York, could do no more. A fresh peace conference was called at Tours in May of that year, and the terms were most disadvantageous for the English king.

These required only a two-year truce and the marriage of Henry VI, now 23, with a princess of France, Margaret of Anjou, aged 16, who would come to the King of England without a dowry. This was not the sort of marriage that bolstered English pride. Marriage apart, the terms of the Truce of Tours called for the English to stay where they were, in all that was left of their conquests: the pale and port of Calais, parts of Aquitaine, Lower Normandy and the valuable county of Maine. The English must refrain from any action whatsoever against the Valois's rule in France. There was, however, a secret agenda which could not be concealed for long.

In this brief pause, other scores could be settled. In 1447 England saw the downfall of old Duke Humphrey, who lost his long battle with the Beauforts. In 1441 the Beauforts had succeeded in getting his wife, the Duchess Eleanor, imprisoned for life on a charge of witchcraft and for conspiracy against the life of the King. It is a measure of the old Duke's declining power that he was unable to prevent this. Then, at Bury St Edmunds in 1447, the court faction went for the kill. The Duke was accused of conspiracy, arrested, imprisoned, impeached by Parliament, and subsequently died under arrest, probably murdered. The newly crowned Queen Margaret was said to have been implicated in his death, which did nothing for her fragile popularity.

Six weeks later, on 11 April 1447, Gloucester's old rival, Cardinal Beaufort, also went to his grave in Winchester Cathedral. Their quarrel, however, was to survive them, passing to the Cardinal's relatives, the Dukes of Somerset, and Gloucester's protégé, Richard Plantagenet, the Duke of York.

William de la Pole, Duke of Suffolk, now stood supreme in the Royal Council but it was suddenly revealed that in return for the Truce of Tours and the marriage of their king, the English councillors, and in particular the Duke of Suffolk, had also agreed to surrender the county of Maine to the King of France. When this news broke, it caused real anger, and not simply of the political kind, simulated to embarrass political opponents. Suffolk's supporters were enraged by his deceit, his opponents furious at his arrogance, everyone amazed at his (and the King's) stupidity. Not only had they accepted a match with a wilful and dowerless lady, they had also paid a heavy and humiliating price for the privilege. This matter of Maine caused a great public outcry and the blame for this further humiliating concession was firmly attached by Parliament to the Queen's favourite, the Duke of Suffolk. When the English garrison refused to withdraw from Maine, Charles broke the truce in February 1448 and laid siege to le Mans. The English had to evacuate Maine, withdrawing to Normandy in June 1448, and from then on one disaster swiftly followed another.

However much odium was heaped on Suffolk, by 1450 Henry VI could not escape a share of the blame for this situation, though 'blame' may not be the right word to attach to a man who was clearly not up to his duties. When Normandy fell in 1450, he had been on the throne for 20 years, and ruling for the previous 13, yet the problems of the realm were worse than ever.

Even if the Beauforts had been right all along, and the war in France was a fruitless struggle, the King was equally ineffective in other spheres of Royal activity. Justice was in pawn to the man with the deepest pocket or the largest pack of bully-boys. Riots, robbery and murder were common; justice, retribution and punishment rare. Every man sought the protection of local lords rather than trusting to security under the protection of the law. It was this, far more than his failures as a war-lord, that wore out men's patience with the rule of Henry VI. Incompetent himself, the King was no more successful choosing subordinates, and lost further ground by his continued support of Suffolk in England and Somerset in France.

By the middle of 1450, the English garrisons had been swept from lower Normandy. Henry V's first conquest, the port of Harfleur, fell to the French in December 1449. In April 1450 an English army under Sir Thomas Kyriel was defeated at Formigny, in Normandy, and the King's Lieutenant in Normandy, the Duke of Somerset, was swiftly hustled out of Rouen and Caen. Three years later, in July 1453, as already related, the last English army in France was shattered at Castillon. Bordeaux, the capital of Aquitaine, surrendered to the French on 19 October 1453, and the Plantagenet rule in France was finally over.

All the English had to show for a hundred years of struggle was the port of Calais. The Hundred Years War was over. The Wars of the Roses were about to begin.

CHAPTER THREE

THE FALL OF SUFFOLK (1440–50)

*Such is the hatred born of contention and desire for
honour and empire: that hath been these many years
increased by mutual bloodshed and slaughter.*

POLYDORE VERGIL OF URBINO (c.1513)

When the remnants of Talbot's army returned from France in 1453, the
struggle between the Dukes of York and Somerset over the prosecution of
the war in France had been going on quite openly for the past three years.
The loss of Normandy in 1450 brought all the barely submerged quarrels
over policy to the surface and the roots of these quarrels, like the earlier
one between Duke Humphrey and the Beauforts, rested on the question
of ability and it is to the differing abilities of York and Somerset that we
must now turn. This means judging between the abilities of King Henry
VI's court and Council and those of the still silent heir-presumptive to the
throne, Richard Plantagenet, Duke of York, who wished to carry on the
policies of Duke Humphrey of Gloucester.

York had emerged as a capable leader, successful in war, popular with
the soldiery, well thought of by the nobility and the people at large as the
natural successor to the murdered Duke Humphrey of Gloucester, but
with little real political support among the magnates of the realm. Like
many good soldiers, York lacked the subtlety to be a good politician and
his position was flawed by the underlying doubts put about by the Queen
and her supporters regarding York's true intentions towards the throne.

Richard Plantagenet, later Duke of York, was born in 1411. He was
therefore just 4 when his father, Richard, Earl of Cambridge, was
beheaded by Henry V on the eve of the latter's departure for the invasion

of France and the successful Agincourt campaign of 1415. Cambridge was attainted for treason, having plotted to put Edmund Mortimer, Earl of March, on the throne. His son was given as ward into the care of Ralph Neville, Earl of Westmorland, who was married to Joan Beaufort, sister of Cardinal Beaufort.

Ralph Neville became fond of his ward, and since attainders did not usually affect the rights of heirs, the young Richard Plantagenet was potentially a good match. In 1424, when Richard Plantagenet was 13, he was betrothed to the Duke's daughter, Cecily, then aged 9. Cecily was already a beauty, known in the north as the 'Rose of Raby'. In 1425, Ralph Neville died and the Countess Joan took over the wardship, Richard then being 14. In 1426 Richard was knighted and in the same year the Earl of March died, leaving Richard as his heir. In 1428 Richard Plantagenet was restored to his father's estates, becoming Duke of York, and was taken from the care of the widowed Duchess of Westmorland and placed into the Royal household, where the young King Henry was one of his companions. A year later he married Cecily. He was now 18 and his beautiful bride just 14.

Richard Plantagenet, Duke of York, was by right and title one of the great magnates of the kingdom, but in spite of his title he had few connections in Yorkshire. His power lay to the west, in the Mortimer lands along the Welsh Marches. The family home of the Yorks was at Fotheringhay Castle in Northamptonshire. York also owned Sandal Castle in Yorkshire and Conisburg Castle in the West Riding of Yorkshire, as well as numerous manors in the South, the Home Counties and the Midlands.

From his Mortimer uncle, the young Duke also inherited vast lands on the Welsh Marches and in Wales. These included the castles at Wigmore and Ludlow, and with his lands there and elsewhere, including Ireland where he was Earl of Ulster, York had the considerable income of some £5,000 a year – a vast sum for the time, though not in itself sufficient to pay all the costs of maintaining his entourage and lands, and his large and growing number of relations, all of whom expected pensions, gifts and wages. York had also spent a great deal of his own money and plunged himself deeply into debt to pay the wages of the King's soldiers in France during his time there as the King's Lieutenant. To cover his debts and costs, York needed Royal appointments.

In the England of Henry VI, York was the man to watch and cultivate. If anything should happen to their childless Sovereign Lord, Henry VI, then York would be heir-apparent to the throne and, even now, was legally the heir-presumptive. Though he never assumed this title, the thought gave many Royal Councillors, especially Suffolk and Somerset, good reason for concern.

It is important to stress that the young Duke of York had no apparent designs on the throne and was very eager to serve his King as a soldier. During the 1430s he was constantly in the field in France. He fought with John Talbot, the greatest captain of his day, campaigning in Normandy and Picardy, where he served his young sovereign loyally and well. By 1437, when the King's minority ended, he was the King's Lieutenant in France, and had practically ruined himself in the King's service, using all the money he had or could borrow to pay his soldiers and prosecute the war.

However, when the young King Henry began to rule as well as reign in 1437, he refused to employ his cousin of York in any capacity. The Duke was ordered home from France and replaced by the elderly Richard Beauchamp, Earl of Warwick, the King's former tutor. When the King drew up the list of members for his first Council in November 1437, the Duke of York was not included. This was a direct insult to York, and all knew who stood behind it. The King was clearly seen to favour his other cousins, the Somersets, and especially the present Earl, later to become the first Duke, John Beaufort, now returned home after 17 years in a French prison after his capture at Baugé. This John Beaufort was a grandson of John of Gaunt by Katherine Swynford. Somerset took Warwick's place in France after old Warwick died in 1439. In this, the young King Henry was badly advised. Somerset proved totally incapable of stemming the French advance and the King, with evident reluctance, reappointed the Duke of York as his Lieutenant in France in 1440. The Duke, accompanied by Duchess Cecily, arrived in Rouen in May 1441, and in April 1442 their son Edward was born in Rouen Castle.

The Duke of York's second tenancy in France during the 1440s was not successful. His expenses were again not paid and he was forced to impoverish himself and his family to pay the wages of his soldiers. In 1443 supplies of men and materials sorely needed for Normandy were diverted to help the Duke of Somerset, who was campaigning in the county of Poitou, between the Loire and Aquitaine, on the orders of the King, who had not consulted York about this venture.

The King was very careful in his orders to Somerset. He stated that Somerset's commission did not apply in any territory in France occupied or administered by the Duke of York, but this ruling was not of great help to either party. York resented the division of his command, the elevation of Somerset to a duchy and the diversion of men and supplies he sorely needed. He also regarded Somerset as an incompetent soldier and events were to prove this judgement correct.

Somerset's campaign was a disaster. He attacked the castle of la Guerche in Brittany, which Somerset thought belonged to the Duke of Alençon. La Guerche actually belonged to England's ally, the Duke of Brittany, who was naturally furious. Somerset's army then wandered fruitlessly about France and the Breton frontier, eventually descending to brigandage. After his forces were dispersed, Somerset returned to England, where he died in May 1444. His younger brother, Edmund Beaufort, took his place, though he did not acquire the ducal title until 1448; he had to make do with being Earl and then Marquis of Dorset, then Earl of Somerset, before finally becoming Duke.

His funds exhausted and deep in debt, York returned to England in 1445, where he was promptly blamed for the continuing run of English set-backs and refused further employment. In 1447 he was given the post of the King's Lieutenant in Ireland, partly because he was Earl of Ulster but mainly, as the Duke was well aware, to get him out of the way while the Dukes of Suffolk and the new Duke of Somerset ruled both King and kingdom. In this, Suffolk and Somerset soon had a new and powerful ally, the King's new wife, Margaret of Anjou.

By the time of his marriage to Margaret of Anjou in May 1445, when the King was 23 and Margaret 16, it was beginning to dawn on most of the people who mattered in England, and that meant the magnates and prelates of the realm, that King Henry was no imperious monarch. Soon after his marriage, it also began to dawn on them that whatever her tender years might imply, Margaret of Anjou, even at 16, was a formidable woman, who quickly exerted her influence on the pacific King Henry and became a power at court after 1454. Though the Dukes of Somerset and Suffolk ruled the council for the moment, Margaret of Anjou was destined to play a leading part in the Wars of the Roses as the prop of the Lancastrian party when all others failed, but she was also a cause of much trouble in the years which led up to the outbreak of civil war in 1455.

Margaret was the daughter of René, Count of Anjou and Duke of Bar, the titular King of Naples, a man known in French history as Good King René. Good King René was an affable prince, much more interested in love and music, hunting and poetry, than in weaponry and war, but the steel in his nature passed to his daughter. To marry the King of England without bringing him a dowry was a very good match for her, though what the new young Queen can have thought of her bookish, monkish husband can only be wondered at. Margaret, however, spent little time in speculation; there was a power vacuum in the realm and this she proceeded to fill.

Within months Duke Humphrey had been arrested and promptly died – perhaps of a stroke, though possibly murdered – and the Queen was at the heart of a powerful Court party, headed by the Duke of Somerset. The Queen's party pursued Duke Humphrey's followers even after the Duke was dead. Five of Duke Humphrey's retainers, including his natural son, Arthur, were arrested, accused of conspiring to make the Duke of Gloucester and Duchess Eleanor, King and Queen of England, although the Duchess had been a prisoner on the Isle of Man for many years. This move was clearly designed to terrorize anyone conspiring against the king and his ever-more powerful councillors.

Margaret quickly perceived that any future threat to the House of Lancaster would come from the Duke of York. She therefore continued the policy of edging him to the margin of state affairs while building up her own band of cronies. Somerset saw to it that the pick of the appointments and rewards went to the Court clique, which Margaret eventually came to dominate. Margaret's other requirement was to produce an heir to the throne, but months drifted into years and the Queen was still not pregnant. Whether the fault was on her side or the King's cannot be known, but when she eventually became pregnant many wondered if the King could be the father, and Somerset was widely supposed to be her lover.

Margaret was in a position to influence the King, who was, in any event, all too easily influenced, and she was openly concerned to represent the interests of her close relative and late sovereign lord, Charles VII of France. Her clique made up the peace party in the Court, a group chiefly composed of the Dukes of Somerset and Suffolk and their adherents, all of whom were opposed to the other great magnate of the realm, Richard Plantagenet, Duke of York, a lord whom Margaret cordially disliked. Margaret had no reason for this, other than personal animosity. York was, and wished to be, a loyal and well-regarded servant of the crown, but Margaret, bred in the intrigues of a French Court still seething in the aftermath of the Armagnac–Burgundian wars, could not see him as anything other than a potential source of danger.

By 1448, three years after the King's marriage, York had assembled a formidable list of grievances. His supporter, Duke Humphrey, was dead, and his enemies, Somerset and Suffolk, were the powers in the land. While they had been building up their position at Court, York had spent his own money to the point of ruin in managing the war in Normandy and ended up posted to Ireland for his pains, though he refused to leave until 1449. In spite of all this, he remained loyal to King Henry.

The time has come to take a closer look at the monarch of this unhappy land. The King had grown up to be a gentle, biddable, yet wilful monarch. By all accounts Henry was the sort of person who finds it difficult to reach a decision and tends to agree with whoever he has spoken to last. Quite early in his reign it became apparent that his abilities were no match for his responsibilities, for the King had no great interest in kingship: he was far more interested in education and religion. He founded both Eton College just across the river from his great castle at Windsor, and King's College, Cambridge, spending a fortune on both foundations, and they remain the most worthwhile relics of his reign. On a personal note, he disliked vulgarity and the rough humour and bad language of soldiers. He also seems to have had a morbid fear of sex and women. He was offended by nudity, even in men, and he was constantly warning Eton scholars, who came wandering up the hill to the castle gates, that his Court was full of sin and wickedness. Even in his youth the King was notably chaste, in spite of the opportunities afforded by his position.

Accounts of the King's life-style are confusing. Some people state that he was careless in his dress, usually wearing round-toed peasant boots and a simple wool tunic, but the Court Rolls reveal another picture, for King Henry maintained a large household which, by 1449, contained over 1,000 servants, and his dress could be lavish. A French embassy to his Court in 1445 went away impressed with the pomp of Henry's Court and the splendour of their reception, and the same comments were made by a Portuguese ambassador who visited Windsor in 1449.

The King's nature is also a complex subject. He was certainly weak and impressionable and too kind for his own good, but he could also be stubborn and vindictive. His support of Suffolk and Somerset, when they were obviously corrupt and incompetent, is a good example of his reluctance to see reason. His relentless pursuit of Eleanor, Duchess of Gloucester, whom he accused of witchcraft and imprisoned for life, is an example of his intolerance. So, too, is his involvement in the death of her husband, Humphrey, Duke of Gloucester, and the threatened execution of Humphrey's followers, who were saved only at the last moment after a terrifying ordeal, which had reached the point of disembowelment. The accounts of the King's goodness are largely based on his devotion to religion, often at the expense of more pressing secular matters concerning the government of the realm.

As he grew older, his religious fervour deepened. He wore a hair shirt on Church festivals and feast days, even ordering that his meals should begin with a bloody piece of meat in remembrance of the wounds of Christ. When he was a youth, none of this mattered too much. A devout prince was an asset. The King was allowed his ways and whims, for his Court hoped he would grow out of them and learn that goodness alone was not enough in a prince. The real trouble began in the latter half of the 1430s when the King came under the influence of William de la Pole, Earl, Marquis and later Duke of Suffolk, who had become a power in the land by 1447, shortly after Duke Humphrey and Cardinal Beaufort were dead.

There is little evidence that King Henry was mentally retarded, at least in his early years, but that his intellect was limited was clearly no secret. As early as 1442, when the King was just 21, a Kent farmer was arrested for saying that the King was as lunatic as his (the farmer's) father was. This sort of remark soon became quite common. The courtiers, who saw more of him than did the common folk, were soon to recall that his maternal grandfather, Charles VI of France, had been definitely mad, even descending into dangerous lunacy from time to time. One of the old French King's delusions was that he was made of glass and, if touched, would shatter. He would therefore lash out at passers-by with a sword and eventually had to be confined. King Henry's madness never got to that stage. He simply faded away and gradually became unable to cope. The best explanation is probably that the King was never very strong mentally and the growing pressures of his office slowly drove him out of his wits, turning away from his cares into a form of stupor.

Richard Plantagenet, Duke of York, the King's cousin, was a quite different kind of man. Richard was more suited to the life of camp and Court. He was educated and literate, skilled in courtesy and the law of arms, a competent soldier, almost the model of a Christian prince. He was also headstrong and always showed poor political judgement. He was also extremely rich, the richest man in England after the King, at least until the failure of the King to refund the money Richard had spent financing campaigns in France plunged him into debt. He had the good sense and luck to marry Cecily Neville, which linked him with the powerful Nevilles who had great estates and as guardians of half the Scottish border were well supplied with professional soldiers. The Salisbury side of the Neville affinity buttressed York in his struggle with the Somersets, but the senior Westmorland Nevilles always remained stout partisans of Lancaster and York's Neville relatives were no help at all in the early years of his struggle with the Somersets.

The nobles and magnates of England were not enjoying great prosperity in the middle of the fifteenth century. Although the yeoman were thriving and the merchant class was doing well enough, the nobility were becoming steadily impoverished. Over the previous half-century, certainly since 1400, the great landowners were having to rely more and more on rents and less and less on ancestral feudal dues. Their lands had been loaned out to their peasants and yeoman farmers as sheep runs, partly because the wool trade was profitable, partly because the loss of manpower caused by the Black Death and subsequent plagues meant that their lands could not be tilled.

The war and the disputes with Burgundy had crippled the wool trade. There was a glut of land and not enough workers or tenants, so rents were static or even fell. The great lords, therefore, found their incomes falling while their costs were rising. The only sources of income were the Royal revenues and appointments, so the root cause of conflict at Court was the need to control the King and get a share of his income.

It is fair to say that the Royal Council and the King's household were making a very good thing out of their allegiance and by 1450 were on the way towards reducing the King to penury, usually with the King's all-too-willing assistance.

In medieval times a king was expected to 'live off his own', supporting the expenses of Court and kingdom from his own estates and from his feudal dues. The latter largely came from taxes on imports and exports, the revenues of Royal wards and the sale of wardships. Financial independence was just possible because the English king had great land holdings, the crown estates – the Lancastrian kings having the added advantages of the lands and wealth accruing to the Duchy of Lancaster. In addition to this, at least while the King was childless, he enjoyed vast revenues from the great estates properly belonging to the Prince of Wales, in Cornwall and Chester. The early deaths of his uncles, the Dukes of Bedford, Clarence and Gloucester, had also increased the Royal income. King Henry should have been rich.

The advantage of this was that a king who could 'live off his own' had no need to call a Parliament. The summoning of Parliament was a Royal prerogative and only exercised when the king needed money from general taxation. The snag here was that over the centuries, Parliament had gradually managed to link taxation to concessions and had slowly whittled away at the king's power. Wise kings, therefore, called Parliament only when they needed money. The chief cause for a shortage of money was war.

There was now another reason. The King was steadily giving away his lands and entitlements and as he did so, his income fell. In 1433 the Royal Treasurer, Lord Cromwell, had to tell Parliament that following the costs of the French coronation and the war generally the Royal expenditure exceeded income by more than £35,000, a huge sum at a time when the total annual Royal revenue was £54,000. Cromwell even had to request an immediate grant of £2,000 to cover the King's private and personal expenses, a shameful situation. To save money the King began to stay in monasteries or with his lords, who then had to bear the costs of maintaining the King and his Court. Where, people asked, had the Royal money gone?

Much of it went in fees or payments to Henry's household, who received money from the King's purse in addition to their own revenues or wages. The Royal revenue was also steadily dissipated by grants of property, nearly 200 of them in the first 13 years of his rule, between 1437 and 1450. Many of these grants went to members of his Council who were in a position to recommend that he make the grant in the first place. Henry gave and gave, and went on giving, until he could not maintain his own state.

In the month of October 1444, for example, the Duke of Somerset was given 13 manors in the West Country which properly belonged to the Duchy of Cornwall. The Duke of Suffolk did even better. During the 1440s Suffolk became Constable of Wallingford Castle, Steward of the Chiltern Hundreds, of Chester, Flint and North Wales, Steward of the Duchy of Lancaster, Captain of Calais, and in possession of four manors, all of them rent free. He also became ward to several rich heiresses. The list of his acquisitions goes on for pages and every penny he gained was a penny deducted from the Royal revenues. Parliament, and in particular the Commons, had little choice but to top up the coffers from taxation, and were most unhappy about it.

By 1444 the situation was so serious that the Royal Council, meeting in the Star Chamber at Westminster, drew up a plan by which all petitions to the crown must first have their grants approved by the Council and then scrutinized by the Keeper of the Privy Seal. The problem was that the grants were usually made to members of the Council or their various hangers-on, and the abuses therefore continued. Eventually Parliament had to pass several Acts of Resumption which aimed to repossess the crown lands and restore their revenues to the King. Until this happened, here was yet another abuse noted by the Duke of York and his friends, who did not share in the Royal bounty and were able to accuse Suffolk and the Somersets of corruption.

The other harmful element in the realm was the growth of noble factions, or 'affinities'. An affinity might be composed of a small group of lesser nobles who joined together to arrange local affairs according to their convenience, as in Wales; or, more often, a large group of local gentry who gave their support to a great lord in hope of his protection – his 'good lordship' – particularly when they put themselves beyond the law.

Every lord of any status soon had a large affinity to whom he gave 'good lordship', protecting them from the consequences of their misdeeds, bribing or intimidating justices on their behalf, obtaining grants or pardons for them at Court. It would have been a bold gentleman who crossed the Duke of Norfolk in East Anglia, as the Pastons were to discover to their cost, or the Percies or Nevilles in the north, the Courtenays in Devon, Somerset in the West Country, the Stanleys in Lancashire, or the Duke of York in the Welsh Marches, where his followers, the Herbert brothers, the Vaughans, Walter Devereux, the Crofts and Baskervilles, made up a powerful affinity. Great lords like York drew their affinity from all over the country, and their affinity was composed of important magnates as well as lesser gentry and simple knights.

The great nobles and their ever-expanding affinities were adept at the threatening or bribery of jurors, and of corrupting justice to suit their own ends. The Royal authority, even when exercised by judges in courts of law, was virtually non-existent and as the 1440s edged towards the 1450s, wise men realized that their best hopes of safety and reward lay in supporting a local war-lord. Chief Justice Fortescue, a prominent lawyer of the time, wrote that while England had a great body of Common Law, whereby the 'King cannot alter nor change the Lawes of the Realme by his pleasure, but governeth the people not only by power but by policy', the rule of law was breaking down because of 'lack of governance' through 'the perils that cometh to our Lord King from overmighty subjects'. This lack of government affected men at every level. In this situation bully-boys wearing a great lord's livery controlled the affairs of shire and state and could commit the most serious crimes with impunity.

These affinities and the practice of granting livery have left England with one colourful reminder of those distant times. Richard II had decreed that every alehouse should have a sign, and as soldiers and roughnecks tended to concentrate in alehouses when not terrorizing the citizens, these 'locals' soon began to display the local lord's cognizance. Hence the 'White Lion' of Mortimer, 'The Bear' of Warwick, the 'White Swan' of Buckingham, and those other signs bearing the 'Arms' of the local lord which swing outside English public houses to this very day.

* * *

One of the other significant features of English life from the early decades of the fourteenth century was the growth of 'bastard feudalism', which was itself caused by the growth of affinities. In the early feudal system introduced by the Normans, land was held by a knight or lord in return for military service, or by a peasant in return for labour. By the early years of the fourteenth century, or even earlier, this system was gradually being replaced by a more convenient system of service in return for wages. During the Hundred Years War, whole armies were recruited by indentures and the soldiers expected to be paid. As feudalism declined, the inefficient feudal levy gradually gave way to the professional soldier. The magnates began to maintain bodies of soldiers, even in peacetime, and this 'maintenance' was not illegal 'unless the lord attempted to support his retainer in outlawry or by influencing a court of law'. By 1450 this fine but critical point had been forgotten.

Bastard feudalism arose where men followed a lord not out of mutual self-interest or because of an oath of homage, but because he could pay them and protect them from justice. It led to the growth of 'livery and maintenance', where every lord began to gather a group of soldiers about him, often rough men who wore his colours, or 'livery', and whom he paid and protected, or 'maintained'. These private armies, maintained by the magnates as part of their affinity were a constant source of trouble not least because 'maintenance' also meant maintaining a suit in a court-of-law, if necessary by force. On the other hand, even the king found these retainers useful. Unlike the King of France, the English King had no standing army. His forces were composed of the contingents provided and maintained by the magnates of the realm. The practice was necessary but it had to be controlled.

Various acts were passed seeking control over the practice of livery and maintenance, but there was no power available to enforce them. Here again, much of the blame for this ineffectual government must be laid at the door of Henry VI or, given the King's limited abilities, on the Royal Council, who failed either to curb the nobles or give the common people common justice. Violence became widespread and the bully-boys, thieves and violent men knew that, provided they had a 'good lord', that lord would protect them from retribution at the hands of the sheriffs and the justices. By 1450 the country was ruled in all but name by the Queen and Suffolk, whose cronies were notoriously corrupt and were certainly not averse to conflict. By the end of the 1440s, violence in town and country had spread even to the door of Parliament where, in November 1450, for example, Lord Cromwell was involved in a violent brawl with one of Suffolk's squires, William Tallboys. The state of affairs in other parts of the realm can only be imagined.

*　*　*

The general depression of the realm in the 1450s was not improved by the ever-wider stream of refugees flowing in from France as one province after another fell to the forces of the French King. Charles VII's army of professional soldiers, equipped with field artillery, was carrying all before it. In one month in 1450, soon after the fall of Normandy, over 6,000 refugees arrived in England to beg in the streets or hang about the Court or seek relief at the castles of the nobility. Even in an age with relatively poor communications, such events did not go unnoticed. It was said openly that Edmund Somerset, the King's Lieutenant in Normandy, having replaced York in 1445, had managed to receive compensation from the King for his losses in France while keeping for himself the compensation intended for others. Parliament, which was supposed to advise the King and check abuses over money, seemed quite impotent.

The House of Commons consisted of 74 so-called 'Knights of the Shires', though the majority were actually either squires or 'gentlemen of coat armour', two from each county. To these were added 190 burgesses, four from the City of London and two each from the other 93 boroughs of the realm. Although these people certainly used their local influence to get elected to Parliament, or were increasingly sponsored by local lords, they were originally elected by the freemen, and the choice of candidate rested with the people – there were no 'parties'. Gradually, however, a property requirement was introduced, not just among the candidates but also for the electorate. By 1445 the right to vote had been removed 'from those of yeoman status or below', which effectively disenfranchised the majority of the population. Moreover, the Court began nominating Members for election, choosing candidates from biddable courtiers. The size of the House of Commons was increased to find them seats. Such actions were a deliberate attempt to undermine the independence of the House of Commons, and this abuse was the first of many.

By the Parliament of 1449, the extent of the catastrophe at home and abroad was beyond the capacity of any king to excuse or any Parliament to overlook. There was piracy in the Channel and the French and Bretons were raiding the south coast ports with impunity. The sea trade with the Low Countries and Aquitaine was in ruins. Lawlessness and economic woes at home and abroad were compounded when the Duke of York stated that, in his experienced opinion, Normandy was lost. The old duchy would soon fall to the French, and all the costs and sacrifices of recent years would be for nothing.

York was in a position to know. He only made the statement to refute an accusation made by Adam Moleyns, Bishop of Chichester and Keeper of the Privy Seal, that York's incompetence in Normandy between 1440 and 1445 was the cause of the impending disaster. Moleyns's claim was undermined by the well-known fact that from his youth York had constantly urged more resources for the French war and by a letter to Parliament from the present Lieutenant of Normandy, the Duke of Somerset, the great hope of the Court party, asking for fresh supplies of men and money. Somerset's demands and the inability of the country to meet them caused a public outcry. A row in the Parliament of 1449 gradually worked round to accusations against the Royal favourite, William de la Pole, Duke of Suffolk, and the whole corrupt edifice which had shielded state affairs from public view began to come down with a rush, with the other members of the Court party happy to let Suffolk take the blame.

Before Parliament could meet to answer Somerset's letter, Rouen fell to the French. Somerset had been forced into a humiliating surrender and he withdrew to Caen. English morale was battered by these continual defeats, which had now gone on without check since the fall of Maine in March 1448 and they culminated shortly after the fall of Rouen with the defeat at Formigny, the penultimate battle of the Hundred Years War.

On 15 April 1450 a small English army under Sir Thomas Kyriel met a French army at Formigny, near Bayeux, and was defeated with great loss of life among the archers and common soldiers. In May 1450, Joan of Arc's old companion, Dunois, the Bastard of Orléans, forced Somerset out of Caen. Fearing retribution at home, the Duke took shelter in Calais. The rest of Normandy then collapsed, with Falaise, Domfront and Cherbourg falling to the French in rapid succession. Cherbourg fell on 12 August 1420, after which a correspondent in Calais wrote to John Paston, 'Shirburg is goon and we hav not now a fote of lande in Normandie and men are ferd that Calys will bee besieged hastily.'

While Normandy was falling, matters were little better at home. In January 1450 a company of soldiers, waiting to embark for Calais at Portsmouth, rioted for their pay and murdered Bishop Moleyns – yet another example of violence by supposedly disciplined troops. Before dying, however, the bishop, who had recently resigned the Privy Seal, reopened old political wounds by accusing Suffolk of direct responsibility for the 1447 cession of the county of Maine. This information was hurried to Parliament, where the loss of Maine still rankled.

On 22 January 1450, Suffolk attempted to avoid the growing wrath of Parliament by a direct petition to the King. In this he declared himself innocent of all charges, which he said were the result of malice, and reminded the King of his long service to the crown. This method of appealing to the King over the heads of his peers had worked three years previously, when the original Maine scandal had come to light, but the Members had scented blood this time and were not to be deflected. On 7 February 1450, pointing out that Suffolk had now publicly admitted the magnitude of the charges against him, they moved to impeach him. Suffolk was arrested and sent to the Tower, where he went in daily fear of his life. When the Bill of Impeachment was brought before the House, it accused Suffolk not just of incompetence, but of the capital charge of high treason.

The list of charges makes a useful record of the misdemeanours and mismanagement of the realm, much of which was laid at Suffolk's door. Suffolk was accused of conspiring with the French in 1447 to kill the King and place his own son, John, on the throne. He was accused of accepting bribes to secure the release of the Duke of Orléans, contrary to the wishes of Henry V. He was accused of having engineered the failure of all the embassies and discussions with France. He was accused of counselling the French against the English interests, and misuse of funds and corruption and bribery and denial of justice . . . the list goes on for pages. Although some of the charges are clearly ridiculous or plainly malicious, the main body was concerned with the government of the realm, the conduct of the French war and the loss of Normandy and Maine. Suffolk was by no means the only one responsible for these disasters, but he was the selected scapegoat, the man to censure instead of the King who, in fact, was very much to blame. Although the King himself was not a war-lord and can hardly be reprimanded for that, he was responsible for the appointment of people like Somerset, who were clearly incompetent, and for failing to support men, like York, who knew how to command armies and how to manage campaigns.

The Commons sent a Bill of Impeachment to the Lords in February 1450 and in March they decided that Suffolk should be brought before the house to answer all the charges and be judged, as was his right and the custom, 'by God and his Peers'. Additional charges were then added to the Bill. These included Suffolk's culpability for the failure of the proposed Armagnac marriage of 1442 and the subsequent loss of the Gascon allegiance. He was also accused of peculation, of stealing from the Treasury and from Royal funds entrusted to his care. To cap it all, he was accused of corruption in that he had accepted bribes for appointing wardships and for appointments to office. Any one of these charges, if proved, could have taken him to prison or to the block.

Fortunately, Suffolk could still rely on the King's sympathy and support. The King demonstrated this by having him taken from his prison in the Tower and lodged comfortably in the Palace of Westminster. Suffolk then refused to ask for the trial before his peers to which his rank entitled him and to which the Lords had summoned him. He placed his fate entirely in the King's hands.

The King did not fail him. On 17 March 1450 he sent for Suffolk and all the peers then in Parliament. In their presence, Suffolk knelt before the King, and after all the charges had been read – a process which took some time – he was asked how he wished to plead. Suffolk denied all the charges, pointing out the obvious fact that even if they were true he could hardly have contrived such a chapter of crimes on his own. The King then gave his judgment. On the capital charges, he found Suffolk innocent. On the second list of non-capital crimes and 'misprisions not criminal', he found him guilty and banished him from the realm for five years. Henry did not ask his lords' advice or seek legal opinion for his judgment, and Parliament was most unhappy with it: the Commons even attempted to bring in a separate bill on the charge of high treason, but to no avail.

Fate had not finished with the Duke of Suffolk. He left England on 1 May 1450, bound for exile in Burgundy, but he did not get very far. His ship was intercepted off Dover by sailors from a Royal ship, the *Nicolas of the Tower*. The sailors hauled the hapless Duke of Suffolk aboard the *Nicolas* and struck off his head, using the gunwale of a boat for a block. The failure of the war in France had claimed its first victim.

CHAPTER FOUR

REBELLIONS (1450–53)

We say that our Sovereign Lord has had fake
counsel. His lands, his merchandise, is lost, his
Commons destroyed. France is lost, and the King so
poor that he may not pay for his own meat and
drink, yet daily traitors muster about him, to wait for
what should come to him, and ask it from him.

MANIFESTO OF THE MEN OF KENT,
CADE'S REBELLION (1450)

The death of Suffolk brought King Henry no relief from the problems of government. Hardly had Suffolk's headless body been dumped on the beach at Dover than the men of Kent were up in arms. Living in the south-east of England, in a county through which travellers streamed to and from France, the Kent folk were better informed than most English people about the state of the realm, and were notably lawless anyway. Kent folk had figured in the Peasants' Revolt of 1381 and were always quick to defend their rights or to engage in insurrection. In June 1450 a great host of Kentish men began to march again on London, under the leadership of a mysterious figure known as Jack Cade, but this rising was very well organized and attended. The rebels produced a detailed manifesto denouncing the state of the country, the corruption of the Court and the incompetence of the King's Councillors – all issues which had been aired recently in the scarcely calmer atmosphere of Parliament.

Jack Cade's rebellion differed in several ways from that of Wat Tyler 70 years before. Tyler had led an army of villeins and working men, while Cade's followers included squires and gentlemen, yeoman farmers and honest citizens. The list of Cade's supporters, over 3,000 in all, makes impressive reading. In the rebel ranks rode Robert Poynings, who became an MP in the next Parliament, and over 70 gentlemen of coat-armour. The Mayor of Queensborough and the Bailiff of Sandwich were there with 53 shire constables from the Hundreds of Kent, each leading a contingent of citizens. There was a great number of other people who were, by any standards, worthy members of society, and their leader, Jack Cade, was among the least of them. Calling himself variously John Mortimer – a significant name – or John Amendall, he claimed to be a cousin of the Duke of York, but was subsequently proved to be plain Jack Cade from Ireland, a thief, a sanctuary man (an evader of justice) and a former soldier.

The rebels' demands included an inquiry into the murder of Humphrey, Duke of Gloucester, back in 1447, while they declared themselves supporters of the policies attributed to Richard Plantagenet, Duke of York, 'late exiled from our Lord's presence.' Other demands included the return of crown property given away on Suffolk's advice, the payment of the King's debts, and the non-interference of great lords in the election of Members of Parliament. All these matters had been discussed in the Parliament at Leicester in early May 1450, when the beneficial effects of any Resumption of the crown lands was largely negated by the king's insistence on exemptions. These exemptions totalled 186 in all, and included everyone who had recently benefited from the King's generosity.

By mid-June the rebels were camped at Blackheath, across the Thames from London, where Henry VI eventually came to meet them. After insisting on reforms, they declared their allegiance to him and then started to disperse. Henry promptly withdrew his offer of concessions and let his guards pursue the rebels into the countryside. This proved unwise. Many of them were old soldiers from the French wars and had their weapons with them. They quickly defeated the Royal forces, killing Sir Humphrey Stafford and several other knights. Henry was forced to abandon London and flee to Kenilworth Castle in the Midlands. Cade's force returned to the capital, and entered the city of London on 2 July, where his men were soon joined by disgruntled apprentices and many of the citizens. Within hours, this alliance of town and country had broken down and the rebels began to hunt down and execute members of the Court party.

The rebels were particularly angry with the King's Chamberlain, Lord Say, the Treasurer of England, a protégé of Suffolk. As Warden of the Cinque Ports and Constable of Dover Castle, he was a man whose abuses of power and privilege were very well known to the men of Kent, and they wanted his blood. Say was accused of interference in county elections, of corrupt taxation, of treason and extortion, in which offences he was aided by his son-in-law, the Sheriff of Kent. In an attempt to placate the rebels, the King had Say arrested and confined to the Tower, but this provided no security. Say and his relative were taken out by force, given a brief trial at the Guildhall, then dragged into the street and beheaded. Such acts and casual murders soon became common, and after several days of looting and riot, the citizens of London rose against Cade's men. Hundreds of people were killed in the subsequent street-fighting, but the rebels were finally driven out of the city and order restored. The rebellion collapsed and on 12 July Jack Cade was killed in a skirmish with the new Sheriff of Kent, Alexander Iden. Meanwhile, the unrest was spreading, and in Wiltshire a mob killed Bishop Aiscough, a Suffolk partisan who had performed the marriage service between the King and the unpopular Queen Margaret.

A general pardon was issued to all the participants who would return peacefully to their homes, but when the King returned from Leicester in July, he once again reneged on the terms. The atmosphere was not improved when Edmund, Duke of Somerset, sailed home from Calais in August, having decided that in the present state of England his loss of Normandy would not be too harshly judged. Somerset was promptly given the post of Constable and slipped smoothly into the role vacated by the Duke of Suffolk. He proved less than capable here and the disorder continued until into September, when the Duke of York, without Royal permission, returned from Ireland with an army. This was the step that moved the country close to war, for it clearly meant a confrontation between York and Somerset for control of the Council and management of the realm.

The events of 1450, at home and abroad, had brought all the inadequacies of Henry VI sharply into focus. To protect Suffolk he had ignored the voice of Parliament, but even the Royal safe conduct had not kept Suffolk from summary execution. Three of his closest advisers – his Keeper of the Privy Seal, Bishop Moleyns, his Treasurer, Lord Say, and his friend Bishop Aiscough – had been summarily murdered by the mob; his capital had seen days of pitched battle and those who had been discontented enough to rise against his rule included the most solid and reliable of the nation's citizens. Having had trouble with Parliament and the common people, the King now faced a further problem with his noble cousin, Richard Plantagenet, Duke of York.

York was 39 and in a difficult position. The King had no heir, so if the Acts binding the succession to the House of Lancaster were set aside, York was heir-presumptive to the throne, though he was aware that Somerset, as a descendant of John of Gaunt, was the heir-male of Lancaster. Here, again, it is necessary to stress that York had no apparent designs on the throne however much this idea was mooted about by his enemies, the Queen and the Beauforts. York saw the kingdom slipping into chaos; he saw the Council abusing the King's weakness, and he wanted to put a stop to it. It would be realistic to add that he probably also wanted his share of anything that was going.

York returned from virtual exile in Ireland in September 1450, a month after his rival, Somerset, had returned from Calais. He landed at Beaumaris in Wales, evaded Sir Thomas Stanley who was sent to arrest him, and marched on London, recruiting men as he came. In the circumstances of civil commotion and York's position *vis-à-vis* the crown, it is hardly surprising that his advance caused considerable alarm. This alarm was increased when two members of the Royal household left the Court and fled to join York's army. The Speaker of the House of Commons, William Tresham, who went to find out why York had returned and perhaps to join him, was cut down and killed on the way by followers of Lord Grey of Ruthin.

In letters to the King, York claimed that he had returned to counter persistent rumours that he had been engaged in treason; but when he entered London at the end of September, the City became virtually an armed camp, full of men from York's affinity, jostling supporters of the Duke of Somerset. In October 1450, while Parliament was assembling, York went to East Anglia for consultation with his supporter, the Duke of Norfolk, and then declared that it was his intention to reform the government of the realm and in particular rid the body politic of the evil and incompetent influence of such people as Edmund, Duke of Somerset. The point to stress here is that on this occasion, and for the rest of the decade, York's quarrel was not with the King but with his Councillors.

York returned to London on 18 November 1450, accompanied by the Duke of Norfolk and a large following, all armed and wearing York's livery. Other lords summoned to Parliament had brought their retainers with them, so the city was full of armed men, needing only the spark of insurrection to ignite the political powder keg.

Then followed a series of private meetings between Somerset and York, all of which ended in violent quarrels. York did not go so far as to impeach Somerset before Parliament, for he soon came to realize that the King and Queen would support Somerset whatever he or anyone else said or did. There were further riots in the City, including an attempt to capture the Duke of Somerset at Blackfriars, which he evaded by escaping in the barge of the Earl of Devon, though he lost some of his baggage. In early December it was necessary for York, Norfolk and the King to march their forces through the streets, to intimidate the citizens and to execute one of the rioters in Cheapside. This calmed things, but when Parliament was adjourned for Christmas, Somerset received the singular distinction of being named Captain of Calais. York, on the other hand, was sent to stamp out the embers of Cade's revolt in Kent, where he was expected to lose much support and gain unpopularity. This sweep through Kent led to a number of executions and was known locally as 'the harvest of heads'.

Clearly, in spite of his failures abroad, Somerset was now firmly established at Court and he had the ear of the King. Equally clearly, York was not yet ready and possibly not even willing to rebel against the King. His offer to advise the King was therefore spurned, but he would not, or could not, work in harness with the Duke of Somerset. After spending Christmas in London, he withdrew to his strong castle at Ludlow to await the spring and whatever events might follow.

York's argument had now been taken up by his nephew, the Duke of Norfolk, and his hand was strengthened still further when Sir William Oldhall, the Duke's chamberlain and one of his leading retainers, was chosen as Speaker of the House of Commons to replace the murdered William Tresham. Evidence of the growing rift between the King and his most powerful subject was also seen about London, where their supporters put up placards of their armorial bearing in opposition to each other, each party tearing down the other's symbols.

On reconvening in January 1451, Parliament settled down to another long discussion on the Resumption by the crown of all those gifts, offices and estates which the King had given away on the advice of the Duke of Suffolk. The petition of Resumption also named people whom the Commons felt should have no place in state affairs and the name which headed the list was that of Edmund, Duke of Somerset. The petition requested that he and many of his cronies should be banished from Court for life, and deprived of all offices. The King received this petition cautiously, but did nothing about it. This Parliament then came to an abrupt end when Thomas Young, the MP for Bristol, presented a petition requesting that the Duke of York be named heir to the throne. This thoroughly alarmed the Court party. Parliament was dissolved and Thomas Young was sent to the Tower.

* * *

Meanwhile, there were fresh disasters in France. Having regained Normandy in 1450, in 1451 Charles VII sent an army into Aquitaine under the veteran Dunois. The great Gascon lords, the Counts of Foix, Albret and Armagnac, promptly joined him, and the English castles and towns of war went down like ninepins. In June 1451 the city of Bordeaux asked for terms and on Wednesday, 30 June, Dunois entered the city in state, to hoist the lily banner over the gatehouse. The shock wave of this capitulation sent a further tremor through England, for it seemed that the Duchy of Aquitaine, an English possession since the twelfth century, had finally been lost.

Back in England, the open enmity between York and Somerset finally flared into armed conflict in September 1451, though at one stage removed from the main contenders. This arose when York chose to intervene in a quarrel between Thomas Courtenay, Earl of Devon, Somerset's brother-in-law, and another local magnate, Lord Bonville. It gives some idea of the state of the realm when it is realized that when York intervened, the Earl of Devon with a small army was besieging Bonville in the town of Taunton. York marched into Somerset with 2,000 men, a considerable force for the time, while Wiltshire and Somerset echoed to the tramp of private armies.

The Bonville–Devon feud is interesting as an example of public affairs and private loyalties in the middle years of the fifteenth century. Thomas Courtenay was the twelfth Earl of Devon, a title of considerable antiquity, though it had not come to him by direct descent from the Conquest. It had once belonged to the de Redvers family, but their line had died out and the title had been revived for the Courtenays by Edward III in 1335. Thomas Courtenay was not a major magnate but he was rich enough and could support a large affinity. He owned some 40 manors and had an income of some £1,000 a year, a considerable sum at the time. He was also an imperious lord, arrogant and violent, and like all too many of his kind, quick to flout the law's authority and take justice into his own hands.

The Bonvilles were less elevated. The family were gentlefolk and could number various knights among their ancestors, but they were of no particular importance, even in local affairs, though William Bonville, the present head of the family, had served in France and been knighted by Henry V.

The cause of their quarrel can be traced to the incompetence of Henry VI who, in 1437, had appointed Bonville to the office of Royal Steward for Cornwall. In 1441, however, the King appointed Courtenay 'Steward of the Duchy of Cornwall', and it was some time before the council realized that the King had given a valuable appointment to two different men. They therefore instructed Courtenay not to proceed with his office, pending some clarification of the position, but the Earl of Devon was not going to hold his hand because of some administrative blunder or in the interests of a mere knight. His partisans were soon in conflict with those of Bonville, and before long Cornwall and Devon were experiencing a form of guerrilla warfare.

In July 1444 Bonville was sent away to Gascony, which brought some peace to the troubled counties, but enabled Courtenay to get his hands on the levers of power. Bonville remained in Gascony until 1448 and in 1449 was summoned to Parliament to become Lord Bonville, a useful jump in status. To maintain his new rank he needed some extra money, and his position as the Steward for Cornwall would have supplied the needed funds.

Bonville was close to Suffolk and to the Court party, so naturally, Devon, seeking support, looked to the Duke of York for his 'good lordship' in their long standing dispute over the stewardship. When York came back to England in 1450, the Earl of Devon decided to take advantage of the times and attack Bonville with his own retainers, mustering some 3,000 men to besiege Bonville at Taunton.

The Courtenay–Bonville feud was no storm in a teacup. It involved senior magnates of the realm and the armies of their expanding affinities. In the course of his campaign, the Earl of Devon led an army across Somerset, fought with the Earl of Wiltshire near Bath, and then besieged Lord Bonville in Taunton Castle, ignoring all attempts and mediation and orders from the Court. York then appeared in arms at Taunton Castle and finally brought the parties to terms, but the fabric of law and order had been severely shaken. Matters worsened when the King refused to accept that York's intervention at Taunton had been solely in the interests of law and order. The King chose to view his actions as evidence that York was seeking to provoke the local magnate, Edmund, Duke of Somerset, which may indeed have been the case. The King summoned all the parties in the Courtenay–Bonville affair to his High Court of Judgment at Coventry, after which several of the participants, including Lord Bonville, were fined or given terms of imprisonment, though York, spared for the moment, withdrew again to Ludlow.

In the event, Devon's insurgency did him no great harm. He was sacked as Commissioner for the Justices of the Peace in Devon and Cornwall in November 1451, which in the circumstances is hardly surprising, and as we shall see, he changed sides later, abandoning York for what he felt to be the more advantageous support of Somerset. Even so, it is worth pointing out that but for the King's incompetence in granting the same office to two men, this dispute in the West Country need never have arisen.

* * *

In February 1452 York issued a declaration from Ludlow, declaring his complete loyalty to the King, offering to swear an oath of loyalty on holy relics if his simple word was not enough, but adding that the constant slanders against him were made by his 'enemies, adversaries and ill-wishers': in other words, by the Duke of Somerset and his cronies at Court. His petition was yet another attempt to demonstrate, on the one hand, his loyalty to the King and on the other, his wish to free the King of corrupt advice and influence.

The King made no reply to this appeal and York then took the field. He wrote to all the towns and counties in his wide domains, asking for their help with arms, men and money for a necessary confrontation with the Duke of Somerset. York then marched for London, gathering men as he advanced, enlisting the support of the Earl of Devon and Lord Cobham, who brought their retinues to serve under his banner.

Copies of York's letters soon reached the King. Henry, or more probably the Queen, Buckingham and Somerset, reacted by summoning the loyal forces of the realm to assemble in force at Blackheath. This summons also declared York a rebel and Somerset a loyal supporter of the King. The Royal army marched out of London on 16 February 1452, but after circling north as far as Northampton it returned to discover York's army entrenched on Dartford Heath, drawn up in battle array with York's men in the centre, the Earl of Devon's men on one flank and Lord Cobham's on the other, all with banners displayed. Several supply ships, full of stores and munitions, waited on the River Thames nearby, and the scene was set for a large and bloody encounter.

According to the Abbot of St Albans, one of the last of the monkish chroniclers, the King's army was much stronger than York's, but both men were reluctant to open hostilities. After a few days of confrontation and parley, a deputation of lords prevailed on York to submit to the King and swear the oath of allegiance which he had already offered to swear in January. York insisted that if he submitted to the King, Somerset should be placed in custody until York's charges were considered before Parliament. This proposal was discussed by a committee, which included the Bishops of Winchester and Ely, and two of York's relatives, Richard Neville, Earl of Salisbury, and his son, another Richard, the Earl of Warwick, and the committee eventually conceded all York's demands.

York then came out of his camp under safe conduct, submitted to the King, and presented a long list of his grievances against Somerset. In this petition, York poured out complaints which had clearly been festering for years. They ranged from Somerset's incompetence in France to his corrupt handling of the King's affairs, his constant slanders of the Duke of York, and his efforts to exclude York from the Royal Councils. Most of these charges were patently true and justified.

The King heard them patiently, then flatly rejected them, and when York entered the King's tent, having disbanded his army, he found Somerset and the King in close conference. Clearly, York had been tricked. Virtually under arrest, York was then taken to St Paul's in London, where he was obliged to swear a most solemn oath that he would never again summon an army against the King nor fail to answer the King's command. He was then allowed to go back to Ludlow, his tail between his legs.

If the King and his adherents posed a problem for York, they were no less perplexed over what to do with him. What we have here, however it was fudged at the time, was a growing confrontation by two magnates of the realm, for the control of the King, his Council, and the Royal revenues. In appearing in arms against the King, York was guilty of high treason, and they might well have wanted to cut off his head, but it was not as easy as that. York *was* the heir-apparent; he was a great lord and he had many supporters, even if not all had yet declared themselves. Somerset was well aware that he must not go too far, and for the moment he was content to see York disgraced and humiliated and banished to his estates.

A general pardon was issued to all those taking part in the field of Dartford, and while York smouldered on his estates, attention switched back again to Gascony.

The Gascons did not find the rule of the French King very much to their liking. The King of England had bought their wine and left them alone, but Charles VII appointed officers from the north of France to rule in Aquitaine, and they set about refashioning the old duchy to suit the French King's fancy. Before many months had passed, the Gascons were in touch with England and on 17 October 1452, John Talbot, Earl of

Shrewsbury, landed again in the Medoc. Bordeaux opened its gates and rang its bells when he appeared before the walls three days later, and as fresh contingents sailed out from England and more towns along the Dordogne and Garonne turned out the French and hoisted the cross of St George, it seemed that the English could look for a renewal of their successes in the realm of France. King Charles, however, was mustering his armies along the Loire, and in the spring of 1453 they came marching south.

*   *   *

In July 1452 the King set out on another Royal progress through the south-west and the Welsh Marches, attempting to restore order to his turbulent nation, hanging a number of men who had been arrested in the recent upheavals and sentencing others to heavy fines or terms of imprisonment. This progress included a visit to Ludlow, but here the King stayed not with his cousin York in the castle, but at the college of Carmelite friars in the town centre, a significant slight to his most distinguished subject.

The King was back in the south for Christmas 1452, which he spent in his palace at Greenwich. In the course of the festivities, he knighted his two young half-brothers, Edmund and Jasper Tudor, appointing them Earls of Richmond and Pembroke respectively, and it was probably here that Queen Margaret at last conceived a child. In February 1453 the King set out on another Royal progress, the last of his reign, returning for the new session of Parliament, which opened at Reading in March 1453.

The last three years had seen a gradual polarization of political affairs in England, for when York first returned from Ireland in 1450 and then marched on London in 1452, he broke the fragile shell of political accord that had so far protected King Henry. It is one thing to be ill-advised, and perhaps manipulated by subtle and devious courtiers; it is quite another to support such people when their corruption and incompetence is common currency. The magnates and people of England were now well aware of the issues which divided York and Somerset, and on the whole their sympathies were with York, unless of course they were part of Somerset's affinity and taking advantage of the weak King's bounty.

York lacked political subtlety. If provoked, he would usually over-react, and his oft-repeated words of loyalty were overshadowed by the fact that he had now risen twice against the King – however much he claimed to be only protesting against Somerset. Throughout the kingdom, rebels and rioters were using York's arguments to justify their actions. It remains an open question as to whether York was behind any of the public unrest, but on balance the answer is probably not. The English were lawless enough without any encouragement from the noble Duke of York.

York returned from Ireland because his enemy Somerset had come back from Calais and, in spite of having lost Normandy, was being openly fêted at Court. This must have driven York to fury, and since the two men were open enemies, he must have wondered how much blame was, even then, being shifted from Somerset's shoulders on to his. Cade's rebellion was simply his excuse for a return; the reason was his growing insecurity as his enemies gathered around the King.

Thereafter, for the rest of the decade, the main thrust of the political argument in England was not about who wore the crown, but between Somerset and York for control of public affairs. For York, the matter was pressing because, while Somerset had been reimbursed for his expenditure in France, the House of York had been reduced to virtual penury. Most of York's income was now devoted to paying off the debts incurred in France, and while Somerset was in power York stood little chance of reimbursement. The continuing campaign against York was also given a little momentum when Sir William Oldhall, York's Chamberlain, who had been Speaker of the House of Commons in the last Parliament, was attainted for treason, for alleged complicity in Cade's rising of 1450 and in York's march to Dartford in 1452.

Meanwhile, matters were coming to a head in France. Fresh reinforcements had been put together in early 1453 and sent out to join Talbot under the command of his son, Lord d'Lisle. So encouraged was Parliament by the return of the Gascon allegiance that it voted a subsidy to pay for a force of 20,000 archers raised for six months' service. The money for the archers was voted, the tax gatherers went out and the rest of the summer of 1453 passed quite pleasantly for King Henry. Queen Margaret was now pregnant and there were prospects of an heir. His favourites were again in power and his worry concerning York had been calmed. Then the terrible news arrived from Castillon and his whole world fell apart.

CHAPTER FIVE

THE OUTBREAK OF WAR (1453–55)

First shall war unpeople this my realm,
Ay, and their colours – oft borne in France,
And now in England, to our heart's great sorrow –
Shall be my winding sheet

HENRY VI

Henry VI was on a progress through his kingdom when the news of the defeat at Castillon arrived from France. Royal progresses were usually undertaken to administer justice, to settle disputes, and to impress on the local lords and justices that the King's writ and the common law took precedence over local pressures and influence. The reason for this particular progress was to head off a potential conflict in the ever-tense relationship between two of his Border families, the Nevilles and the Percies. The two families had been at loggerheads for generations, so the King could only have hoped to paper over the cracks and enforce a temporary peace.

The Nevilles and the Percies had held lands along the Scottish border for centuries, competing for the influential and profitable posts of Warden of the East and West March, which most sovereigns, for the sake of peace and quiet, usually shared between them. In recent years though, the balance of power in the north had slipped towards the Nevilles, who had gained fresh advantages through marriage.

To trace this advantage, we must go back a little. Ralph Neville, first Earl of Westmorland, had been married to Margaret Stafford, and from this marriage came the line of the Earls of Westmorland. Ralph had then married Joan Beaufort, daughter of John of Gaunt. He thereby gained both the patronage of her brother, Cardinal Beaufort, and Joan's rich dower lands in Yorkshire. Their son, another Richard, became Earl of Salisbury by his marriage to Alice Montacute, daughter of Thomas Montacute, Earl of Salisbury, who had been killed at the siege of Orléans in 1428. The Nevilles knew all about the benefits of matrimony, for all Salisbury's brothers and sisters married well, the men taking wives from the baronies of Abergavenny, Fauconberg and Latimer, the sisters marrying the Dukes of York, Norfolk and Buckingham. Another brother, Robert, entered the Church, where he was rapidly elevated to the powerful see of the prince–bishops of Durham.

The policy of marrying well continued with Salisbury's son, another Richard, who married Anne, daughter of Richard Beauchamp, Earl of Warwick, sometime tutor to Henry VI. With her hand, young Richard acquired the title to the Earldom of Warwick and it is as 'Warwick the Kingmaker' that this member of the family has come down in history. The important point is that the Nevilles, at this time, were supporters of the Lancaster dynasty. They had sided with the King against York in 1450–52, and the senior branch of the family, the Westmorlands, remained partisans of Lancaster even after the wars began, thus splitting the Neville clan in two.

The King knew all this. He should also have remembered that however important it was to have a balance of power in the north, the Neville's continued support depended either on his opposition to their ancestral rivals, the Percies, or at the very least, on his even-handed treatment of both families. King Henry, however, was a fool.

The Percies could also forge marriage alliances, even with their rivals. Henry Percy, the second Earl of Northumberland and the son of Harry Hotspur, had married Eleanor, the Earl of Salisbury's sister. As we shall see, the Somersets and Nevilles were also related by marriage, though little good came of it, and family ties proved no bar to strife.

The King's attention was drawn to the north in 1453 by an outbreak of lawlessness between two of the younger sons of these families, Thomas Percy, Lord Egremont, the Earl's second son, and Sir John Neville, a scion of the rival House. Frequent commands to cease disturbing the King's peace were ignored, and having formed a commission of 'oyer and terminer', the King proposed to ride north and settle the matter in person. However, before he left Reading, another and more serious problem arose in the west, also concerning the Nevilles and involving Salisbury's son, Richard Neville, Earl of Warwick, and Edmund, Duke of Somerset, the King's favourite. The matter was one of inheritance and the circumstances are complicated, but since they present a useful portrait of fifteenth-century family entanglements, they are worth unravelling.

Richard Beauchamp, the deceased Earl of Warwick, Henry VI's old tutor, had married twice. His first wife was Lady Elizabeth Berkeley, by whom he had a daughter, Eleanor, and Lady Eleanor had married Edmund, Duke of Somerset. Soon afterwards, Elizabeth Berkeley died. Beauchamp then married Isabel Despenser, widow of the Earl of Worcester, by whom he had another daughter, Anne. This lady, Anne, was now married to the present Earl of Warwick, Richard Neville (the Kingmaker). The present dispute arose over Isabel Despenser's lands which had been divided, half going to her daughter, Warwick's wife Anne, half to George Neville, Isabel's grandson by her first husband, the Earl of Worcester. George was still a minor and a Royal ward, but Warwick had acquired the wardship in 1450, and thus gained control of all the Despenser lands.

However, it will be recalled from the previous chapter that in 1451 the Parliamentary Acts of Resumption reclaimed any wardships for the king. Although Richard Neville remained in physical possession of the Despenser lands, the Right of Ward reverted to the king, and in June 1453 George Neville's wardship – which included the right to half the Despenser lands – was granted to Edmund Somerset. Somerset then demanded that Warwick hand over the Despenser lands, which included the town and castle of Cardiff and large areas of Glamorgan. Warwick flatly refused. He then garrisoned Cardiff Castle and prepared to hold the Despenser lands against Somerset by force of arms.

At the end of July 1453 Henry called a Council at his palace at Sheen, after which he ordered Warwick to hand the castle and lands over to Somerset. This was hardly an impartial judgement, for Somerset had been present at the council, while Warwick had not even been invited to state his case. As the above account makes clear, Somerset had no right whatsoever to the Despenser lands, and only obtained his leverage against Warwick because the King, not for the first time, had set these two lords in contention. If the King had deliberately intended to upset the Neville clan, he could hardly have chosen a more obvious way of doing so.

The effect of this decision was to drive the Nevilles into the affinity of York, while the Percies naturally joined that of Somerset. With Warwick in arms in the west, the King suddenly abandoned the idea of a visit to the north and decided to ride into Wales and dislodge Warwick from Cardiff. By early August he was at the royal hunting lodge at Clarendon in

Wiltshire, close to the city of Salisbury. There, some time in the first week of August, he received the catastrophic news that Talbot had been defeated and killed at Castillon. Such news might have stunned a stronger spirit, but the effect on King Henry was disastrous: he went mad and remained that way for the next year and a half.

Henry's madness did not assume any violent form. He seems to have suffered a total mental collapse, withdrawing completely from the world, unable to speak or hear, understand what he was doing, or what was going on about him. Modern psychiatric opinion concludes his illness to have been a depressive stupor or some form of recurrent schizophrenia. Given the King's impressionable nature, his vagueness, his poor judgement and his inability to make or stand by his decisions, all of which indicate a man without strong mental reserves, this collapse is hardly to be wondered at. Henry's reign had been anything but tranquil, and a relentless succession of problems, conflicts and disasters, even if most of them were his own fault, indicates that some form of nervous breakdown must have been inevitable sooner or later. It could hardly have occurred at a worse time.

The onset of the King's illness was compounded by the fact that the doctors of the day had no idea how to treat him, and their suggested remedies could not have helped. While the rest of the Court and kingdom mourned the defeat and considered the effects of Castillon, the Royal physicians plied the King with purges, hot baths, leeches, bleedings, potions and emetics. None of them had the slightest effect. The King was beyond all help and his kingdom was effectively leaderless. His Council ruled in the King's name and it lacked any other authority.

This situation flung the whole responsibility for the management of the realm on to the Royal Council. It tried to give effect to measures already decided by issuing writs against Lord Egremont and Sir John Neville, ordering them to stop brawling. These orders were ignored. The archers originally destined for Gascony were sent to reinforce the garrisons of the Calais pale, where a French assault was awaited daily. Meanwhile, the fragile rule of law in England fell apart.

On 24 August 1453 the quarrel between the Nevilles and the Percies developed into open warfare when a 700-strong force of men-at-arms in the Percy livery fell upon a party of Nevilles, including the Earl of Salisbury, his wife and sons, returning from a wedding between Thomas Neville, Salisbury's second son, and Matilda, niece and heiress of Ralph, Lord Cromwell. The wedding party was armed (another indication of the state of affairs) and a battle raged across the Yorkshire Moors for several hours, with a number of people being killed and many wounded, while the Neville ladies rode for shelter at the manor of Sheriff Hutton.

As if this were not enough, the Percies were involved in another dispute which also concerned Lord Egremont and Henry Holland, Duke of Exeter, a young man with some claim to the throne by his descent from a daughter of John of Gaunt. Both men had quarrels with Lord Cromwell, Salisbury's new brother-in-law, so Egremont and Exeter decided to combine their forces for a struggle against Cromwell and the Neville affinity in the north.

By October 1453 the kingdom was rapidly slipping into chaos, although the King's illness was a well-kept secret. The Royal Council decided that some leader must be found to give clear directions to the ship of state, and given the King's known preference, the obvious choice was the Duke of Somerset, who had the support of the Queen. Knowing that York and Somerset could not work together, the Council decided to avoid any conflict by simply not inviting York to meetings. However, a small group of bishops, supported by the Earl of Worcester and the Prior of the Order of St John, sent a message to the Duke of York at Ludlow, urging him to attend the Council. This message was made more urgent by the fact that on 13 October 1453, Queen Margaret had given birth to a son, Edward. This child displaced York from his role as heir-presumptive to the throne and made him of equal status with the Duke of Somerset. If Somerset and the Queen had their way, life would now become very difficult for the Duke of York. The Duke would also have noted that one of the young Prince's godparents was his rival, Edmund Somerset, who was widely rumoured to be the baby's father.

At this point, it is useful to look at the peerage of England in the middle years of the fifteenth century. The House of Lords did not then exist, though a man became a lord by being summoned to attend the king in Parliament. The lords attending were composed of peers and bishops, and at the start of the century the bishops were in the majority. More peerages had since been created and by 1436 there were 51 peers in England and about 2,000 armigerous gentry, knights, squires and 'gentlemen of coat armour', who together made up the aristocracy. The lords consisted of about 100 peers, lay and ecclesiastic, but as a rule only about 30 or 40 bothered to attend a Parliament. Their power rested with the Royal Councils, though (at least in theory) when Parliament was sitting, *all* the peers replaced the Royal Council with a 'Great Council', which served as the King's advisers while Parliament was in session.

The Royal Council – best imagined as the equivalent of the modern Cabinet – consisted of about 20 peers, lay and ecclesiastic, who usually met in the Star Chamber at Westminster. The Members of the Council could and did change, but all the great lords considered they had a right to be included, and the great officers of state, the Chancellor, the Treasurer, the Keeper of the Privy Seal and the Chamberlain, were there by virtue of their office as well as by right of rank. The Council was there to advise the King, not merely to rubber-stamp his whims and actions, but King Henry was always prey to his cronies. He was, therefore, continually at odds with at least part of his Council for making decisions which he was to regret and of which they were often unaware. Ideally, the Council would debate matters and present solutions to the King for his approval, and in practice most Council meetings took place without the presence of the King.

Duly advised of the situation concerning the King, York arrived in London on 12 November 1453, accompanied by his eldest son, Edward, Earl of March, then aged 12, and a large retinue. His mood at the Council was far from conciliatory and his wife's nephew, the Duke of Norfolk, once again raised the question of Somerset's culpability for the loss of Normandy. York also claimed, with good reason, that he had been deliberately kept from his rightful role in the affairs of state by a conspiracy between Somerset and the Queen, and that other peers had been warned not to associate with him. York, therefore, required the Council to issue a statement declaring that all men were free to meet with him or serve him. Only Somerset and his ally, Lord Beaumont, abstained from signing this statement. The union of York and Norfolk was clearly powerful enough to make the Council act against Somerset, who was committed to the Tower on 23 November 1453, pending specific charges which would be laid before Parliament not later than January 1454. York had, therefore, gained all he had asked for at Dartford in 1452. While Parliament was assembling, the magnates began to muster their supporters.

The Dukes of York and Norfolk ordered their retainers to come south from their lands in the north-west and East Anglia. Humphrey Stafford, Duke of Buckingham, ordered armour, weapons and badges of the Stafford Knot for the 2,000 men of his affinity who were called to attend him in London. The Duke of Buckingham had a personal affinity of 10 knights and 26 squires, and held manors in 26 counties, so this force of 2,000 armed men is an interesting example of the personal power at the command of one member of the peerage.

Buckingham had so far kept aloof from the disputes between York and

Somerset, but his aid was worth having. In terms of wealth, he was the third magnate of the kingdom after York and Warwick, with an income of more than £4,000 a year.

Somerset, on the other hand, was not rich in land or revenues, which may account both for his avarice towards others in a better position and his need to retain a position at Court and the perquisites that went with it. He had, however, plenty of paid retainers at his command.

From his quarters in the Tower, Edmund Somerset commanded men of his affinity to seek lodgings in the City close by and await his orders. Even Cardinal-Archbishop Kemp, Chancellor of the Realm and Archbishop of Canterbury, was mustering forces. On the political front, Queen Margaret suddenly stepped into the arena, making a claim for the regency of the realm during her husband's illness, with control over all appointments. Meanwhile the Council, and in particular the Duke of Buckingham, who had no wish to see this dispute escalate, were urging the doctors to effect the King's recovery.

Parliament was due to assemble at Reading Abbey on 11 February 1454, before moving to London on the 14th. On 13 February the Great Council, which consisted of all the peers at Parliament, nominated York as the King's Lieutenant, charging him in particular with presiding over the opening of Parliament. Most of the Duke of York's opponents, including Somerset and Northumberland, were not present at this meeting. York duly opened Parliament and took his place at the head of the Council which, in mid-March 1454, passed a Bill to Parliament recognizing the infant Prince Edward as Prince of Wales, Duke of Cornwall, Earl of Chester and heir to the throne.

This Bill again underlines two points. Firstly, that York had no designs on the throne at this time. Secondly, that his quarrel was with the Queen and Somerset, who had kept him from playing his part in government. His loyalty to the King should never have been doubted. The Court party still nursed suspicions that York had a secret agenda concerning the succession to the throne, while York may have suspected that the Queen and Somerset would eventually conspire to bring about his death. Mutual trust had long since fled from the higher councils of state.

Although the facts of the King's illness were by now widely known at Court and in London, and could, indeed, hardly have been concealed for long, no official announcement had been made. The reasons behind York's sudden elevation were, therefore, unknown to the country at large. At the Parliament of Reading, York obtained the release of Sir

William Oldhall and the imprisonment of the new Speaker, Thorpe, who had seized some of York's goods in the previous Parliament. The Commons demanded Thorpe's immediate release, and the judges, in the person of the Chief Justice, Sir John Fortescue, declared that he should be released from Newgate to fulfil his duties in Parliament. The Lords, however, declared that since Thorpe's offence had been committed and himself sent to jail in 'tyme of vacation . . . and not in Parliament tyme', the judgment that Thorpe should remain in prison must stand, 'the privileges of Parliament notwithstanding'. Giving in, the Commons elected a new Speaker, Sir Thomas Charlton, the MP for Middlesex.

In March 1454, Archbishop Kemp died. As Chancellor, he had kept the great Seal of England at the pleasure of the King, and with the King mad and the Chancellor dead, the Royal Seals were unusable. The business of government could not be carried on and when a deputation of lords went to see the King at Windsor, it was unable to break his silence. It became clear that York's powers as Lieutenant would have to be increased.

Two days later, on 27 March 1454, York was appointed Protector of England and Chief Councillor to the King. He was granted a substantial salary of 2,000 marks a year, which he must have found most useful, but his powers were still carefully restricted by Parliament. He could not amend or alter the King's previous decrees; he could not tinker with the rights or property of Queen Margaret or Prince Edward, and the deed noted that only the present circumstances had forced Parliament to make this appointment at all, an appointment which was to be in force only during the King's pleasure. York accepted these conditions but insisted on the addition of an extra codicil: that he had not sought the position. This was a grudging Protectorate on both sides, but the powers it granted were sufficient for York to act.

Somerset was swiftly stripped of his lucrative post as Captain of Calais, which went to the Duke of York, though Somerset's lieutenants, who actually commanded the Calais garrison, were left in their posts for the moment. York's brother-in-law, the Earl of Salisbury, was appointed Chancellor of the Realm, the first layman to hold the post, and Buckingham's half-brother and York's brother-in-law, Thomas Bourchier, became Archbishop of Canterbury and Primate of England. Other lords, including the Earl of Wiltshire, a Court noble, were ordered to raise ships and clear the sea of pirates, and funds were devoted to pay the wages of the Court servants, which had been outstanding for nearly six months. In May, York set out to implement the decisions of King Henry's last Council and settle disputes in the north, where the Egremont–Neville brawls were still continuing. Egremont was now in open alliance with the Duke of Exeter and they were attempting to raise the north against the King, with Exeter even claiming to be the rightful heir of Lancaster. For this, he and his affinity were condemned rightly as traitors. In November 1454, Egremont was brought to battle by Sir Thomas Neville at Stamford Bridge, captured and imprisoned in Middleham Castle before being taken to London and lodged in Newgate gaol. The Duke of Exeter, that half-crazed claimant to the crown, then fled for sanctuary to Westminster, from where he was forcibly removed by the Duke of York's men and sent under guard to Pontefract Castle.

Having settled the troubles in the north, the Protector was back in London by mid-July, where he proceeded with the reorganization of the Royal household. The King's household was severely reduced, most of the horses being sold off and many servants dismissed: the number of household knights falling from 300 to 24, though the Queen and Prince Edward, now aged six months, were allowed their full establishment of servants and guards. The King's resources could not afford to maintain a large Court, and York seemed determined to reduce the expenses of government before he could be accused of failing to do so. The imprisoned Somerset remained a problem because although removed from the post of Captain of Calais, he refused to accept his dismissal, claiming he held his post from the King alone. His Lieutenants, Lord Rivers and Lord Welles, continued to hold Calais in his name and refused to admit York's officers.

York was still in command of King and kingdom at Christmas 1454 when the King began to recover his wits. His recovery was gradual and his memory uncertain. When told of the birth of Prince Edward, he remarked that the Prince 'must have been fathered by the Holy Ghost' as he had no recollection of doing so, a remark which caused comment and hilarity all over Europe, and led to rumours that the Prince's real father was the Duke of Somerset.

York's last Council decision was taken on 30 December 1454. A month later, on 3 February 1455, the King sealed an order removing the Duke of Exeter from Pontefract to softer quarters in the castle at Wallingford. This can only have been done to spite and denigrate the Duke of York, since Exeter was a declared traitor to the King. Somerset was released from the Tower by 4 February 1455 and on 4 March, King Henry presided over a meeting of the Royal Council at Greenwich, where he proceeded to undo or reverse all the decisions of the Protector.

He took back the Captaincy of Calais from York and returned it to Somerset, 'Our faithful liegeman', binding both men over to keep the peace. He dismissed the Earl of Salisbury from the post of Chancellor and appointed the new Archbishop of Canterbury, Thomas Bourchier, probably to ensure the support of the Duke of Buckingham. A week later York's ally, the Earl of Worcester, John Tiptoft, was replaced as Treasurer by the courtier Earl of Wiltshire, who owed his title to the Queen's favour. The King was making it more than clear where his sympathies and interests lay, and in doing so made enemies unnecessarily. By uniting York and the Nevilles, he sealed an alliance against Somerset and eventually his own House. All this was done by the end of March 1455. The first battle in what history came to call the Wars of the Roses took place just six weeks later.

* * *

Following the Royal Council in March 1455, the Duke of York, the Earl of Salisbury, and the young Earl of Warwick, now aged 25, left London with their retinues and returned to their estates in the north and west. On 21 April a council writ was issued, calling Parliament to assemble on 21 May at Leicester, a favourite Lancastrian stronghold. The main item on the agenda was 'to discuss the safety of the King'. This was seen by York and his adherents as a repeat of the humiliations forced upon the Duke in 1452 – a view confirmed when York and Salisbury were not summoned to the Royal Council which called the Parliament, and were ordered to disband their retinues on pain of treason.

Moreover, it was soon clear that this was to be no normal Parliament. There was no previous election of Members among the burghers or the knights of the shires, and the writs of summons only went out to a carefully selected group of York and Neville enemies, all avowed supporters of Somerset, telling them to bring all their retainers, fully armed, to the Parliament. The Duke of York, perhaps with good reason, sensed the beginnings of a trap. These were the sort of proceedings which had led to the arrest and sudden death of Humphrey, Duke of Gloucester, at Bury St Edmunds eight years before. York, Salisbury and Warwick mustered their affinities and began to march on London.

King Henry left London for Leicester on 21 May, the day when Parliament was to meet, but he had gone no distance from the city before he and his Chancellor were handed a message from York, Salisbury and the other Yorkist lords, complaining that they had been excluded from the

Council of 21 April and that the forthcoming Parliament at Leicester was designed to threaten and humiliate them. This allegation was followed by the demand that the King should dismiss the traitors about him – which meant the Duke of Somerset – and call a truce and representative council. If the King would do that, then they would disband their followers. It should be noted that York's party now included Lord Bonville, while the King's party contained York's former ally, the Earl of Devon.

While the King and his council were digesting York's message, the Yorkists – as we can now call them – were advancing to Ware, in Hertfordshire. Their force amounted to some 3,000 men, all members of their direct affinities, all fully armed and wearing livery. From Ware, York sent his personal cleric and confessor, William Willifleet, with another message to the King who had now arrived at Watford. This restated York's complete loyalty to the King but repeated his demands for justice and the removal of Somerset. York's army laid siege to the town of St Albans, which lies astride the main road to the north. They took up positions in the fields east of St Albans, around dawn on the morning of 22 May 1455.

Back in Watford, the King was dithering. Somerset, who as Constable of England was in command of the royal forces, proposed digging in where they were at Watford and waiting out events. This was not the advice Henry wanted, so the King promptly dismissed Somerset from office and appointed the Duke of Buckingham as Constable. Buckingham then led the Royal army out towards St Albans, where they arrived at about 9 o'clock on the morning of 22 May 1455, a few hours after the Yorkists.

The composition of these armies is worth a closer look. Charles VII of France had realized the need for a paid professional army as long ago as the 1440s, and it was his *gens d'ordonnance* and the skilled artillery of Jean Bureau which had blasted the English armies out of France. The English King was without a paid, professional army of any kind, though he was normally responsible for paying the gunners and miners who made up an increasingly important part of his army. The rest of the force was composed of archers and men-at-arms raised by his lords from their affinities, the difference being that everyone, from mailed and mounted lord to foot-slogging archer, expected to be paid.

The unwieldy feudal levy had not been called out in either country for decades, but the King of England was dependent on his barons for raising and commanding his armies. Other than the garrison at Calais, the gunners in the Tower and some palace guards, the King of England had no soldiers at all, so the raising and retaining of large armed retainers by his magnates had to be tolerated, for in times of war these retainers combined to become the Royal army.

The two armies, now set on a collision course at St Albans, were typical of the forces that the great magnates of England could put in the field. The armies which fought the battles of the Wars of the Roses comprised well-paid, professional soldiers in the affinity of some great lord. Heavily armed and, in the case of the gentlemen and men-at-arms, heavily armoured, they fought for pay and to keep their lord's protection and 'good lordship'. The lords and knights wore complete plate armour, which was extremely expensive but virtually impervious to arrows and crossbow bolts, though the latest steel crossbows could and did penetrate plate armour at close range. The armour was, therefore, increasingly sloped and fluted to offer a glancing surface to any missile.

Archers were still the dominant force in the English army; indeed they had increased their percentage compared with men-at-arms from about six to one at Agincourt in 1415, to about ten to one in the baronial retinues of 1455. Their arrows could stop any cavalry charge, so most battles were fought on foot, though all who could afford a horse rode to the encounter. At St Albans and later in the wars, since both sides had archers, the effect of the arrow storm which had ravaged the armies of France was largely nullified. Both sides now relied on field artillery to 'soften up' the other side before the hand-to-hand encounter. Hand-guns, like the hackbut, a primitive form of harquebus, were in use on the Continent by 1450, especially among castle garrisons, but these weapons were still too unwieldy for use in the field. The artillery was mainly used for the defence of castles or in sieges, though light culverins (long cannon) were now being trundled along behind the marching foot, and had recently defeated Talbot's army at Castillon.

The tactics might vary slightly but the typical strategy for a battle was to draw up the armies in opposing lines, arranged in three divisions, or battles – centre, left and right – which on the march would be the vaward (or vanguard), the centre and the rearguard, each commanded by a great lord. The word 'battle' is the forerunner of the modern 'battalion'. These lords might remain mounted, the better to view the field or get about, but most would dismount for the actual onslaught, when they were expected to play their part in the hand-to-hand fighting.

The battle would commence with an artillery duel and an exchange of arrows and crossbow bolts, after which the dismounted men-at-arms and knights would advance under a forest of banners and lay into each other with sword, axe, mace, battleaxe and a variety of bludgeoning weapons, helped by the foot-soldiers armed with bills and halberds, and the archers loosing arrows at close range into the opposing line. The archers could also join in the fighting with swords and daggers or their own favourite battering weapon, the lead-shod mallet, or maul. Shields were no longer carried by the men-at-arms, though the archers in defence often employed a large shield, or *pavaise*, which could be planted in the ground to afford some protection from enemy arrows and crossbow bolts.

The common people had kept out of the struggles so far and continued to do so whenever possible. The lords' retinues had expanded rapidly in recent months, for as more and more professional soldiers returned to England after Castillon, they were quickly snapped up by the lords' recruiting officers. Every lord was anxious to secure experienced men 'of the war of France', for however primitive the actual encounter might be, men were aware that war was an art where good leadership, fighting skills, experience, and a tactical sense were essential.

Among the lords present at St Albans for the House of Lancaster, were: the Dukes of Somerset and Buckingham, Edmund Tudor, Earl of Richmond, and the Earls of Northumberland, Wiltshire and Devon; lesser lords included Lords Clifford and Dudley. The eldest sons of Somerset and Buckingham were also present. With the Duke of York were the Earls of Warwick and Salisbury, and Viscount Bourchier. The King had the greater number of lords, but York had the greater number of fighting men, though the Duke of Norfolk had not yet arrived with his forces from East Anglia. Estimates vary, but the King probably had around 3,000 men, and York somewhat more.

Buckingham had assumed from York's repeated declaration of loyalty that York would not face the Royal Banner in the field, for to do so would be treason. Henry's army entered St Albans and made its way over the bridge across the River Ver and up the hill of Holywell Street, past the great abbey of St Alban, England's protomartyr, into the wide market-place of St Peter Street. Here the army halted and displayed its great square banners, while barricading the side-streets with carts and market stalls. The Yorkist army had now deployed for battle in the Key Field, east of the town, and the critical moment had arrived. Heralds went to and fro with various demands, but when negotiations broke down around 10 o'clock in the morning, the Yorkist army advanced on the town.

John Whethamstede, Abbot of St Albans, observed the battle from the tower of the abbey church and has left a record of the encounter. The centre of St Albans has changed very little in the last 500 years and it is easy to work out what happened where, for the first Battle of St Albans was hardly a battle at all: it was a brief, short-tempered street fight, fought out by archers plying their bows at short range, and by heavily armoured men on foot, hacking at each other with sword and axe, mace and pole-axe. The bulk of the action took place in the market-place, St Peter Street, or in the side-streets to the east of it and the whole affair cannot have lasted more than half an hour.

Battle commenced when Warwick led his contingent through the gardens east of St Peter Street and attacked the barriers blocking the side-streets. Here they were stoutly resisted and checked for a while, until the King's forces, assembled behind the barricades in St Peter Street, began to suffer from arrows flying over the roof-tops into their close-packed ranks – one of these arrows may have wounded the King. Checked in the streets, Warwick's men began to break into the houses on either side and climb over the garden walls into the houses along St Peter Street, where their archers had a large target to loose arrows into at close range.

Flights of arrows streaked across the tree-lined market-place, and as the King's front crumbled, heavily armoured men crashed through the flimsy barricade of carts and stalls and lumbered towards each other, a fierce mêlée breaking out in the square as the two forces clashed.

The great square banners and emblazoned surcoats of the lords made for easy identification of the more obvious targets. As more of Warwick's men began to flood into the market-place, certain of the King's men were singled out for attack. The Duke of Somerset was bludgeoned to death outside the Castle Tavern and both the Earl of Northumberland and Thomas, Lord Clifford, were pinpointed and cut down by their Neville enemies. King Henry, standing under his banner in the centre of the market-place, was slightly wounded in the neck, and his standard-bearer flung down the Royal banner and deserted him. Buckingham and the Earl of Wiltshire fled for sanctuary into the precincts of the abbey, where Wiltshire promptly threw off his armour and made his escape through the gardens; but Buckingham was forced from shelter by York and taken prisoner. The rest of the Lancastrian lords fled and took horse for London as their army collapsed. In an hour it was all over. The King's men were fleeing across the Hertfordshire countryside, the townspeople and monks were emerging cautiously from their hiding-places, and York's army was contemplating the uncertain outcome of its victory.

CHAPTER SIX

THE RISE OF YORK (1455–60)

From Ireland thus comes York to claim his right,
And pluck the crown from feeble Henry's head:
Ring, bells, aloud; burn, bonfires, clear and bright;
To entertain England's lawful king.

HENRY VI

When the last of the barricades blocking the streets came down after the first Battle of St Albans, more and more Yorkist knights, men-at-arms and archers, came spilling into the market-square, thronging the narrow alleys off St Peter Street. There was little jubilation. There were too many unpleasant sights littering St Peter Street. 'Here you saw a man with his brains dashed out,' wrote Abbot Whethamstede. 'Here one with a broken arm, another with his throat cut, a fourth with a pierced chest...the whole street was full of corpses.' It was no light matter to take up arms against your king, and King Henry was there too, sitting on the ground by his fallen banner, bleeding from an arrow wound in the neck.

After that sight, the main feeling among the ranks of the Yorkist army was one of shock. York was sent for and came hurrying up with Warwick at his heels. The Duke and the Earl fell on their knees before the King, and a surgeon was summoned to staunch his wound, which fortunately seemed to be slight. The wound was dressed in the house of a tanner, and the King was then led respectfully downhill, through the silent ranks of the soldiery to the Abbey of St Albans. There the victors and vanquished spent the night, while Masses were said for the souls of the dead, who numbered no more than 60.

Henry's army had scattered far and wide across the countryside, though there was no pursuit. Most of the King's supporters simply returned to their estates and kept their heads down. One of these was the King's standard-bearer, Sir Philip Wentworth, who had abandoned the King and his charge at St Albans. According to Paston, 'Sir Philip Wentworth was in the field and bore the King's Standard but cast it down and fled; my Lord of Norfolk saith he should be hanged therefore and so he is worthy. He is in Suffolk now and dares not come about the King.' Norfolk's comment is curious, for he was a Yorkist and took no direct part in the street fight at St Albans, though his herald was there and joined in the negotiations between the factions before the fighting started.

Abbot Whethamstede of St Albans had watched the battle from the abbey tower and afterwards he received the Duke and his followers with as much Christian charity as his Lancastrian sympathies would allow. There was aid for the wounded and unction for the dying. Apart from Somerset, the loss among the nobility had been small but included some particular enemies of the Nevilles. Henry Percy, the second Earl of Northumberland, and Thomas, Lord Clifford, another Border magnate from Westmorland, were among the slain. Like Edmund Somerset, both these lords had sons to succeed them and carry on their quarrel. Among the wounded were the Duke of Buckingham, the Earl of Devon, York's former ally, and Somerset's son, the Earl of Dorset.

On the following day, York, Warwick and Salisbury led King Henry back to the capital. Once in the City they paraded their forces through the streets on the way to the Tower, taking care to show the King every obvious mark of respect, an indication to the citizens that in spite of recent events they were not and never had been traitors and rebels. The Duke of York was particularly keen to make this point, for not three years before, in St Paul's Cathedral in this very city, he had sworn a most solemn oath not to instigate a rising against the King's Majesty. If appearing in arms, fighting a battle and killing some of the King's loyal supporters was not a rising, a rebellion, and by that count, treason, it is hard to think what is.

However, the sight of the King chatting easily with his foes seemed to calm the citizens. People soon came to accept York's claim – one he had made before – that he and his party came not to seize the throne but to defend it, the country and the King against the influence of unworthy and corrupt advisers. On the following Sunday, the King formally wore his crown in St Paul's, where, once seated on his throne, he insisted on receiving it directly from the hands of the Duke of York.

Even with this achieved, York was not at ease. At the next session of Parliament at Westminster in July, a session to which the Yorkists went 'daily down the Thames, their barges filled with armed men,' he introduced an Act offering Royal pardons to all those who had fought at St Albans, while reaffirming their loyalty to the King. At the end of the month came a general amnesty, one embracing even old Duke Humphrey of Gloucester, stating 'he had lived and died a true liege'. With this act passed and his legal position assured, York proceeded to garner the victor's due – the spoils.

In November 1455 York became Protector of the Realm again, for the King was slipping into another bout of deep depression, perhaps induced by the shock of his slight wound at St Albans. Warwick took up the lucrative post of Captain of Calais. York and his party also proceeded with a further round of Resumptions, retrieving more of the King's possessions from his greedy Councillors and henchmen. A firm hand was needed, for law and order had broken down in many parts of England, especially in Devon, where Lord Bonville and the Earl of Devon were at each other's throats again.

Even so, the opposition was not silent, especially from the lords. In the face of the King's growing inability to rule, the Lancastrian interests had come more and more into the control of his Queen, Margaret of Anjou, who was now the centre of a large Court party, whose members were cemented together by their implacable hostility to the House of York. Chief among these were the new Duke of Somerset, Henry Beaufort, John, the new Lord Clifford, and Henry, third Earl of Northumberland. All these men were young, hot-blooded and vengeful, eager to settle accounts with their fathers' enemies.

By November 1455, York was signing decrees as Protector and Defender of the Realm, though, as in 1453, he was very careful to act only with the agreement of the Council. This was not sufficient to keep him in power. Early in February 1456 York heard that he was to be dismissed from office. On 9 February he and Warwick and the other Yorkist lords arrived at Westminster fully armed and accompanied by a large contingent of soldiers. Paston records that York might have been arrested had he arrived without such a force, so clearly the Court party had regained confidence and had mustered men. As it was, Parliament reduced his powers from Protector to chief Councillor and Lieutenant... 'all this at the Queen's instigation'. Two weeks later, on 25 February, the King, in a lucid moment, again dismissed York from his service. This was done with the full approval of the Council and Parliament, though together with Warwick and Salisbury, York continued to serve on the Royal Council.

It seems clear from this that Henry VI's sanity came and went. After St Albans his lapses were never deep and rarely prolonged. He was certainly capable of making decisions or concurring with those taken in his name, but ever weak-willed, he left the hard decisions to others.

Egged on by his Queen, Henry did not stop with York's demotion from office. The extent to which Henry was responsible for his actions, let alone his Acts, is debatable, but he proceeded yet again to promote and favour those lords least acceptable to the Yorkist faction and replaced York's men with his own or the Queen's favourites. The one exception to this was the Earl of Warwick, who was left in his post as Captain of Calais. The advantage here was that Warwick actually took up his post instead of appointing a lieutenant, as was customary. To leave him in office, therefore, had the effect of keeping him out of the way. Warwick left for Calais in March 1456 and finally obtained access to the town on 20 April, after a prolonged argument with the garrison over their unpaid wages.

The Court party's next move was to dispatch York to the northern borders where the Scots were in arms and raiding south across the Tweed, and in May 1456 York prepared to march north. This was an unexpected development because James II, King of Scots, had already offered support to the Duke of York in his struggle with Somerset and had openly declared that, in his opinion, York was the rightful King of England. York arrived in Durham in August 1456 and the Scots promptly withdrew across the border.

The King's – or more likely the Queen's – clear intention was to move York and his friends to the margin of political affairs, but the pace proved too slow for Queen Margaret. In August 1456, with York away on the border, she gathered up the King and a large quantity of cannon from the Tower and took both to the Royal castle at Kenilworth, away from London, which she believed, rightly or wrongly, to be a hotbed of Yorkist supporters. Leicester, on the other hand, was central to the kingdom and a place to which forces could be summoned quickly from Lancaster and Cheshire. Meanwhile, Court appointees had moved into Yorkist offices across the spectrum of public affairs. The courtier Earl of Shrewsbury replaced Viscount Bourchier as Treasurer, while Archbishop Bourchier was replaced as Chancellor of the Realm by William Waynefleet, the Bishop of Winchester, to the great annoyance of the Duke of Buckingham.

Rumours of further rebellions and outbursts of lawlessness continued to flourish, keeping everyone on edge. Rather more perturbing, especially to the Court party, was the curious affair now taking place on the March of Wales, an area where lawlessness was endemic, and a stronghold of York through his Mortimer connections. Here Devereux, the Constable of Wigmore Castle, was up in arms. The recent Parliament had just pardoned Devereux for his treason against the crown following the Dartford affair in 1452, and here he was in the field again. Devereux was a long-time member of the Duke's affinity, having served with York in France, and Wigmore was a Yorkist castle, the ancestral stronghold of the House of Mortimer, which Devereux had held during York's abortive rising of 1452. In the summer of 1456 Devereux and the garrison suddenly descended on the city of Hereford, where they took the mayor and the justices captive. Devereux then brought several local men before them, whom the justices were obliged to condemn to death; he then had them hanged. This done, Devereux mustered a force of 2,000 archers from Gwent and marched on the castles at Carmarthen and Aberystwyth. These he took by assault, afterwards declaring a commission of 'oyer and terminer' to judge and condemn more people whom he believed hostile to York. Among his prisoners were Edmund Tudor, the king's half-brother, and Robert Rees, Keeper of the Welsh Seal and an influential court official.

Devereux had scant regard for the law, for though he was clearly a good soldier, his attainder for assisting York in 1452 had only just been lifted by Parliament. There was, inevitably, a political dimension to all this. The Royal castles at Carmarthen and Aberystwyth had been held by the Duke of Somerset as Constable. Although they had since been granted to the Duke of York, the garrisons had refused to hand them over and were still refusing to do so when Devereux appeared before the walls. The snag was that, possibly unknown to Devereux, when the King regained his senses in 1456, he had taken the castles back from the Duke of York and given them to his half-brother, Jasper Tudor, Earl of Pembroke.

What possessed Devereux to do all this can only be guessed at. Perhaps he was just another turbulent Marcher lord; perhaps he simply thought it a good idea to take advantage of the times. However, even in the lawless 1450s it was not every day that a simple knight raised an army and went about hanging citizens, besieging castles and imprisoning royal officials and the King's relations. There were those who thought, perhaps with good reason, that York put him up to it – he certainly knew about it. Perhaps he even authorized the seizure of the castles, but Devereux exceeded his instructions by hanging the citizens of Hereford.

Queen Margaret, who needed no excuse to suspect the worst of the Duke of York, certainly thought so. Devereux's action was her excuse for fortifying Kenilworth, supposedly to prevent such attacks against the King himself. By withdrawing to the Lancashire heartlands in the Midlands, and summoning men from Lancaster, Cheshire and other Lancastrian areas, she had soon surrounded herself with a considerable army, all wearing her livery and the young Prince Edward's badge of the Swan. When York returned from Scotland in the autumn of 1456, he found the country once again set on a course for war, and the King again insane.

It is necessary to point out, yet again, that the King's insanity was not of the raving variety. By all accounts it manifested itself in the form of either a complete mental collapse and withdrawal from the world, or as a profound depression. Letters relate how the King spent whole days in prayer or contemplation and needed great amounts of sleep, sometimes not moving from his bedroom for days at a time. Whatever the cause or nature of the illness, he was obviously unable to rule and his role was taken over by his Queen, Margaret of Anjou, and her various adherents. It has been said that the government effectively lapsed when the King and the Court abandoned London for Kenilworth, though orders and instructions still flowed from the council. The Queen's view of the King's interests and the country's needs did not usually coincide with those of York.

* * *

The next two years, from August 1456 to August 1458, saw England dividing into two factions and public affairs slipping steadily out of anyone's control. There never was a confrontation in the Temple Gardens as described by Shakespeare, where Somerset and York each chose a rose – red for Lancaster, white for York – as a badge for their affinities, but the split, if less theatrical, was no less real. The problem for the rest of the nobility was that they could not ignore it, even if they wished to. Everyone needed a 'good lord' to advance their interests and the stakes were obviously high. Those on the winning side could expect high office and preferment; the losers could expect insult, neglect, banishment, or even the block. The *Chronicles of London* recall that by August 1458, anxious provincial lords, who might well have preferred to stay neutral, were meeting the Yorkist Lords, Salisbury, Warwick and York, at Blackfriars in the morning and making their way in the afternoon to Whitefriars to discuss the problems of King and kingdom with the Queen's partisans, Somerset, Clifford and Northumberland. These were the sons of the men who fell fighting at St Albans, so the quarrel of York and Somerset had already spread to the second generation. The King's contribution to this debate was slight and usually unhelpful.

There were more riots and disturbances throughout 1457. Lucid again by March 1458, the King decreed that as a fine for sowing faction and to atone for the deaths of St Albans, York and his affinity should pay out £45 per year for Masses to be sung in St Albans Abbey. This judgement was followed by a 'love-day' on 25 March 1458, when the leaders of both parties, York and the Court, attended a service of reconciliation in St Paul's. York walked in procession through the streets of London hand in hand with the Queen, while Salisbury and Somerset followed, walking together behind the King, who was sane for the moment and wearing his crown. The smiles on that occasion must have been very stiff and formal.

The central problem afflicting the country was that King Henry could not rule. He regained his senses from time to time to overturn previous decisions, spread well-meaning dissent and support his Queen; but sane or not, he could not rule in any real sense. This fact was known and accepted by Parliament, if not yet publicly admitted, but that fact led inexorably to two dangerous questions. If the King could not rule, who should? If the answer was either Margaret of Anjou or Richard of York, what happened then? They and their affinities hated each other. Margaret was determined to keep King Henry on the throne, at least until her son, Prince Edward, could rule in his place. York was equally determined to control the kingdom if the King could not. There was room for compromise because York had no apparent designs on the throne, although he was unacceptable to the Queen's adherents, Somerset, Clifford and Northumberland.

The position of Richard, Duke of York, was particularly difficult. He had a good claim to the throne by right of descent from Edward III. He was competent in peace and war, and he had been, and perhaps still was, loyal to Henry and the young Prince, in spite of great provocation. If only Henry could rule and rule well, he would have been content. He was certainly content to support the King and the infant Prince as Protector of the Realm, but the Queen and her supporters would not let him. One can imagine York sitting with his friends over their wine in the evenings, the Duke waiting for the question which probably ended every quiet debate: 'What are you going to do about it?' York's answer, for the moment, was: 'Wait.'

Nobody wanted war. The country, fractious as it was, could not afford it, for then as now, the outcome of war was uncertain. Then as now, war had its own dynamic, but though nobody wanted war, war was coming because compromise was impossible. All-out war, not just a skirmish like the first Battle of St Albans, finally came to Lancaster and York in the autumn of 1459.

* * *

The Lancastrian cause had not been helped by Queen Margaret. Since arriving in England in 1445, she seems to have spared few efforts to make herself unpopular with the common people, the merchants and the uncommitted peerage. The English have an inbuilt sense of right concerning their sovereign, a feeling that loyalty is a virtue and due even to an unworthy king. Such tolerance is not usually extended to consorts, especially foreign consorts – particularly French consorts. By 1457 many people were saying openly that the troubles of England really began when Queen Margaret set foot on this side of the Channel.

Margaret did not appreciate this. She thought that respect and obedience were her due, a privilege that came with her rank, not something that must be earned. Out of politeness and loyalty to their King, the lords and courtiers accepted her demands but her arrogance made her few friends and often drove people to support the Duke of York. The Queen made more enemies as she went about the country; she did not improve on acquaintance. Margaret demanded Royal honours and large gifts from towns. She attempted to have the King abdicate in favour of her infant son, the Prince of Wales, whom many believed was not the King's son at all. She mustered men, extracted loans and taxes, exceeded the bounds of propriety and made enemies on every side – or so it is said. She certainly drove many potential allies into the Yorkist camp. The problem with such tales is that when goodwill and trust are missing, people are willing to believe the worst of their enemies and can entertain suspicions of their friends. In such an atmosphere, rumour can be a potent force for the fuelling of conflict. Among the rumours one fact was certain. The Queen was set on the destruction of the Duke of York and would do anything to achieve that end.

It is perhaps worth remembering that Margaret's background was the Court of France, where faction ruled. The wars of Armagnac and Burgundy had ravaged the country for years, and her childhood must have been filled with tales of overmighty subjects, ignoring the Royal writ to pursue their own advantage, of which the Duke of Burgundy was a visible example. Arriving in England and discovering that her husband was in pawn to his relatives and courtiers must have seemed an all-too-familiar situation and one which she was not prepared to tolerate. The fact that England was a very different kind of country seems to have escaped her notice. Her idea of the role of Parliament was that filled by the French *Parlements*, or Assembly of Estates, bodies called together to hear the King's will and do his bidding, not to comment on or interfere in affairs above their station.

By December 1458 the Lancastrians, as we may now fairly call them, were arming. In early December 500 pikes and as many lead-bound mallets (mauls) were ordered to equip the Royal retainers against 'certain seditious persons'. At the same time the Tower armouries cast three great siege cannon which, according to the Master of the Ordnance, John Judde, would enable the King to 'subdue any rebel castle or place held against him'. Five months later, in May 1459, 3,000 bows and many sheaves of arrows were removed from the Tower into the keeping of Thomas Thorpe, Keeper of the Wardrobe, 'for use against the enemies appearing by sea and land'. News of these acts, and scores more like them, got back to the Yorkist camp and increased their feelings of unease.

Having secured arms for her army, the Queen then moved to put the Yorkists in the wrong. In April 1459 a Great Council of all the peerage was summoned to Coventry, a Lancastrian stronghold, for the following June. Among those summoned were the Duke of York and the Earls of Warwick and Salisbury, the Archbishop of Canterbury and various other Yorkist supporters, and they viewed the summons with some trepidation. Quite apart from their reluctance to appear at any council held deep in Lancastrian territory, they would have been alarmed by the news that private Privy Seal writs had been sent out to certain lords of the Lancastrian affinity, instructing them to appear in arms at Leicester in May, well before the Council met, with forces equipped or 'defensibly arrayed' for two months' service. Against whom?

The Yorkist lords, therefore, declined to enter the trap. They were duly indicted for their non-appearance at the Parliament and the rival armies began to move. The Lancastrians assembled at Coventry; York was then at Ludlow Castle; Warwick in Calais, and his father, the Earl of Salisbury, at Middleham Castle in Yorkshire. Consequently, the Yorkists decided to concentrate their forces at York's great stronghold in the west, Ludlow Castle. Warwick arrived in Kent, sailing over from Calais with part of the garrison, marching hard for the Midlands to muster men; while Salisbury set out across the Pennines from Yorkshire. The next battle of the Wars of the Roses took place between the forces of the Earl of Salisbury marching

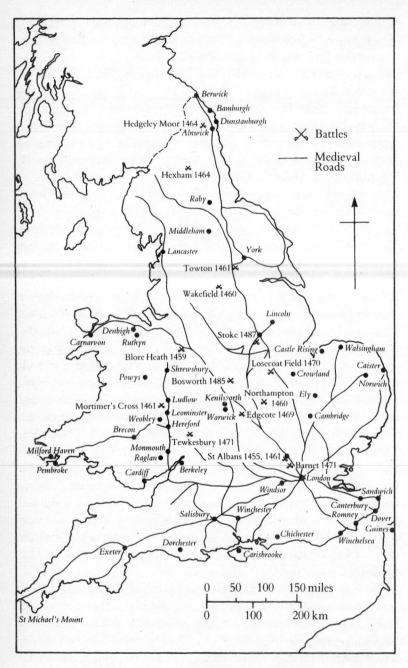

England and Wales during the Wars of the Roses.

for Ludlow and those of two Lancastrians, Lord Audley and Lord Dudley, who attempted to intercept him. The two armies collided at Blore Heath, near Market Drayton, on 23 September 1459.

The fight at Blore Heath did not last long, from 'one of the clock until five after noon', according to one account, but it ended in defeat for the Lancastrians. Blore Heath lies in rolling open country, and although Salisbury had fewer men than the Royal army, his men were more experienced and enjoyed the advantage of fighting on the defensive. Salisbury drew up his forces in line on the slopes behind the Hempmill brook, and when Audley and Dudley came up, they crossed the brook on horseback and charged up the slope, easy prey to the sweeping arrows of Salisbury's lines of archers. The pursuit went on until nightfall and the only major loss to Salisbury was his two sons, Sir John and Sir Thomas Neville, who went too far in pursuit and were cut off, surrounded and taken prisoner. The Lancastrians, however, lost heavily.

Lord Audley was killed in the field (a stone now marks the spot where he fell) and his deputy, Lord Dudley, captured. Night came on before Salisbury could round up his men and march on, and his position was still dangerous, for the main Lancastrian army was nearby. However, aided by a drunken friar who 'shot gounes all night', he was able to disengage his force and slip away to the west. On the following day the Duke of York met the Earls of Warwick and Salisbury at Worcester, where they again swore oaths of loyalty in the cathedral and sent them to the King. No reply came. With the approach of the Queen with a much larger force, the three Earls drew off towards Ludlow, where they arrived on 12 October.

Blore Heath dismayed all parties and there were further attempts at a peace. The King sent a writ offering a full pardon to anyone who submitted and joined his banner in six days, but this proposal for an amnesty was rejected by York and his followers, who pointed out that the amnesty of 1455, after St Albans, had not prevented the Queen moving against them in the years since. This probably refers to the secret attempts to gather armed men at Coventry in May, before the Yorkists arrived for the Great Council meeting.

The Royal army followed the Yorkists to Ludlow, collecting men as it came, until its numbers were said by the chronicler Gregory to exceed 25,000 'harnessed' men. This may be a considerable exaggeration, but it certainly far exceeded the size of the Yorkist host. The two armies confronted each other at Ludford Bridge, just south of Ludlow, where the Yorkist army lay entrenched. The Yorkist position, though strong – 'a great ditch fortified with carts, guns and stakes' according to Gregory's *Chronicle* – lacked enough men to man it. Their resolve and ability to give battle weakened on the evening of 12 October when Warwick's Calais troops, 600 skilled, professional soldiers under their leader, Andrew Trollope, left the Yorkist trenches and went over to join the Lancastrians. Trollope left behind a reason for his defection, stating that while he was aware of the dispute between the great lords, he had not been told that he would have to confront his sovereign 'in the field with his banner displayed'. To do so would be treason.

York and the Earls were dismayed by the desertion of the flower of their army, and when dawn came on 13 October, the Yorkist trenches were deserted. Their army had dispersed and the leaders had flown: York to Ireland; Warwick and Salisbury to Calais, which was held by their relative, Lord Fauconberg, taking with them the young Edward, Earl of March. The Royal army entered Ludlow that morning, hanging any Yorkist soldier foolish enough to remain, looting shops and raping women. In the castle they found York's Duchess Cecily and her two young sons, George, aged 10, and Richard who had just had his seventh birthday. The Duchess was given a pension of 1,000 marks (£666) to maintain herself, as was then the custom, and placed in the care of her sister, the Duchess of Buckingham, in her castle at Wallingford where, according to Gregory's account, she was kept 'full strait, with many a great rebuke'. This seems unlikely as the Duchess of Buckingham was Cecily's older sister.

Queen Margaret now assumed control of affairs. She summoned a Parliament at Coventry, where draconian measures were employed against York and his adherents. The entire family of York in exile – York, his sons, the 17-year-old Earl of March and the 16-year-old Edmund, Earl of Rutland, together with their supporters, the Earls of Warwick and Salisbury, Lord Wenlock and Lord Clinton and the rest – were accused of high treason. The Act of Attainder proclaimed: 'Richard Duke of York, Edward, Earl of March, Edmund, Earl of Rutland, Richard, Earl of Salisbury, Richard, Earl of Warwick, for their traitorous levying of War at Ludford be declared attainted of High Treason'. Their offices were taken from them, their lands seized and distributed among their opponents, or let off on payment of rents to defray the costs of campaigning against them.

The Act of Attainder threw in everything. York was accused of complicity in the rising of 'Jakke Cade' nearly ten years before, and for persistently trying to diminish or curtail the King's prerogative and authority. The field of St Albans came as the next indictment, with a passing reference to the subsequent amnesty, and covered the reconciliation in London in 1458 and the pledges given by York and Warwick in 1456. The matter of York's obligation to respect the succession also came up. Although York had never put forward a claim to the throne, the thought that he might clearly rankled in the minds of the court party. The Attainder embraced almost everyone with any connection to York, Salisbury and Warwick, 23 lords, ladies and gentlemen of quality in all. The King signed the Act on condition that he should be 'free to shew grace and mercy to any person or persones' and the loyal lords then again swore their allegiance to the House of Lancaster.

Parliament acquiesced to all this, but uneasily, for York and the Earls had always insisted, and were still insisting, that they were loyal subjects of King Henry. This quarrel, they maintained, as they must have got weary of maintaining, was with the Queen and her advisers who, said York, were ruining the kingdom, ruling the King, sunk in corruption and plotting against the life and lands of the Yorkist affinity, who were all loyal servants of the crown.

The Lords and Commons were well aware that public opinion in England was by no means convinced that York and the Earls were traitors, rogues who must be caught and killed, their families ruined, their heirs disinherited. In this last point alone, Queen Margaret went too far. It was the practice in England that ancestral lands, even those of attainted traitors, were entailed for their heirs who eventually enjoyed them. Besides, most attainders were eventually reversed. Many lords had seen their fathers at odds with the crown, yet their ancestral lands and titles had come down to their descendants who had then served the King loyally. By proceeding so harshly against York, Margaret was setting a new and unhappy precedent, and the English have no love of precedents. Besides, even though Parliament might attaint the Yorkists, the Yorkist lords were still in the field and might soon return.

The Irish Parliament, for one, supported and protected York, granted him men and money and refused to accept writs sent against him from England. Warwick, Salisbury and March were soon established in Calais, where the garrison, rejecting Andrew Trollope's action at Ludlow, refused to admit the newly appointed Lancastrian Captain of Calais, the young Duke of Somerset. They even sent a detachment to besiege him when he occupied the nearby castle of Guines in the Calais pale. Given all this, whatever decisions were forced on Parliament by the Queen, many

English lords preferred to wait and see. The power in England rested with whoever held the person of King Henry, and that could change at any time.

* * *

By 1458 the English had held Calais for over a hundred years, since it had fallen to Edward III in 1346. The port and the country which surrounded it, the Calais pale, including two outlying castles, Hammes and Guines, had all originally belonged to the Count of Flanders, a great feudatory of France. By the 1450s Calais was vital to England's economic well-being, as it had become the trading centre of the kingdom. Calais held the wool staple, and was the only continental market for the fleeces of East Anglia and the Cotswolds, but this was just a part of it. Through Calais flowed England's vital exports of tin, leather and, in times of plenty, fish and grain. Rich continental merchants, who would not risk the gales and pirates of the Channel and the barbarous English beyond, came happily to Calais to trade with the Merchants of the Staple, riding on to Calais from the great fairs of Champagne. Next to London, Calais was the most important and wealthy city in the kingdom, protected even in peacetime by a permanent garrison of 2,000 men . . . and in 1459 the Yorkist lords held it and all that it contained.

The three Earls, Salisbury, Warwick and the young Edward of March, spent eight productive months in Calais, raising money, mustering men, putting their side of events across and raiding the coast of Kent. No one made better use of his time here than Edward, for it was here that he, freed from family restraints, began to make his way in the world. In Calais he began that familiarity with the wealthy merchant classes which was to prove so useful to him later. From them he learned the importance of trade and the value of money; he learned to talk the language of commerce and could discuss business, making the merchants easy in his presence. He apparently made himself more than easy with their wives and daughters, too, but that was the way of a prince, and no one held it against him.

Edward's life and character has been overshadowed in history by that of his younger brother Richard, Duke of Gloucester; but Edward is an equally interesting man, a very different kind of ruler, but a man to watch. At this time, perhaps overawed by his older and more worldly relatives, Salisbury and Warwick, Edward seems to have been regarded as a frivolous youth with a taste for low company. The real man had yet to appear but the boy was learning fast and was to put his new-found knowledge to good use. He was now 17, a golden-haired young man, six feet three inches tall, very well built, handsome and affable like his father. He was also remarkably intelligent and willing to learn. Apart from endearing himself to the Merchants of the Staple, he learned a lot about the day-to-day business of soldiering from the professional men-at-arms of the large Calais garrison and he was able to hone his fledgling military skills a little by raiding the English coast.

In January 1460, for example, a detachment of the Calais garrison swooped on the port of Sandwich, where an expedition under Lord Rivers was assembling for an assault on Calais. Rivers was taken totally by surprise while asleep in bed with his wife, the Duchess Jacquetta, who had previously been married to no less a person than Henry V's brother, John, Duke of Bedford. They were taken prisoner, together with their son, Anthony Woodville, and hustled back to Calais, where Rivers and Woodville were reviled by the three Earls as low-born traitors. This is the first appearance of the Woodville family in the wars of York and Lancaster, but they were to appear again. A few months later, a Lancastrian force coming to the aid of Somerset was driven into Calais by gales and its commander, Lord Audley, son of the man killed at Blore Heath, was taken prisoner, only to fall under the spell of the young Earl of March and join his party for the new games that were afoot in England.

As the campaigning season of 1460 drew near, Warwick sailed to Ireland for a conference with the Duke of York. There it was decided that the three Earls should campaign in England, while York remained in the comparative safety of Ireland until King Henry was in their hands. The details of their conference are not known, but York may have decided to make a diversionary landing, once the three Earls were ashore, and gather troops from the Neville lands in the north, or he may have been advised by Warwick to stay in Ireland until the situation in England was resolved.

York felt very secure in Ireland. As Earl of Ulster he was an Irish peer and sensible behaviour during his time there as the King's Lieutenant had made him popular. His son George, later Duke of Clarence, had been born in Dublin Castle in 1449 and the Irish felt that York understood them and had put down roots there. Even so, the decision to leave him in Ireland, or for him to stay in Ireland, is unusual, for on both military and political grounds his presence in England was desirable. His troops could have created a diversion by landing on the west coast or joined Warwick and the rest in Calais for the invasion. His presence in England could have brought waverers and sympathizers over to his side. If there really was a definite reason for his absence, then the histories gloss over it.

The finer details of this conference are not known, but with a course of action now agreed on, the three Earls set off for the coast of Kent, with Lord Audley and a useful ally, the Papal Legate, Francesco Coppini, the Bishop of Terni, in their party.

They crossed the Channel on 26 June 1460 and landed at Sandwich. They were met on landing by Archbishop Bourchier and a large force of armed men from Kent, led by Lord Cobham. The purpose of this invasion was spelt out in a manifesto addressed to Coppini but which was distributed in England as the Earls came ashore. This (yet again) stated their loyalty to the King while requiring the reversal of the Attainders of Coventry. This was accompanied by a manifesto from York, probably one concocted during Warwick's visit to Ireland. This too went over the same old ground and demanded the removal of the King's evil Councillors, though it added charges of violence done to the Church and excessive taxation of the Commons. York was clearly attempting to present himself as the champion of Church and State against the corruption of the Court. His specific charges included, for the first time, the accusation that the death of Duke Humphrey in 1437 was murder.

On 2 July the Yorkists entered London, to be greeted by a huge crowd of cheering citizens. The Lancastrians, then in the City under Lord Hungerford and Lord Scales, withdrew to the Tower, from where Scales ordered his artillery to fire upon the City, interrupting the service in St Paul's where Warwick was issuing York's statement and reaffirming his loyalty to the King.

The Lancastrians had been anticipating a landing, perhaps from France, perhaps from Ireland, and had therefore mustered at Coventry, in the centre of the kingdom, close to the centres of Lancastrian power in the East Midlands and the north-west. On hearing of the landing on 1 July, the Royal army broke camp and moved south to Northampton. The Yorkists left Salisbury and Lord Cobham to hold London and besiege the Tower, while Warwick and March took the rest of the army north to find the King. They must have marched fast, for the two armies met at Northampton on 10 July 1460, less than a week after leaving London.

The Yorkists had mustered a considerable army which contained many experienced soldiers from the Calais garrison. The Archbishop of Canterbury and the Papal Legate rode in their ranks, along with former loyal supporters of the King, like Lord Audley, and Salisbury's brothers, the Lords Fauconberg and Abergavenny.

Warwick commanded the army and deployed his force in three battles, with the young Earl of March on the left, Lord Fauconberg on the right, and himself in the centre. As at the first Battle of St Albans, the two sides were reluctant to engage and all that morning envoys, notably Richard Beauchamp, the Bishop of Salisbury, trudged to and fro between the armies in pouring rain, trying to patch up a peace and get the quarrel settled by mediation. It was early afternoon before Warwick finally gave the order to attack.

The Lancastrians has also deployed in three battles behind a deep ditch and a palisade, fortifying their front with cannon, but the whole field was now a quagmire. The morning rain had long since drenched the powder and slackened bow-strings, so the customary opening exchange of arrow and artillery fire either failed or fell short. Then Warwick advanced his banners and the armies came to hand strokes, but only briefly, for Lord Grey of Ruthin, previously a staunch Lancastrian who commanded the King's right, turned traitor and elected to change sides. His men were soon seen helping the Earl of March's force up the slippery side of their protecting ditch and over the embankment. To cries of 'Treachery!' from the King's men, Ruthin and March united to roll up the Lancastrian centre and left. The whole battle then became a rout and inside an hour it was all over. Four Lancastrian lords, the Duke of Buckingham, the Earl of Shrewsbury, Lord Beaumont and Thomas Percy, Lord Egremont, were cut down in the battle or before they could gain their horses; while hundreds of common folk were killed while fleeing from the battlefield across the muddy plough, or drowned in the River Nene. The total death toll was still quite small, at between 300 and 500.

Warwick had given the word to spare the common folk, but to cut down everyone in coat armour and the slaughter of Lancastrian lords here, either in the actual battle or the subsequent rout, was to set a precedent for other encounters in this increasingly bitter war. A number of country knights and squires were killed, while King Henry was discovered sitting quietly in his tent and taken back into captivity. Margaret and Prince Edward fled into Wales and took shelter with Jasper Tudor, Earl of Pembroke, while their supporters elsewhere either lay low or hastened west to join them.

Taking King Henry with them, Warwick and the Earl of March returned to London and other Yorkist successes followed. The Tower surrendered to Salisbury on 18 July, after which some Lancastrians of the garrison, including Lord Scales, were murdered by a mob of watermen in the streets of the City. The Duke of Somerset was starved out of Guines early in August and with Andrew Trollope went to join the Queen's forces.

All Lancastrian appointees in England were swiftly replaced by Yorkists. The Bishop of Exeter, George Neville, became Chancellor, Lord Bourchier became treasurer, and Robert Stillington, Dean of St Martin-le-Grand, one of the great sanctuaries of the kingdom – who was also Archdeacon of Wells and later Bishop of Bath and Wells – became Keeper of the Privy Seal. This is the first appearance of Robert Stillington in this story, but as with the Woodvilles, we shall hear of him again. More important than all these moves were the first Acts of the new Parliament which was summoned in Henry's name to Westminster on 7 October 1460. This reversed and repealed the Acts of Attainder against York and his affinity of the previous year, declaring them to be 'the work of covetous persons bent on the destruction of King Henry's loyal and noble lords'.

The Duchess of York was released from her captivity at Wallingford and arrived in London with George and Richard, moving into a house in Southwark, owned by one of the Pastons. The Duchess soon left to join her husband who had come over from Ireland and was mustering his men at Chester. She left her two young sons in London where, according to Paston, 'My Lord of March comes every day to see them.'

King Henry's 'loyal and noble lords' were to receive a great shock on 11 October, when the Duke of York arrived in London. York entered Parliament in state, with his trumpets sounding and his banner displayed, while 500 soldiers cleared a path for his procession. A naked sword of justice was borne before him and his banner bore not the arms of York but 'the arms of England without difference', or without any mark of cadency. After years of loyal service, York's patience had finally run out. This time he came to London not as the loyal Duke of York but as the rightful King of England. Accompanied by his forces, York then proceeded to Westminster to lay his rough hands on the throne.

CHAPTER SEVEN

A YEAR OF BATTLES (1460–61)

This conflict was of all unnatural for in it son fought
father, brother against brother, nephew against uncle
and tenant against lord.

ON TOWTON FIELD, EDWARD HALL (1569)

The reaction of the Yorkist lords to the Duke's claim speaks volumes, for until this moment there seems to have been no intention to deprive King Henry of his throne. York and his friends certainly wished to control his person and dominate his Councils partly because the King himself was unable to rule, partly to keep the government out of the hands of people they felt were corrupt or incompetent. The King's dignity or person had not been at risk – until now.

The reaction of Parliament, the earls and the bishops to York's claim was one of shock. After all, the earls and the Duke himself had sworn an oath of loyalty to Henry less than a year earlier. Their loyalty to the King had been one of the planks of their platform, the reason for asking for and getting the support of the common people of England. Everyone was stunned; some were disgusted. Warwick, Salisbury, even his own son and heir, the Earl of March, remonstrated with the Duke of York and begged him to withdraw his claim, which clearly had little support among the nobility.

York, however, was adamant. He laid his claim before them by his descent from Lionel, Duke of Clarence, second surviving son of Edward III, and by that token down a senior line to the Lancastrian 'Henry of Windsor' who was descended from John of Gaunt, the third surviving son. This claim was perfectly valid and all men knew it, so when York demanded that they either support it or refute it, the Lords were in a quandary. They decided to put York's claim to the highest authority in the land, the current incumbent on the throne – Henry VI. Henry must have been in one of his more rational periods, for he returned the claim to the Lords, requiring them to find a way to refute it.

Baffled, the Lords then laid York's claim before the judges, who after two days of discussion also refused to touch it, declaring such a great matter 'beyond their competence' and fit for discussion only by the higher nobility, the Royal Family and the Princes of the Blood. The lawyers also refused to get involved in a matter which 'must needs exceed their learning'. The buck was being passed around rapidly before returning to the Lords. Had it not been so serious, this hot-potato handling of the issue might have seemed almost comical.

The Lords in Parliament, lay and religious, then withdrew into a secret session. During this, unable to refute York's title, they drew up a list of objections, not only to York's claim but towards any move which might depose King Henry. These included the fact that the Lancastrian line had now produced three successive kings since 1399, all of them crowned, anointed with holy oil and given willing oaths of homage by the peerage. These three Lancastrian kings had also given their assent to hundreds of Parliamentary Acts, which could not now be declared invalid. Besides, in 1406 Parliament had freely entailed the crown to 'the Heirs of the House of Lancaster,' an entail not questioned for the last half-century.

Coming to the present, all the Lords, including York, had themselves sworn oaths of loyalty and homage to King Henry VI, either at his coronation or subsequently, or both. The Lords also pointed out that York's claim was a new and novel one since he had previously taken his descent from his father, the Earl of Cambridge, and from his grandfather, Edmund of Langley, Duke of York, the fourth surviving son of Edward III; not as now, through his mother's line to Lionel, Duke of Clarence, the King's second surviving son.

This argument went on in public and in private for the next two weeks. It was gradually borne upon the Lords that, come what may, York would press his claim. In turn, it was impressed on York that the Lords and Parliament were most unhappy about it. York's position hardened under this opposition, for his situation was unique. The other Lords could probably come to terms with the King, the Queen, and the Lancastrian lords at any time. Many had changed sides several times in the last few years to take advantage of the political climate, but York was fully exposed. He was the head and the cause of the opposition to Lancastrian rule. If he failed or faltered now, his head was off – and he knew it. A compromise was clearly needed to end the present impasse, and one was eventually found.

On 21 October 1460, a proposal on behalf of the Lords was made to King Henry and the Duke of York by the Chancellor of the Realm, George Neville, the Bishop of Exeter. The Lords' proposal was that Henry should stay on the throne until his death or until he willingly abdicated, but that he should disinherit his son, Prince Edward, now aged 6, in favour of the Duke of York, who would now become his heir.

This compromise was accepted with relief by all those present. On 31 October York and his sons swore fresh oaths of loyalty to the King, who, in turn, bound himself to keep the agreement. By Act of Parliament, York, now the heir-apparent, was given immunity from charges of treason and granted all the lands and revenues which rightly belonged to the heir to the throne, including the Duchy of Cornwall and the Earldom of Chester. At the same time, Parliament repealed the Lancastrian entail on the crown of 1406. Parliament then dissolved and all men returned to their estates to raise men, arms and money.

The matter of York and Lancaster would not be settled in Parliament. What one Parliament decided, another could revoke. Besides, there was the small matter of the Queen and Henry's heir, Edward, Prince of Wales; his interests would surely be advanced by his party as soon as possible, and the Queen was even then mustering her forces in Scotland, in Wales, and in the Lancastrian heartlands. The issue of York and Lancaster could only be decided on the battlefield.

* * *

Queen Margaret and the young Prince Edward had fled west after the rout of Northampton to seek refuge with Jasper Tudor, Earl of Pembroke, who was then besieging the strong Yorkist castle of Denbigh. This fell to Jasper Tudor soon after the Queen arrived. There she began to gather her forces and more supporters came to join her. These included the Duke of Exeter, while Somerset, the Earls of Pembroke, Northumberland, Devon and Wiltshire, and the Lords Roos and Clifford, plus hundreds of knights and squires with their affinities all with armed retainers in close attendance, began to assemble in Yorkshire.

While the lords in the north began to harry York's lands, Margaret took ship from Wales for Scotland, where the powerful Queen-dowager, Marie of Guelders, and the young King James III promised her arms and money – on terms. The terms were a marriage between Prince Edward and one of King James's sisters and the ceding to the Scots of the Border town of Berwick-on-Tweed. These were harsh terms which would tie the Queen's hands and infuriate the Percies, but before they were agreed, her lords had won a notable victory at Wakefield in Yorkshire, and snuffed out the life of·Richard, Duke of York.

Very little is known about the circumstances surrounding the Battle of Wakefield. After obtaining all he wanted in London, York had placed King Henry in the Tower and sent his supporters out to muster men for the forthcoming campaign. Warwick stayed in London to hold the city, guard the King and raise forces in Kent. Edward of March rode to Shrewsbury and began recruiting along the Welsh border while York, with the Earl of Salisbury and his son, Rutland, went north into Yorkshire. Here they spent Christmas, feasting at York's castle of Sandal, near Wakefield, and while they were celebrating, the Lancastrian army, led by Somerset, Northumberland and Andrew Trollope, entered the Royal castle of Pontefract just 10 miles away.

In the circumstances, York's best course would have been to stay in his castle either until reinforcements arrived or the Lancastrians rode north to meet the Queen. In the bitter winter weather, no army could stay in the field for long. Some accounts say that Sandal fell by subterfuge, others that York was tempted out by an attack on his foragers who were out attempting to restock the castle larders after the Christmas feast. Perhaps they had run out of food and were in no state to withstand a siege. All that can be certain is that York did leave the castle and his small force of about 5,000 men was defeated outside the walls by the larger Lancastrian army. York fell about 500 yards from the castle; while Rutland, aged 16, was caught and killed, supposedly by Lord Clifford, outside the sanctuary chapel on Wakefield bridge, Clifford shouting as he cut him down, 'By God's blood, thy father slew mine and so shall I slay thee.' Also killed in the battle or the rout were Salisbury's son, Thomas Neville, Edward Bourchier, son of Viscount Bourchier, and a dozen more Yorkist knights. Salisbury himself was captured in the field and taken to Pontefract Castle, where he was beheaded the next day. The heads of York and Rutland were also struck off and, with Salisbury's, mounted over the Micklebar gate of the city of York where, to mock his pretensions, York's head was decorated with a paper crown.

While the Lancastrians were scoring this success in the north, York's heir, the young Earl of March, was being equally successful in the west.

On 3 February 1461 he met the forces of Jasper Tudor, the Earl of Pembroke and the Earl of Wiltshire at Mortimer's Cross, near Wigmore on the Welsh Marches. Edward had left London after his father and ridden to Wales in the company of the new Sir Walter Devereux, son of the old warrior who had died in 1459, and the other Marcher lords. With him also were Lord Audley and Sir Humphrey Stafford, his prisoners at Calais but now his friends. They spent Christmas at Shrewsbury and were still there when news of his father's death arrived from the north.

Here we have our first sight of Edward's intelligence and maturity. His instinctive reaction must have been either to march north to avenge his father or to return to London to join Warwick for their mutual comfort and support, or even to flee abroad. He did none of these things. He went on with the task in hand, mustering men to defeat the Lancastrian army in Wales which was coming down upon him, led by that formidable fighter, Jasper Tudor, Earl of Pembroke, the King's half-brother, and James Butler, the Earl of Wiltshire.

Jasper's army was made up of the affinities of these two lords, plus a number of Irish, French and Breton mercenaries brought over by the Earl of Wiltshire. The size of their force is not known, but Geoffrey Hodges in his recent and comprehensive account of the battle estimates it at between 2,000 and 3,000 men. The monument at Mortimer's Cross, erected in 1799, gives a figure of 4,000 men for the fallen alone, while other accounts refuse to give an estimate at all. Whatever the numbers involved, the battle at Mortimer's Cross was a bloody affair.

Edward, now aged 19, had completed his muster and was marching east to join Warwick when he heard that Pembroke and Wiltshire were in the field and coming up behind him. Edward had a number of other experienced soldiers in his army. Apart from the Herbert brothers, who were the grandsons of Henry V's famous squire, Dafydd Llewellyn, or Davy Gam, there was Sir Walter Devereux and Sir John Wenlock, another soldier of the war in France, and Edward's closest friend, William, Lord Hastings, and his new friend from Calais days, Lord Audley. More than twenty of Edward's knights or squires were local men.

The armies met at Mortimer's Cross on 3 February 1461, the feast day of St Blaise, the patron saint of wool combers. On the previous day, Candlemas Day, while Edward's army was assembling in the usual three divisions, they were struck by a curious apparition through the morning fog: three suns rising together – a parhelion – an effect caused by the sun refracting on ice crystals in the frosty air. This was taken as a good omen following the death of York, who had left three sons, Edward, George and Richard, to carry on the fight. Edward himself declared the sight to be a sign of support from the Trinity and afterwards took the 'Sun in Splendour' for his personal banner.

Edward had an army of some 2,000 men, including many knights from Herefordshire. Jasper's army, though less cohesive and homogeneous, probably mustered a similar number, though this force had been on a forced march over the wintry hills and the foreign contingent must have grown uneasy as the distance from the coast increased. The Lancastrian force formed up soon after dawn at their camp by the present monument, and in the usual three-battle formation began to advance across the frozen fields towards Edward's waiting army, drawn up on level ground between the River Lugg and a steep slope which gave his flanks some protection on open ground, 4 miles south of Wigmore Castle. Edward's position was probably close to the present Bluemantle Cottage and his force was drawn up in depth, three lines of deployed men-at-arms, fronted by knots of archers. The presence of so many lords in Edward's ranks indicated that his force was more professional and better armed than those of Pembroke and Wiltshire, with their Irish, Welsh and Breton allies. Certainly, when the battle began the Yorkists were quick to seize the initiative.

The Yorkist arrow storm ravaged the ranks of the unarmoured Welsh foot, and ever quick to seize an advantage, Edward then advanced his banners, flung his right flank forward and hustled the crumbling Lancastrian force back against the brimming banks of the Lugg. This was no secure position, and the Lancastrian front began to crumble. Details are scanty but the battle did not last long. Within half an hour the Lancastrians were fleeing across the meadows, harried on their way by the armoured Yorkist knights.

As at Wakefield and too many of the other battles of this war, the details of the battle at Mortimer's Cross are few and vague but it is certain that Edward smashed the forces of the two Lancastrian earls and sent them fleeing headlong across the countryside, 'telling his forces to kill the lords and spare the common soldiers'. The Earls of Pembroke and Wiltshire escaped, but the Yorkists did capture old Owen Tudor, Pembroke's father and the King's stepfather, husband of Henry V's widow, Catherine of Valois, who had come to help his son in the battle.

Owen Tudor was taken to the market-place at Hereford where, says Gregory, 'trusting that he would not be beheaded until he saw the axe and block...not even until the headsman tore the collar from his doublet . . . then he said, "That head shall lie on the block that was wont to lie on Queen Catherine's lap," and full meekly took his death.'

According to another eyewitness, his head was mounted on the market cross in Hereford where, 'an old mad woman got to it, combing his hair and washing off the blood by the light of candles she set about it, more than a hundred.'

* * *

After Wakefield and Mortimer's Cross, honours in the battles were even. All the affinities of York and Lancaster were now in the field and concentrating for the great battle that should settle this conflict once and for all: Margaret and Somerset in Scotland and the north; Warwick and March – now Duke of York – in the south and west.

Greatly encouraged by the deaths of York and Salisbury, the Lancastrians, reinforced by their Scots allies, were marching south. Other historians have remarked how the common people of England were not greatly inconvenienced by the Wars of the Roses, which was largely fought out by the nobility, using their private armies of professional soldiers. There may have been some truth in this, but not a lot: soldiers had to sleep and eat and it was hardly likely that many paid for meals or shelter, regarding such matters as the civilians' contribution to their lords' campaigns. Forage for horses used up crops and emptied storehouses, armies required food and lodging, and demands for a levy to pay the troops all took their toll, and if the common people managed to stay out of the actual fighting, this was surely at the expense of paying the lords to take their men away and do the fighting elsewhere.

The Lancastrian army, now marching on London, plundered as it went, leaving a swath of destruction across the East Midlands as it came down the north road to the fateful town of St Albans, where the Earl of Warwick stood ready to meet them. This encounter, the second Battle of St Albans, took place on 17 February 1461, two weeks after Mortimer's Cross.

Once again, there is the usual difficulty over numbers. Margaret left Scotland with a large army and as she marched south more men would have joined her. On the other hand, many of her Scots and northern allies, weighed down with booty and anxious not to march too far from home, almost certainly slipped away. Her final force at St Albans can hardly have exceeded 10,000 men, and Warwick, who opposed her, probably had slightly less.

Warwick left London on the afternoon of 12 February, taking with him an army of some 8,000 men and his prisoner King Henry, whom he dared not let out of his sight. It is curious that Warwick and Edward made no attempt to consolidate their forces. They had more than a week to do so, and yet Edward remained in the west and was marching east at a leisurely pace when Warwick fought the Lancastrians at St Albans. Warwick's army contained the Dukes of Norfolk and Suffolk – the latter the son of York's old enemy – the Earl of Arundel and the Lords Bourchier, Bonville, and Warwick's brother Montagu. Also present was that old soldier of the French wars, Sir Thomas Kyriell, who had been so soundly defeated at Formigny in 1450.

Warwick had several days to prepare the town for the Lancastrian assault and he proceeded to fortify his position with ditches, barricades, a plentiful sowing of caltrops (small spiked objects), and nets sewn with nails to cripple men and horses. His archers and crossbowmen had thick pavises (large shields) to fire through and, a novelty, his army contained a number of men, probably Burgundians, armed with hackbuts, an early form of harquebus which could fire lead shot or arrows – the first recorded instance of hand–guns being used in England. He also had a number of cannon taken from the Tower arsenal and used them to create, not a continuous line, but a series of strong points, or redoubts, along the ridge between St Albans and Nomansland Common.

Warwick departed from convention and from wisdom by not concentrating his forces. The surviving reports are, as usual, vague and contradictory, but it appears that his army was deployed over a 4-mile front from the town centre in the south to Nomansland Common to the north, in four clearly defined and defended positions, but with a strong body of archers left to hold the town centre and, most probably, guard the baggage. Warwick had too many men to deploy in the town and little time to entrench this large force, but even so, to split his forces like this was an act of folly. It is also likely that details of his positions had been passed to Andrew Trollope, the 'Great Captain' of the Lancastrian army, by some traitor in the Yorkist ranks. Trollope must have had a good idea of Warwick's deployment before he launched his own most original attack.

The Lancastrians arrived at Dunstable, 12 miles north-west of St Albans, on 16 February, wiping out the small Yorkist garrison. On the following night they marched east, down the old Roman road, called Watling Street, thus turning Warwick's position by advancing into the town from the west, to fall on the left flank of Warwick's army in St Albans town centre. Here the Yorkist archers made a spirited resistance and brought Trollope's men to a halt. The fighting spread between rival groups of archers and men-at-arms who fought hand-to-hand over the market-square and up and down the streets of the town.

The second Battle of St Albans, now hardly begun, had already produced a series of then-startling innovations. The use of hand-guns, the establishment of fortified positions on a wide front, a night march, a flank attack: all almost unthinkable at a time when a skilled commander was one who could get his men-at-arms in a long line against his opponent's front and settle the issue with sword and axe.

Now there was street fighting from house to house in St Albans, and the Yorkist archers could only have maintained the fight so long by using the vast store of arrows in the baggage park. While they fought on, there came another innovation. Trollope disengaged his rear troops and sent them round to turn and assault Warwick's other positions. While the Lancastrian vanguard and Warwick's left flank were engaged in St Albans, the Lancastrian centre moved on to engage the Yorkists mustered on Bernard's Heath, just to the north of the town.

The Second Battle of St Albans went on for most of the day as the various divisions of the Lancastrian army came on round the town to

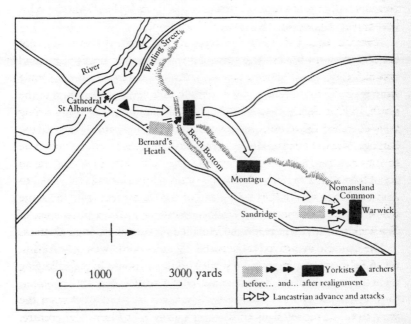

The second Battle of St Albans (1461).
The Lancastrians roll up Warwick's army.

engage the Yorkist contingents now spread out between St Albans and Sandridge. Overall control on Warwick's side seems to have been conspicuous by its absence, but Trollope was fighting his army with considerable skill. All Warwick's precautions and complicated entrenchments and entanglements were made useless by this flanking attack, which might have rolled up and destroyed his entire army had the Lancastrians been able to disengage earlier from the centre of St Albans and bring the full force to bear. Those gallant archers holding out in the town bought the Earl of Warwick precious time.

There was, as at Ludford and Northampton, treachery. This time it came from a Kentish squire called Lovelace, who may have betrayed Warwick's plans to Trollope and certainly brought his men over to Lancaster at the crux of the battle. Warwick's central position at Bernard's Heath then collapsed, but Warwick held on at Nomansland until nightfall, after which he was able to disengage and withdraw with about 4,000 of his men still fit to fight, and ride for the safety of the Cotswolds.

The Lancastrians captured a number of Yorkists, including Lord Montagu, Lord Bonville and Sir Thomas Kyriell, while King Henry as another battle ended was again found sitting quietly in his tent. The Lancastrian field commander at St Albans, Andrew Trollope, was wounded in the foot by a caltrop and was knighted after the battle boasting to the Queen that even thus incapacitated he had managed to kill 15 men. The killings went on after the battle, for though Montagu was spared and sent captive to the city of York, Lord Bonville and Sir Thomas Kyriell, who had stayed to protect King Henry and been promised safe conduct by the King, were promptly brought before the Queen and Prince Edward, now aged 7, and flung on their knees.

'Fair son,' said the Queen to the Prince, 'by what manner of means shall these knights die?' 'Let their heads be taken off,' replied the Prince, and it was done. This was the Prince's introduction to affairs of state. Though the Earl of Devon had probably willed the death of Bonville, it was the Prince and his mother who ordered the deed done.

Very few Lancastrians of note were killed: their plate armour made them almost invulnerable, but the death of one Lancastrian knight was to have consequences later. Sir John Grey of Groby, who was killed fighting in the town, left a widow, Elizabeth Grey, formerly Elizabeth Woodville, the daughter of Lord Rivers and the Duchess Jacquetta. This lady had children and a number of relatives and little left to sustain her but her wit and beauty. The chronicles say that something over 2,000 men on both sides were killed in the battle, but very few were gentlemen of coat-armour. The Yorkist archers and the foot-soldiers of both armies must have made up the bulk of the slain.

* * *

London was now in turmoil, and hurriedly sent envoys to Queen Margaret, offering to open its gates if she would dismiss the Scots and keep her followers from plundering. This was not a guarantee the Queen could easily give. York's widow, the Duchess Cecily, sent her two younger children, George and Richard, to the court of the Duke of Burgundy, where they were made very welcome.

Queen Margaret was in a dilemma and uncertain how to exploit her victory. The Scots in her army were deserting in droves with their plunder, and Edward and Warwick were still hovering in the Cotswolds with an army that grew stronger every day. With hindsight it is easy to see that she should have marched on London and given whatever guarantees were required to get within the walls of the Tower. As it was, she hesitated and by that hesitation she was lost. She had the King and was content with that, but that strategic mistake at St Albans spelt the downfall of her House.

She should have marched on London if only to secure the Tower and its artillery, as well as the City, the centre of power, which contained the wealth of the kingdom. Some of her people had already entered the City in pursuit of Warwick's men, and the aldermen would do anything to save the City from sack. Her army still contained far too many unpopular plundering Scots, Border raiders who had gained the victory at St Albans but had since ransacked the town and the abbey and were even now pillaging and burning the London suburbs of Southwark and Westminster. The thought of what might happen if they entered London must have made her pause, and before she could decide what to do, the Earl of March acted. On 26 February he entered London with the Earl of Warwick, and on 4 March he was proclaimed King as Edward IV.

Thousands of Londoners turned out to cheer Edward on his way to Westminster. Among those of the nobility riding at his side were the Earl of Warwick, the Duke of Norfolk, Thomas Bourchier, Archbishop of Canterbury, and from the Marches of Wales, Sir William Herbert and his comrade, Sir Walter Devereux, both of whom were soon to be elevated to the peerage. Thwarted, the Queen and her forces drew off to the North.

The Yorkists were now enjoying popular support because Edward's claim to the throne was seen as at least equal to that of Prince Edward, the heir of Lancaster. King Henry, by the actions of his Queen and her supporters at Wakefield and St Albans, had broken his solemn compact to protect the Yorkist succession. The fact that this pledge had been forced from him made no difference. York might be dead but the compact lived on in his son and gave legitimacy to his succession. Besides, the young Edward IV, now aged 18, was personable and showed signs of becoming a formidable soldier, a great change after the pacific Henry. His first task was to engage the main Lancastrian army in the field and defeat it; this he now proceeded to do.

Edward began by mustering men, summoning all men between the ages of 16 and 60 to join his array: more men than an English king had ever put in the field before. He raised the money to arm them in the City; that Calais touch with the merchants came in handy here and the City fathers loaned him £12,000, a vast sum for the time. By the time the Yorkists assembled by Pontefract Castle on 27 March 1461, they had amassed a mighty army, including another contingent of Burgundians under the Seigneur de le Barde, who came to join the Earl of Warwick.

Queen Margaret had also assembled a mighty force, which gathered in Yorkshire. The Duke of Somerset was now in command, probably because in spite of his inexperience, he outranked Andrew Trollope, a mere esquire. All the Lancastrian lords were there including the Duke of Exeter, the Earls of Devon and Northumberland, plus a number of disaffected Nevilles from the Westmorland branch of the family, for this war, like all civil wars, split families down the middle.

Recent accounts of the battle at Towton have reduced the numbers of combatants considerably to the customary 10,000 men, but all the contemporary evidence indicates that on this occasion at least, much larger forces were in the field. It must have been very clear to everyone that this must be the decisive encounter, and Edward certainly made every effort to gather every fighting man he could find. As is usual in accounts of medieval armies, the actual numbers are not known but a fair estimate would be that the muster of each army would be around 40,000 men, a vast force for the time. With some 70,000 to 80,000 men engaged, the battle at Towton was, in terms of numbers, the largest battle ever fought on English soil. Edward Hall calculated the 48,000 soldiers in Edward's army from the pay and muster role, an accurate method of computation, though not all these would have been combatants.

Advancing north from Pontefract, Edward found the Lancastrian army drawn up along a ridge above the plain of York, between the villages of Towton and Saxton, with a forward detachment under Lord Clifford guarding the only bridge over the River Aire at Ferrybridge. King Edward began his attack on Friday, 27 March by sending Lord Fitzwalter ahead to take this position. On arriving at the river, Fitzwalter found the bridge destroyed but the crossing unguarded. Fitzwalter therefore crossed the river and got his men repairing the bridge to permit the passage of the main army and their cannon. This work went on during the Friday afternoon, the men working waist-deep in the freezing river on a day of piercing cold, when the fields were dusted with snow flurries. The work went well but at dawn the next day, Lord Clifford swept down on the bridge with a force of Lancastrian knights, overran the outposts and hustled the Yorkists back across the river. In the confused fighting, Lord Fitzwalter was killed and by some accounts the Earl of Warwick was slightly wounded.

Fugitives from the fight brought the news of the bridge's recapture to Edward who therefore sent his vanguard, under Lord Fauconberg, to cross the Aire 4 miles upstream at Castleford and take Clifford in the rear. Fauconberg pursued Clifford's men into the Dintingdale valley, near Saxton, where Clifford and Sir John Neville, brother to the Earl of Westmorland, were killed in the fight. Meanwhile, the Yorkist army had crossed the river unopposed and advanced towards the Lancastrian host, who they found drawn up in their battle array along the 100-foot high ridge above Towton Dale, nearly half a mile south of the village of Towton, their right flank secured on the bridge which ran down steeply to the Cock beck, a tributary of the Aire.

The Lancastrians were in the usual three battles, with Northumberland and Trollope commanding the right-hand division, the Earl of Devon and Lord Dacre commanding on the left flank, and the Duke of Somerset as commander in the centre. The Yorkist army was not complete, for Lord Wenlock with the rearguard had not yet crossed the river and the Duke of Norfolk's large contingent had yet to join the army at all, though his harbingers had arrived. The Yorkists, therefore, spent that freezing night in Saxton village, just south of Towton vale, drying their clothes and preparing for the morrow, while the Lancastrians stayed bivouacked in the open. It was very cold, with snow flurries sweeping out of the dark and white frost freezing hard on the grassy slopes.

The battle began about 10 o'clock on the morning of Palm Sunday, one of the most holy days of the Christian calendar and not usually a day for the shedding of blood. These were not the chivalrous days of Edward III and the two armies, or at least the commanders of the two armies, were itching to get at each other's throats, though the Yorkists were still short of the Duke of Norfolk's large contingent, still half a day's march (say 10 miles) behind, but coming up fast.

The disposition of the armies is unclear, with some historians stating that they fought in columns of battles, which would be unusual at this time though a sensible way to control the abnormally large numbers in the field. Whatever their tactical arrangement, the battle began with the usual exchange of arrow volleys and probably with cannon fire.

The battle commenced when Lord Fauconberg had his vanguard of archers begin volleying shafts into the Lancastrian line. This done, he had them retire to the ranks of the men-at-arms, and here the Yorkists had an advantage, for the piercing wind was at their backs and carrying their shafts well forward, while the returning Lancastrian arrows fell well short. The continued Yorkist arrow storm, to which they could make no reply, soon persuaded the Lancastrians to advance. The distance between the two armies was little more than 200 yards. The Lancastrians left their position on the Towton ridge and marched down into the shallow valley between the armies. Except on their right flank, Towton vale is little more than a brief depression, and the slope beyond was no obstacle to their advance as they came towards the Yorkist line, a forest of banners and pennons slanting into the falling snow and snapping in the chill wind. Within minutes, the two lines of armoured men had clashed together and the slaughter began.

In such a battle as Towton, there was no room for elaborate sword play. The main work was done by bludgeoning men to the ground and there was no great skill in it. Most of the actual killing was done with a variety of weapons, the battleaxe, mace or pole-axe dealing heavy blows to crush a skull, break an arm or shoulder and get a man down. Then a swift thrust with a sword or dagger through the eye slits of his helmet would finish the job. War cries were soon replaced by screams and groans, but the main sound on the battlefield was the clang and clash of weapons on armour plate, the swish and thud of arrows, the screams of men and horses.

The initial burst of fighting went on for three hours. There must have been pauses, when the men drew back, panting, to lean on their weapons and draw breath. Then they hurled themselves forward again, ever more exhausted, until the battle became a vast scrum or shoving match, each side hoping to break the other's line, each surge forward or back being made across the bodies of the dead or injured. The battle hung in the balance until some time before 1 o'clock in the afternoon, when the Duke of Norfolk's strong battle arrived and flung their fresh power and weight on to the Lancastrian's left.

This may have been fortuitous, but at Northampton and at Mortimer's Cross Edward had seen the advantage of reinforcing one flank in order to break through the enemy line at one point, and then roll it up. This tactic, as at Mortimer's Cross, could prove partially effective if the enemy line could be forced back against some natural obstacle, like a river or, as here, the foaming River Cock. Wary of being forced into the river, the Lancastrians began to leak away to the left and rear.

Slowly the Lancastrian army began to crumble, but the battle did not end quickly. The fighting went on into the late afternoon. There was an increasing leakage to the rear as more and more Lancastrians realized that they were losing, as their line was pushed back, little by little, down into the steeper part of the vale and into the area by the River Cock, which from all the slaughter that took place there, later came to be known as Bloody Meadow.

With the river close at their backs, the Lancastrian front suddenly gave way and the great slaughter of Towton began. The Yorkist knights, now too exhausted to run, mounted their caparisoned war-horses which their pages brought running forward. This, plus the elation of victory, gave the Yorkists fresh strength to roam among the fleeing Lancastrians and cut them down by the score, the hundred, the thousand. Many drowned in the swift-flowing river, which soon became choked with bodies. Others were knocked down and trampled into the marshy ground round about. Sir John Wenlock and Sir John Dinham led the pursuit almost to the gates of York, from where Queen Margaret, King Henry and the Prince of Wales had already fled, warned of the disaster by the first survivors to arrive.

No one knows how many died at Towton but the numbers were certainly large and well spread between the armies. One of the Paston letters states: 'among the knights, Sir Andrew Trollope and twenty-eight thousand more, as numbered by the heralds,' and this is one of the lowest estimates. The *Croyland Chronicle* suggests over 38,000 and Edmund Hall over 36,000. These figures are very large, perhaps on the high side, but the battle did last all day, and the slaughter was considerable in the rout and in the River Cock. The grave pits tend to confirm the figures which do, for once, display remarkable unanimity, though it is possible that the totals include the wounded as well as the dead. Modern estimates of the dead do not exceed 9–10,000.

Sir Andrew Trollope was not the only one of note to fall. On the Lancastrian side, the Earl of Northumberland died of his wounds. Lord Welles, Lord de Maulay and Lord Clifford succumbed too. Lord Dacre was killed when he took off his helmet to take a drink of water and was struck by a crossbow bolt in the throat – he and his horse were buried at the parish church at Saxton, where his tomb can still be seen. Among the knights, Andrew Trollope, Sir Richard Percy, Sir John Heyton and many more perished. The Dukes of Somerset and Exeter again escaped and fled after the Queen into Scotland. After the battle was over, the executions began: Thomas Courtenay, Earl of Devon, was found sick or wounded at Clifford's Tower in York and beheaded, as was the Earl of Wiltshire, who was captured a few days later at Newcastle.

Edward IV and his victorious army entered York on Easter Monday when the King and Warwick were greeted by the grim, crow-pecked heads of their fathers, York and Salisbury, displayed on spikes over the main gate, together with that of Edward's young brother, Rutland. These heads were taken down and replaced by those of Devon, Wiltshire and the other Lancastrian lords.

King Edward IV now ruled in England and the sun of Lancaster had set – or so it seemed.

CHAPTER EIGHT

EDWARD AND WARWICK (1460–64)

Wherefore warn princes not to wade in warre
For any cause except the realm's defense.
Their troublous titles are unworthy for
The blood, the lyfe, the spoil of innocence
Of Friends and foes behold my first expense
And never the need: lest therefore tarry time
So right shall reign and quiet calm each crime.

A Mirror for Magistrates (1539)

Edward IV, sometime Earl of March, heir to Richard Plantagenet, Duke of York, was crowned in London on 28 June 1461. He was born on 28 April 1442 in the castle at Rouen, while his father was the King's Lieutenant in Normandy. This allowed his enemies to claim later that Edward IV was not a true-born Englishman. Some even said worse things, claiming that his true father was not Richard Plantagenet at all, but an archer in the Duke's retinue. This story spread and in some of the courts of Europe Edward IV was referred to in later life as '*le fils d'arblatier*', the archer's son. This was a disgraceful slur on Duchess Cecily, a lady known for her piety and rectitude.

Edward's nurse, Anne of Caux, came from Normandy, and Edward, unlike many Englishmen of his class, grew up to be relaxed in the company of foreigners, and following his time in Calais, with men of the rising middle and trading classes; with their ladies, he was frequently over-familiar, and noted throughout his rule as a great womanizer. Edward was a tall, fine-looking man, handsome in his youth, energetic in knightly pastimes, affable and easy-going, but like all the Plantagenets, relentless in pursuit of his rights: not for nothing was '*Dieu et mon Droit*' – God and my Right – the Plantagenet family motto.

Edward's early years followed the conventional path for any scion of a noble House. Most of his childhood was spent in his father's strong castle at Ludlow, though he and his brother Rutland spent part of the time in the nearby castle of the Croft family, where they were sent to be 'nourished', or trained in the duties and responsibilities of their class, in the management of horse and hound, in the knowledge of arms and in chivalry. Edward could read and write with ease, knew the classics and spoke good French. In 1459, after the rout at Ludford Bridge, when Edward was 17, his father was driven from Ludlow into Ireland and Edward was forced to flee to Calais. So began a long association with his cousin, Richard Neville, Earl of Warwick.

Although Richard Neville is one of the best-remembered figures in English history and generally known as 'Warwick the Kingmaker', he remains a shadowy person: no contemporary portrait has survived, no physical description is available, and the closest we can find to a likeness is a small carving of him as a 'weeper', or mourning figure, on the tomb of his father-in-law, Richard Beauchamp, at St Mary's Church in Warwick. However, enough is known to place Warwick firmly on the upper rungs of English society, and in a strong position to influence public and political events, which he was to do for much of his adult life.

Warwick was the eldest son of Richard Neville, first Earl of Salisbury, the brother-in-law of York. Warwick was born in 1428, so he was 14 years older than Edward of March – a significant gap – and when they fled to Calais in 1459, Warwick was 31 and Edward 17. In 1434 Warwick had married Anne Beauchamp, the 9-year-old daughter of Henry VI's tutor, Richard Beauchamp, Earl of Warwick, and assumed the title and the Earldom of Warwick when Richard Beauchamp's male line died out in 1449. The marriage had always been seen as a profitable alliance, but with the death of Anne's brother, she became sole heir to the vast Beauchamp estates and revenues which her husband Warwick then came to control. There was, however, a snag. Anne had half-sisters and one of them, the Lady Eleanor Beauchamp, was married to the avaricious Edmund Beaufort, second Duke of Somerset, who was not unnaturally furious that his wife had been excluded from any share in his father-in-law's estate.

Even so, by this fortunate matrimonial stroke, at the age of 20, Warwick found himself one of the richest men in England, second only to York among the magnates but an enemy of one of the most powerful, the Duke of Somerset. This, as much as anything else, drove his family into the camp of Richard, Duke of York. This was a powerful gain for York because

Alice Chaucer,
Duchess of Suffolk

Richard Beauchamp, Earl of Warwick

Warwick Castle

Heraldic pub signs:
The Bear of Warwick

*and the Sun in Splendour
of Edward IV*

This pedeftal is erected to perpetuate the Memory of an obstinate, bloody, and decifive battle fought near this Spot in the civil Wars between the ambitious Houfes of York and Lancaster, on the 2nd Day of February 1461 between the Forces of *Edward Mortimer*. Earl of March, (afterwards *Edward* the *Fourth*) on the Side of York and thofe of *Henry the Sixth*, on the Side of Lancaster.

The Kings Troops were commanded by *Jafper Earl* of Pembroke. *Edward* commanded his own in Person and was victorious. The Slaughter was great on both Sides Four Thousand being left dead on the Field and many Welfh Perfons of the firft diftinction were taken Prisoners among whom was *Owen Tudor* (Great-Grandfather to *Henry* the *Eighth*, and a Defcendent of the illuftrious *Cadwallader*) who was afterwards beheaded at Hereford

This was the decifive Battle which fixed *Edward* the *Fourth* on the Throne of England who was proclaimed *King* in London on the Fifth of March following.

Erected by Subfcription
in the Ye...

Tewkesbury Abbey

*Micklegate Bar,
York*

Left: *Memorial,
Mortimer's Cross*

Lord Dacre's Grave

*Bloody Meadow,
Tewkesbury*

Richard III

Bosworth Field

King Richard fell here
Bosworth

Warwick maintained a large affinity, with scores of archers and men-at-arms under command. During his alliance with York, his fortunes waxed as he became Captain of Calais, when successful piracies against French shipping from Calais made him popular in England, only to wane again when Henry VI returned to his senses and to power and dismissed all York's adherents from office.

The flight to Calais in 1459 cemented the relationship between Edward and his cousin Warwick, but there seems little doubt that at that period in their lives, and for some time afterwards, Warwick was the dominant figure. It was Warwick who led the troops and made the decisions, while young Edward was seemingly content to go along with the Earl's decisions and enjoy himself with the citizens of Calais and their ladies. It was Warwick who went to Ireland in March 1460 to confer with the Duke of York; Warwick who ordered the raids on Sandwich; Warwick who commanded the expedition to England in June 1460, and Warwick who commanded the army which thrashed the Lancastrians at Northampton in July of that year. Warwick was very much York's deputy in England, and his most valued subordinate. Edward was merely the Duke's son and the Earl's favourite cousin, thought of by many as a lightweight.

Matters moved on to a different plane when, on 9 November 1460, Richard became heir-apparent to Henry VI. By that step the young Edward became next in line after his father, gaining several degrees in status over his cousin of Warwick. Then at the end of that year, York and Salisbury were killed. The two Earls of March and Warwick suddenly found themselves fatherless and leading the opposition to the Lancaster party. When their fathers died, the Earls were not together; Edward was on the March of Wales, while Warwick was in London. Both had to fight a Lancastrian army, but the results of their separate battles were very different. As we have seen, on 3 February 1461 Edward of March, now Duke of York, defeated a Lancastrian force at Mortimer's Cross. Two weeks later Queen Margaret and Andrew Trollope broke the Earl of Warwick's army at the second Battle of St Albans and Warwick was forced to flee west and take shelter with the forces of his young cousin, now advancing on London. Though Warwick again took the lead when Edward was proclaimed King, as Edward IV, on 4 March 1461, he had lost status and reputation and he and Edward both knew it.

The King was not yet 19 at his coronation, while the Earl of Warwick was a mature 33, but it was the young King Edward who now gave the orders. Before the month was out, the Yorkist army, under the direct command of King Edward IV, had shattered the huge Lancastrian army at Towton. In this battle, the Earl of Warwick was clearly in a subordinate position and the glory of the victory went to the young King Edward.

This brief resumé of their lives to 1461 is necessary because of what followed. Up to Edward IV's coronation and the victory at Towton, Warwick, by virtue of his age, experience and wealth, had been the senior partner, commanding attention and respect by the force of his experience and personality. After the events of March 1461, all that subtly changed. Edward was now a king, while Warwick remained an earl. Warwick had been defeated by Andrew Trollope at St Albans and forced to flee; Edward had defeated Trollope and a great Lancastrian force and left his enemies dead upon the field. From allies, the King and the Earl had become master and man: bending the knee to his cousin, the new young King, cannot have been easy for the great Earl of Warwick.

The delicate relationship between the King and the King's most mighty subjects had bedevilled the political life of England for centuries and was to continue to do so for generations to come. It is possible to find similarities in the relationship of the Percies to Henry IV, the Beauforts to Henry VI, Cardinal Wolsey to Henry VIII, Strafford to Charles I: all these were people who wished, perhaps for the best of motives, perhaps for reasons of self-interest, to rule the kingdom while the king merely reigned.

Warwick wanted to serve Edward as York would have served Henry VI, as the greatest man in the kingdom next to the King. He expected to be consulted on all things and have his decisions accepted. He also wanted rights of patronage and such power, wealth and privilege as his efforts for the House of York had earned him.

The snag was that King Edward was not King Henry. He had no need of such a prop to his throne and could make his own decisions. He was grateful for his cousin's help in the past and for his present advice, but he had no intention of letting the Earl make up his mind for him, or run his kingdom.

Following his coronation in June 1461, honours were distributed among the King's followers. Walter Devereux became Lord Ferrers of Chartley. Warwick's brother, Lord Fauconberg, became Earl of Kent, and Viscount Bourchier Earl of Essex; while Wenlock and Herbert were elevated to the peerage, and the King's brother, George, became Duke of Clarence. The Earl of Warwick remained an earl, but received a great number of profitable lands and appointments.

Given their combative natures and the difference in their ages, conflict between the King and the Earl was probably inevitable. Over the next months and years, Edward attempted to ease away gradually from any dependence, real or imagined, on the Earl of Warwick. In September 1461 he appointed John Tiptoft, Earl of Worcester, as his Constable, and granted lands, titles and responsibilities to Warwick's brother, Montagu. He began to deal directly, and not through Warwick, with the other great magnates of the realm. He forgave Lancastrians who submitted, even those who were sworn enemies of Warwick, and reserved the rights of high justice to himself alone.

Failing to take the hint, Warwick insisted on remaining at centre stage, as the King's chief Councillor. All men could approach the King, but wise men deferred to the Earl of Warwick, and even if all men in England soon learned who ruled the country, the Earl's reputation remained high abroad – a not unusual state of affairs in politics. Embassies paid their respects to the Earl before seeing the King, and the courts of foreign kings and lords buzzed with stories of King Edward's 'fleshy wantonness', stating that while the King enjoyed himself, the Earl of Warwick actually ruled the kingdom. As late as 1464, the Seneschal of Abbeville could remark in a dispatch to King Louis XI: 'They tell me they have two rulers in England – Monsieur de Warwick and another, whose name I have forgotten.'

Looking back over the centuries, the positions of Edward and Warwick are easy to understand, even to sympathize with, though Warwick's is the most clear-cut. He had risked everything in the wars and remained loyal to York in triumph and adversity. His father had been executed, his lands seized, his wealth spent, all to place King Edward on the throne. For all his good points, Edward IV was, in Warwick's eyes, just a lucky lad with an eye for the ladies.

King Edward saw things differently. He too had lost a father and risked his life and while, like all young men, he might sometimes be foolish, he knew he was not a fool. He had demonstrated the first necessary quality for a medieval king: the ability to lead men into battle and emerge victorious; that apart, he was the King, not Warwick. He was no Henry VI, a prisoner, a fool and a fugitive. He had no intention of being a puppet in anyone's hands, not even in those of his mighty cousin Warwick. To let that happen would indeed place him on the same level as that poor imbecile, Henry of Windsor; the very idea was laughable. The situation was full of danger, for sooner or later the two men would fall out.

King Edward still relied on Warwick, for at the time of his coronation and from long habit, Warwick was his closest confidant. They had been through a lot together and Edward had the gift of friendship. Besides, who else could he rely on? Of the King's brothers, Edmund, Earl of Rutland, had died at Wakefield, and the other two, George, made Duke of Clarence at the King's coronation, and Richard, later Duke of Gloucester, were still too young – Clarence being just 12 and Gloucester 9. Edward, therefore, had to rely on his Neville relatives, who were quickly appointed or reappointed to positions of power in the kingdom. George Neville became Chancellor, Keeper of the Great Seal; John Neville, Lord Montagu, became Captain of the North, while the Earl of Warwick picked up a generous number of appointments and commands – Captain of Calais, Constable of Dover Castle, Lord Warden of the Cinque Ports, Warden of the East and West Marches. Warwick took over the military power of the kingdom and was charged to hold it for the King. He did not, however, become a duke.

King Edward now gave his attention to constitutional, political and economic affairs, beginning with a series of Royal progresses through his newly won kingdom, putting its affairs in order. The land was still noticeably lawless, the Scots were harrying the Border and besieging Carlisle, and French pirates were attacking English shipping in the Channel. From September to November 1461, the King was progressing through the west and up the Welsh Marches from Bristol to Ludlow, granting charters, attending law courts and attempting to restore order to the most restless regions of his land. The smack of firm government had come to England, not before time, and with that trade began to recover.

A king's major responsibility was to 'provide good governance' in the form of law, order and justice, so the King sat on the Bench with the justices to see justice done, which kings had not done for decades. Edward's first Parliament met in Westminster in November 1461 and stayed sitting for the unusually long time of six months, being adjourned with a good deal of business accomplished and a general atmosphere of satisfaction, not least because the King had not asked the Commons for any money. A great deal of time was devoted to sorting out the lands of those nobles variously attainted or executed in recent years, or granted since the Lancastrian 'usurpation' of 1399. The King also heard petitions and urged the passing of various measures against the practice of livery and maintenance.

While the new King was progressing through England, his loyal Lieutenants were nailing down the frontiers of the realm in Wales, and with rather less success in the north. Lord Herbert, newly elevated by King Edward, was slowly taking over the Lancastrian castles in Wales, among them Pembroke, the home of the Lancastrian Earl of Pembroke, Jasper Tudor. Jasper was away with the Queen, but Herbert did capture an interesting toddler, the 4-year-old Henry Tudor, son of Margaret Beaufort and the late Edmund Tudor, Earl of Richmond, half-brother to Henry VI. This Royal connection even gave the young Henry Tudor some slight title to the throne. Edward IV sold the wardship of Henry Tudor to Lord Herbert for £1,000, for Herbert had several daughters and if Henry Tudor, Earl of Richmond, were married to one of them later, any future ideas about taking the English crown from Edward or his heirs would be quite out of the question.

In February 1462, the list of Royal appointments was extended by the elevation of John Tiptoft, Earl of Worcester, to the office of Constable of England. The role of Constable was a French appointment and the Constable of France was usually responsible for the raising and command of the French armies if the king was not present. Tiptoft's role was more judicial, and in his hands gradually became that of Lord High Executioner. This Tiptoft was an interesting man. Born in 1437 and Earl of Worcester since 1449, he had been married to Cecily Neville, the widow of Henry Beauchamp. Cecily had died in 1450 while Tiptoft was in Italy studying the life and politics of the Italian city-states and the first stages of the Renaissance, for John Tiptoft had cultured tastes. He had been educated at University College, Oxford, owned a fine collection of books and paintings and preferred the company of scholars to that of soldiers. He had made the pilgrimage to Jerusalem and was said to be devout. He appears as the archetype of the Renaissance lord: cultured and cruel; pious yet vengeful. His piety and learning apart, Tiptoft's main asset to the King was his ruthlessness in dealing with the King's enemies, and perhaps even his cruelty. Tiptoft was a cold, killing machine, and lost no time in demonstrating that fact.

Shortly after his appointment, a plot was discovered against the throne, involving John de Vere, the twelfth Earl of Oxford. The de Veres had come over with the Conqueror and were an ancient, well-connected House, but this did not protect them from Tiptoft. The Earl and his eldest son were arrested, attainted, tried by Tiptoft and executed, not in the seclusion of the Tower but by the axe on Tower Hill before a largely sympathetic crowd. With men of lesser blood, Tiptoft gave his nature full rein, hanging, drawing and quartering his victims, and decorating the gates of England's cities with dismembered corpses. He also introduced the Byzantine practice of impaling bodies on stakes, the first time this had been employed in England and a sight which came as a great shock to the citizens.

The next de Vere, another John, now aged 18, eventually obtained the reversal of his father's and brother's attainder and became the thirteenth Earl. He then married Margaret Neville, Warwick's youngest sister, but he never forgot what had happened to his father and brother. This Earl of Oxford became an implacable foe of the Yorkists and, when the chance arose, of Tiptoft personally.

De Vere's plot had been supported by Queen Margaret who, with the young Prince Edward, was still in Scotland. When it failed, she took ship for France in April 1462, landing first in Brittany, where the Duke Francis passed her on hurriedly into the care of her father, René, Count of Anjou. Count René was getting on in years and had no wish to become involved in his daughter's brawls, but the new King of France, Louis XI, was anxious to meet her. His father, old Charles VII, had died on 22 July 1461, starving himself to death for fear that his meat was poisoned, as mad at the end as his father had been. King Louis feared that the new King of England might be thinking of further adventures in his realm of France, and was interested in any scheme that would keep Edward at home, while he settled accounts with his former ally, the Duke of Burgundy.

The Queen and King Louis met at Chinon in March 1462 and struck a bargain. In exchange for the town of Calais, Louis would provide Margaret with a small force of soldiers, commanded by the Grand Seneschal of Normandy, Pierre de Brézé. The Queen did not actually hold Calais and de Brézé, who was suspected of conspiracy with the Duke of Burgundy, was currently being kept in a cage at the castle of Loches, south of Tours, but that could be sorted out. For the moment the Queen's word would suffice. The King was less keen to support Margaret's venture with money, and most of the funds for her expedition were, in fact, provided by de Brézé, who was probably glad to get out of France for a while. This meant that her final force was rather small, just 300 soldiers and a few Lancastrian lords and supporters, including Jasper Tudor, Earl of Pembroke, and Dr John Morton, a wily cleric but a stout Lancastrian who was in time to become Archbishop of Canterbury, Chancellor of the Realm and a Cardinal. There was some discussion on where to land and the final decision, to head for Northumberland, turned out badly. Going first to Scotland to collect King Henry and the Duke of Somerset, they came ashore at Bamburgh on the Northumberland coast on 25 October 1462, where they were soon in possession of the three great castles of Bamburgh, Dunstanburgh and the Percy stronghold, Alnwick.

When Warwick, as the King's Captain in the North, marched against them, Margaret and Prince Edward sailed back to Scotland with the foreign mercenaries, leaving Pembroke and Somerset to hold the three castles; but this retreat turned into a disaster. Their ships were wrecked on Lindisfarne, and although Margaret and the Prince escaped to Scotland, all the French mercenaries were killed or captured.

King Edward came north to command his army but was struck down with measles and for several weeks commanded the royal army from his bed in Durham. By Christmas 1462, both besiegers and besieged were tired of campaigning in the harsh northern winter, 'being grieved with cold and rayne' and an accommodation was arrived at. On Christmas Eve 1402, Jasper Tudor surrendered Bamburgh and returned to Scotland. Somerset opened the gates of Dunstanburgh, abandoned Queen Margaret, and swore an oath of loyalty to Edward, as did the Lancastrian Constable of Bamburgh, Sir Ralph Percy, who was then given charge of both castles. The other Percy stronghold, Alnwick, continued to hold out.

This agreement lasted only for a few months. In the spring of 1463, the Lancastrians rose up again. Sir Ralph Percy promptly threw off his brief Yorkist allegiance and Queen Margaret came south with de Brézé and King Henry to reoccupy Bamburgh. A Scots army came over the border in the summer, but by then Warwick and his brother, Montagu, were in the field and drove them back again. Margaret then went to Burgundy, while King Henry remained in Bamburgh, closely besieged by the Yorkists under Montagu. The siege cannot have been well kept, for the King was soon joined by the Duke of Somerset, who had also renounced his oath of loyalty to Edward IV.

These alarms and excursions, with constant skirmishes and sieges of the three castles, went on to no great effect for an entire year, until the spring of 1464. In April 1464, Somerset was in the field when Montagu rode north to meet the Scots Border lords and discuss a truce. Montagu was attacked at Hedgely Moor by a force commanded by Somerset and Sir Ralph Percy.

The battle at Hedgely Moor was brief, little more than a skirmish, but Percy was killed and Somerset fled from the rout, while Montagu proceeded to the border with most of his force intact. Somerset rounded up more men and a month later, on 14 May, Montagu met Somerset again at Hexham. Somerset, who seems to have been no soldier, had drawn up his army in the confines of a field called the Linnels, where they were unable to deploy. Some even fled before the armies clashed and the rest were swiftly overwhelmed as Montagu broke into the field and drove the survivors into the Tyne. The losses in the battle were not great, but Somerset was captured and immediately beheaded, as were Lord Roos and Lord Hungerford. Other Lancastrian prisoners were executed in York after a brief appearance before the implacable Tiptoft. Tiptoft later executed the wounded Sir Ralph Grey, the commander of Bamburgh, captured when the castle fell to cannon fire and infantry assault in May 1464. By mid-1464 the Nevilles had wiped out all Lancastrian opposition in the north of England, executing captive Lancastrians from Newcastle to Yorkshire. King Henry, however, was still at large.

In the first three years of his reign, the young King Edward had done very well. He was now recognized as King of England by all the foreign powers, and had kept friendly with his overbearing cousin, the Earl of Warwick. Lancastrian attacks had been thwarted in the north, and his rule had been recognized and legitimized by Parliament. His kingdom was still disorderly, for the rule of law was ignored by those with the power and influence to do so, but the King was working on that. For the moment, he was building up his own power-base and restoring the royal finances, for he knew, better than most, how much money fed the sinews of power. If a clash came, he would be ready for it, and in the meantime, if certain people paid excessive deference to cousin Warwick, that was not something the King felt concerned about.

One of Warwick's brothers, George Neville, now became Archbishop of York and, as a reward for his efforts in the north during the past year, in 1465 Warwick's brother Montagu was given the title and lands of the Earls of Northumberland; the last Earl of Northumberland had been killed at Towton and his heir was still a prisoner. At the time this seemed a sensible decision and a just reward, but it had unforeseen consequences. Not all the English were as self-seeking as their lords, and the people of Northumberland preferred the familiar rule of the Percies. This action also had the effect of granting the whole Border to the Nevilles, a course considered unwise, but for the moment everyone except the common people seemed content. Anyway, the court in London had other matters to concern it apart from these skirmishes in the north, for their King had married, neither wisely nor too well, and the Earl of Warwick was furious.

In the Middle Ages, and for a long while after, a royal or noble marriage was much more than the joining together of a happy couple. Whether the couple were happy hardly came into it. Marriages were an opportunity to heal a breach, cement an alliance, conclude a treaty or make a fortune. Marriage, in short, was an opportunity, and an opportunity was not something to throw away lightly. This was especially so when the male part of the bargain was that handsome bachelor, Edward IV, King of England, the catch-of-the-season for any princess. What prospects and opportunities such a marriage might provide could only be dreamed of.

Edward IV, aged 22, was in no hurry to marry. He was now rich and becoming richer, powerful, very good-looking and a great lover of the ladies. According to the Croyland *Chronicles*, Edward was 'fond of companionship, vanities, debaucheries, extravagance and sensual enjoyments'. This reputation, if true, did him no great harm. He was expected to be a bit of a lad and the common people loved him for it. Given half the chance, they would have done exactly the same. His lords, on the other hand, in particular his tiresome cousin Warwick, thought that it was time King Edward turned his attentions to a profitable marriage. That done, he could continue to play the field if he wished, but meantime he must marry. The question was, who?

Warwick might have forced one of his own daughters on the King – the thought of a scion of the House of Warwick on the throne must have made his head reel – but both of them were still very young. Besides, Edward was not interested and Parliament would have been against it. It was then suggested that a marriage to Marie de Gueldres, Queen-dowager of Scotland, might be advantageous. The lady was no longer young (in fact she died in the autumn of 1463) and her morals were doubtful, but such a match might stop the Border wars and deny a base to the Lancastrian rebels. Besides, Marie de Gueldres was a relative of Philip the Good, Duke of Burgundy, with whom England now had every reason to forge good commercial relations. This idea, too, came to nothing. If forced to choose a foreign alliance, Warwick would certainly opt for one with France, and here there was another opportunity, for King Louis had a sister-in-law, the Lady Bona of Savoy, who was eligible and available and not entirely ill-favoured. Before long, both King Louis and Warwick were pressing for the match.

Edward was less than enthusiastic. He felt that the wool trade with Flanders was more vital to England's interests than any alliance with France, and was well aware from his own experience how much the world of politics is ruled by faction. An alliance of any sort with France could only bring England into conflict with Burgundy which, he shrewdly suspected, was the secret thought in King Louis's head. That point had to be considered carefully, so here again the division between Edward and Warwick was soon obvious. Edward leaned to Burgundy, Warwick to France.

Edward's public image as a youthful, sensual lightweight, now worked against his interests. When serious matters, like a royal marriage, came to be considered, people preferred to listen to the Earl of Warwick. The great Earl had *gravitas* and a better grasp of affairs of state. It was said openly that he ruled while the King played. People were less aware of the fact that King Edward was perfectly capable of making up his own mind in this as in all other matters, and the news that the King and his chief minister were at odds over this delicate matter only confused them.

By the end of 1463, Warwick was deep in correspondence with King Louis, negotiating the terms for a marriage between his King and the Lady Bona. (The title of 'Princess' was not used until the next century, and is even missing from Shakespeare's text.) He continued to negotiate with France and eagerly supported Edward when, in early 1464, the King declined to consider marriage with Isabella, the 12-year-old Infanta of Castile, who eventually married Ferdinand of Aragon. Before long though, the King and his most senior Councillor were clearly set on a collision course. Conflict became certain from May 1464, for by then the King was nursing a secret. He kept it from everyone until the great council at Reading on 14 September 1464.

The peers of the realm assembled in Reading Abbey with just two items on the agenda. Firstly, some questions concerning the new currency; and secondly, the name of the lady whom the King would marry. The question of the currency was the major issue, for Europe was very short of gold and silver for the coinage, and continued to be so until the treasures of Mexico and Peru flowed in during the next century. Periodic reform of the coinage was a serious economic measure, and the new coins, the rose noble, worth ten shillings (50p), and the angel, worth half a mark (six shillings and eight pence; 34p) were to be displayed for approval before general issue. This done, the news of the King's forthcoming marriage and the name of his bride-to-be would serve as light relief. According to Warwick and his clique, this bride would be the Lady Bona, for the Earl had made up his mind and the matter was closed. After the Royal announcement of betrothal, Warwick would leave for France to conclude the wedding arrangements with the King of France, and thereby score a great political coup, and no doubt – though the matter was unspoken – the King of France would richly reward him for his support in this matter. Given all this, the King's announcement came like a thunderbolt.

Having gathered all his nobles close about him, Edward rose from his throne to say, blandly, that, alas, he could not marry the Lady Bona. He was already married and had been for the last four months – not to a princess of France or Spain, but to the Lady Elizabeth Grey, daughter of Lord Rivers and Duchess Jacquetta, widow of that Sir John Grey of Groby who had been killed at St Albans, fighting for the Lancastrians. If the King had set out to shock his council and affront his cousin Warwick, he could hardly have done more.

CHAPTER NINE

THE RISE OF THE WOODVILLES (1465–70)

What other pleasure can the world afford?
I'll make my heaven in a lady's lap,
And deck my body in gay ornaments,
And witch sweet ladies with my words and looks.

HENRY VI

The Woodvilles were respectable country knights from Northampton-shire, holding a manor at Grafton, near Stony Stratford. They had made their first step up the ladder to nobility when Sir Richard Woodville married Jacquetta, Dowager-duchess of Bedford, widow of John, Duke of Bedford, the brother of Henry V, and the late Regent of France. Bedford had been married to the sister of Philip the Good, Duke of Burgundy, and when she died in 1433 he hurriedly married the 17-year-old Jacquetta, who was a daughter of Burgundy's principal vassal, the Count of St Pol. This hurried remarriage, so soon after the death of his sister, apparently gave the Duke of Burgundy great offence – or so he maintained. In fact, Burgundy was racking his brains to find some reason to quarrel with the English and this marriage was a good excuse.

The Duke of Bedford died in 1435. A year later, Jacquetta married Sir Richard Woodville, a member of her late husband's household and a man of no connections at all. There was, inevitably, a scandal. The marriage, and Sir Richard, were rejected by Jacquetta's French relatives and for marrying without the permission of the Royal Council, the Duchess was fined a thousand pounds, a trifling sum to her as she was very rich. In the minority of the King, she was the leading lady at the court of Henry VI and remained so until the arrival of Queen Margaret in 1445.

This may have been the time when the Woodville family first began to irritate the old nobility. The magnates may, at a pinch, have been prepared to tolerate the Duchess Jacquetta, who was from very grand *noblesse* in France and the widow of the famous Duke of Bedford, King Harry's brother. The English nobility had always felt nervous in the presence of the French nobility, who carried the whole business off with much more aplomb, but they found no difficulty at all in dealing with one of the lower orders foolish enough to get above his station. Sir Richard had rather a thin time of it around the court, though he did the King good service and was a thoroughly decent man. Fortunately, Jacquetta got on well with Margaret of Anjou and in 1448 Sir Richard Woodville was summoned to Parliament and became Lord Rivers. In 1450 he became a Knight of the Garter and a Privy Councillor. Their son, Anthony Woodville, Lord Scales, was popular with the knighthood of England for his prowess as a jouster; he was also a skilful soldier who had fought the Moors in Spain, and had made the pilgrimage to Santiago de Compostela. The Woodvilles, then, were a happy, confident and united family, typical, save that one aristocratic connection, of many of the country gentry.

King Edward's new wife, Elizabeth, was the eldest daughter, but even if the match had been suitable, there were several snags in the alliance. All the family were partisans of Lancaster and the Lady Elizabeth had been married before, to a Lancastrian knight, Sir John Grey, who had been killed fighting for the Lancastrians at the second Battle of St Albans. By Sir John she already had two children: Thomas, later Marquis of Dorset, then aged 9, and Richard Grey, who was probably 5 or 6.

Sir John Grey – Grey of Groby – was a near neighbour of the Woodvilles, living at Groby Castle near Leicester. The family were also close friends of the Hastings family, whose eldest son, William, now Lord Hastings, was a close friend and comrade-in-arms of Edward IV. Hastings may even have introduced Edward to Elizabeth, though legend – and Shakespeare – has it that they met when Lady Elizabeth Grey came to beg the King for the return of her attainted husband's lands. According to Shakespeare, Edward offered to return the lands in exchange for her virtue, an offer the lady rejected. He continued to press her and she continued to refuse, but they continued to meet until, rather to their mutual surprise, they fell in love.

This love-match put the King in a quandary. He knew that his Council, and especially Warwick, would be dead-set against such a worthless match, and with a Lancastrian family to boot. On the other hand, short of rape, he could have the lady on no other terms. Even kings cannot always have what they want, but he was, after all, the King and could arrange matters. It is not likely that Edward actually hesitated, though the secrecy which subsequently surrounded the marriage is surprising, not least in that it lasted for so long.

Edward left Windsor Castle after the Garter service on St George's Day, 23 April 1469, and rode north into Leicestershire, ostensibly to go hunting. He left Stony Stratford early on the morning of 1 May and rode across to Grafton, where the pair were married later that day. Passions must have been running high, for the King and his bride retired to bed immediately after the service and stayed there for several hours. By nightfall, however, he was back at Stony Stratford where, apart from a few close friends, probably including Hastings, no one was any the wiser. The King was now 22, his new wife 25 or 26. He returned to see and sleep with Elizabeth on several occasions over the next few weeks, but their secret was kept for four months, until the King himself broke the news to the council at Reading in October.

If the council was stunned and shocked (and all the evidence says that it was both), the Earl of Warwick's reaction goes unrecorded. There can be no doubt that he was furious, but under the circumstances he concealed it well. He was the first to come forward with congratulations, and when the Lady Elizabeth appeared at Reading at the end of October to be formally introduced to the council as Edward's wife, she was led in by the Earl of Warwick and the Duke of Clarence, and by all accounts both made her very welcome.

Public faces are one thing, private thoughts another. The King's marriage had made the Earl of Warwick look a fool, not merely in England but in France and Burgundy. The Earl had gone so far down the road towards engaging his King to Bona of Savoy that he hardly knew how to let King Louis know that, while they had been negotiating over her hand, her prospective bridegroom had been married for months to someone else. King Louis had long ears and by early October he had heard the news and begun badgering Warwick for an explanation. He also expressed his surprise that Warwick's first reaction was not to take up arms against the King. This, Warwick declined to do, but as more and more Woodvilles appeared at court and slipped into profitable appointments, he began to change his mind.

The Woodville family was not highly regarded or widely accepted by the other magnates of England. This is rather curious because the family had been gentlefolk for a long time and knighthood was, anyway, supposed to create a bond between all gentlemen of quality. The Duchess Jacquetta had been a very high-born lady, daughter of a count and wife of a duke, and if her husband, Lord Rivers, had started life as a simple knight, he had been a good soldier in the French wars, a fact now generally acknowledged. He had now been Lord Rivers for six years and a Knight of the Garter for four, and he was a Privy Councillor. Others may have thought the Woodvilles low, but the Woodvilles thought, quite rightly, that they were a match for anyone.

On the face of it, there could have been little for any lord to object to, but this: the Woodvilles were representatives of the 'new nobility', who had risen recently by royal preferment. Edward and his father, York, had been against the elevation of favourites, like Suffolk or Somerset, and yet here was the same cycle, starting again among the King's relatives to the detriment of his proven friends, the old magnates of the realm – like Warwick. Even worse, not only were the Woodvilles Lancastrians, but there were also far too many of them.

Elizabeth had 12 brothers and sisters, who all now sought preferment. Edward's rapid promotion of his new relations, if understandable, was too rapid and somewhat unwise. Elizabeth's father, Lord Rivers, became an earl and took up the post of treasurer, a role which he filled at least adequately, for the King prospered. Her brother Anthony, Lord Scales, was a well-known figure about the court, and indeed, in knightly circles all over Europe. Edward rewarded him with the lordship of the Isle of Wight. Her other brothers received only minor offices – grants of manors or the constableship of royal castles – for Edward, if fond, was too clever to create another powerful family in his kingdom when trouble was already brewing with the Nevilles.

Where Edward really did show favour to the Woodvilles was in the marriages he arranged for the daughters. Elizabeth's sisters were soon married to peers or the sons of peers. This caused general offence because, apart from elevating the upstart Woodvilles, it prevented profitable marriages for other members of the old nobility. Anne, daughter of the exiled Henry Holland, Duke of Exeter, was retrieved from the son of Warwick's brother, Lord Montagu, and married to Thomas Grey, Elizabeth's eldest son. Mary Woodville married William Herbert, son of the new Earl of Pembroke; Margaret Woodville married Lord Maltravers, heir to the Earl of Arundel, and Anne Woodville married William Bourchier, heir to the Earl of Essex.

Catherine Woodville was married to Henry Stafford, the second Duke of Buckingham, while in a match which caused a great scandal, John Woodville, Elizabeth's younger brother, was married to the King's aunt, Catherine Neville, Dowager-duchess of Norfolk, who was at least 66 while John was just 20. The Dowager-duchess had already had three husbands and her children were not too pleased with their new stepfather. By these alliances Edward did two things. He began to create his own affinity, separate from that of the Nevilles, and he forged links with a cross-section of the nobility, who would adhere to him, he hoped, by virtue of their wives. The Earl of Warwick must have viewed these arrangements with interest.

The new Queen was crowned at Westminster on Whit Monday, 26 May 1465, amid considerable celebrations, although Warwick and William, Lord Hastings, were not there, being engaged in a round of talks with the envoys of France, Burgundy and Brittany. The Queen seems to have taken her new rank very seriously, obliging even her close relatives to kneel when speaking to her. This affectation was noted by the old nobility, already smarting from the rash of Woodville marriages. The Woodvilles were swift at making enemies, and their enemies now looked to Warwick for some redress of their grievances.

In February 1466, Elizabeth gave birth to their first child, a girl, who was christened Elizabeth after her mother; a child who grew up to become the wife of the Tudor monarch, Henry VII. Other marriages were now in the air, for the second wife of Charles, Count of Charolais, son and heir to the Duke of Burgundy, had died and a new wife had to be found for him. Edward saw this as a chance for another alliance and he proposed that Charles the Rash should marry Edward's sister Margaret, while Charles's daughter by Isabelle of Bourbon, Mary, should marry the King's brother George, Duke of Clarence. The negotiations were handled by Warwick, who clearly still enjoyed the King's trust but who had no particular interest in a Burgundian alliance, and they soon broke down. To soften the blow slightly, Warwick came back with a number of suggested suitors for the hand of the infant Lady Elizabeth – all of them French lords, loyal to Louis XI.

* * *

While all these exciting manoeuvres were exercising the minds and tongues of the English court, the exiled House of Lancaster was having another round of bad luck. After the fall of the Northumbrian castles, King Henry had fled to Scotland, but by the spring of 1465 he was back in the north of England, being secretly passed from house to house, sheltered among his Lancastrian supporters. In July 1465 he was discovered and captured at Waddington Hall, near Clitheroe, and brought in slow stages to London. The Earl of Warwick met him at Islington and paraded the King, now aged 44, through the streets of the city before taking him to the Tower, but there were no royal honours on display this time; the ex-King's ankles were lashed to his stirrup leathers and armed guards rode at his elbow.

Henry was to remain in the Tower for the next five years, but his imprisonment was neither hard nor strict. He had plenty of visitors, was allowed his own servants and a choice of guards, and a weekly sum of five marks was allotted for his maintenance. He even seems to have been happy. Wine was supplied to him from King Edward's own cellars and velvet cloth from the Royal wardrobe. The only thing missing, apart from liberty, was the Royal dignity, for Henry was no longer referred to as King. The captive in the Tower was Henry of Windsor, nothing more.

His Queen, Margaret, and the relics of her Court were now at the castle of St Michel-en-Barrois in France, living on the slender resources provided by René of Anjou. With her were the young Prince Edward, the Duke of Exeter, Lord Roos and Dr John Morton, among a collection of fugitives amounting to around 200. Some of her knights soon drifted away to serve other lords, and Comines the chronicler recalls seeing 'the Duke of Exeter following the Duke of Burgundy's train barefoot and begging his bread from door to door'. The Duke of Burgundy eventually gave Exeter and the other Lancastrian lords a small pension to live on while they awaited better times.

★　★　★

In June 1467, a question which had vexed the noble minds of Europe for many years was finally put to the test. Who was the finest jouster: Anthony, Bastard of Burgundy, the eldest son of Philip the Good, or Anthony Woodville, Lord Scales, the champion of England? The matter had been debated for years and cheerful challenges had been sent to and fro across the Channel many times, but now at last the stage was set for a decisive encounter. The Bastard was coming to London anyway, to revive the negotiations over the marriage of Edward's sister Margaret to Charles, Count of Charolais, heir to the Duke of Burgundy, and the chance was too good to miss. It was agreed that the Burgundian lord would come to London with his retinue in June 1467 and there engage his rival, Anthony, in the lists. The aristocracy of Europe thrilled to the event and talked of little else.

Jousting, which had been falling out of favour, again became a passion with the nobility and the castle yards echoed to the thundering hoofs of knightly destriers. Any knight displaying talent in the lists rode to London or Dijon to help the gallants practise or to lend them items of equipment. It promised to be a jolly affair and Edward, who had now been on the throne for six years, was very much looking forward to it, both as a celebration of his reign to date and as evidence of his kingdom's growing prosperity.

On the surface, at least, all was going well for King Edward. There had been no fighting since Hexham and the wounds of war appeared to be healing. Henry of Windsor was in the Tower, while his Queen and her brat were enduring genteel poverty in Anjou. The King's interests in trade and his investments in commerce saw the royal coffers filling steadily, and his own Queen was pleasant to live with. The only cloud on the horizon was the King's brother, George, Duke of Clarence.

Clarence had been born in Dublin Castle in October 1449. He was now 18 and had recently become a close confidant of the Earl of Warwick, and the two were plotting advancement. Their scheme was for Clarence to marry Warwick's eldest daughter, Isobel Neville, a marriage that would have the effect of moving the Nevilles one step closer to the throne, for until the Queen produced a son, Clarence was the King's heir. Such a marriage would require a papal dispensation since the two were cousins within the limits of consanguinity, but that obstacle had been overcome before and they saw no difficulty there. The problem was the King: following the convention, since made law after the marriage of Catherine of Valois to Owen Tudor, a member of the Royal family could not marry without the express permission of the sovereign. Warwick and Clarence considered it most unlikely that the King would attempt to bar a match between his brother and the daughter of his long-time friend and supporter, for such a denial would be an insult to both earls. Unless, that is, the King had decided to prefer the Woodvilles to the Nevilles.

This seemed possible at the Parliament of June 1467, a few days before the eagerly awaited tournament, when the King made two announcements. The first was that his finances were so much restored he could now 'live off his own' and would have no need of grants. This meant he would have no need to call Parliaments. The second was to dismiss his chancellor, the Archbishop of York, George Neville, and pluck the Great Seal of the Realm from his hands, giving the post to a man the King favoured, Bishop Stillington, now elevated to the See of Bath and

Wells, a man whose abilities were obvious to no one but the King. Edward had gone to Archbishop Neville's house, with Lord Herbert at his back, to demand the Great Seal and to dismiss the chancellor, while Warwick was away in Burgundy. The news of this insult to his brother simply added to Warwick's growing fury with the King.

While the old nobility was digesting this move, the great tournament came and suddenly went. On the first day, Thursday, 11 June 1467, the two lords managed one joust on horseback before the King stopped the fight and there was an argument over Scales's jousting saddle. On the second day, they fought for an hour with axes, knocking each other down from time to time, but without injury and to no very definite conclusion. Then a herald galloped in to tell the Burgundian champion that his father, Duke Philip, had died. The Bastard hurriedly departed and the entire court went into mourning. Then, to cap it all, the plague returned and was spread about the country by spectators trailing home from the tournament. An event that had promised a lot of innocent enjoyment had ended in misery, and worse was to follow.

The next two years passed without great events, but there was a noticeable increase in the tension between the King and Warwick. In June 1468 the King's sister, Margaret, set out for her marriage to Charles the Rash, the new Duke of Burgundy. The arrangements went ahead in spite of the united efforts of the Earl of Warwick and King Louis, who were trying to get the Pope to ban the match on the usual grounds of consanguinity. When that move failed, rumours were spread about Burgundy and Paris that the Lady Margaret was no lady but actually the mother of an illegitimate son. Duke Charles quashed this merry tale by proclaiming that anyone caught spreading it would be wrapped in chains, put in a sack and thrown into the river.

In Ireland, there were the usual troubles with the turbulent kerns, and in 1467 the formidable Tiptoft gave up his constableship of England and went to Ireland as the deputy lieutenant. The post of Constable of England went to the King's father-in-law, Earl Rivers.

In 1468 the Duke of Brittany sent envoys to Edward, asking for aid to counter hostile actions along his frontiers by troops of Louis XI. Edward declined to intervene directly, but urged Duke Charles of Burgundy to do so, offering him money and archers. On 18 July 1468 this growing alliance between England and Burgundy was sealed by the Duke's marriage to the King's sister Margaret, but the King of England could not attend the wedding at Damme: he had enough problems at home.

In England, matters were slipping out of the King's control. The cracks in the alliance between him and Warwick had now been widened into a considerable breach by the King's preferential treatment of the Woodvilles, and by Warwick's gradual recognition that Edward was a king who would be ruled by no man. By June 1468 this breach between the old friends and allies was getting too wide for past goodwill to span.

The most powerful argument used by Bolingbroke against Richard II and by York against Henry VI was that they were weak monarchs, pawns in the hands of their corrupt supporters and court sycophants, who were bleeding the royal coffers and usurping the role of the King's traditional props and councillors, the great magnates of the realm. According to Warwick and his supporters, the latter role was currently being played by the Woodvilles, who were seen as enjoying undue preferment, while the King wasted his energy in the pursuit of pleasure and other men's wives.

There was just enough truth in this to provide a fragile alliance between the Earl of Warwick and the easily affronted 'old nobility' of England: the Norfolks and the Nevilles, the Duke of Buckingham and other lords with ancient quarterings on their blazonry. Warwick was able to declare – or at this stage, murmur softly – that he was not interested in the crown for himself (perish the thought!) but perhaps for that upright prince, George, Duke of Clarence, who was the second son of the late protector, Richard of York, or perhaps even his first son, if those old stories about Duchess Cecily and the archer of Rouen were correct. In this activity Warwick had a willing tool in the Duke of Clarence.

Clarence had grown to be a weak, spoilt, vacillating man, jealous of his brother, Edward, a hater of the Woodvilles, and easy prey for a manipulator like the Earl of Warwick. Warwick could lay before him an alliance where both could profit. Warwick had no sons to take on his vast inheritance, which was lure enough in itself, but he would also use his power to place Clarence on the throne as he had done for Edward, and he had a pair of nubile daughters, a catch for any prince. For Clarence, he had in mind his eldest daughter, Isobel, now aged 15.

If this plot to replace Edward worked, Warwick's descendants through Clarence and Isobel would be Kings of England. Warwick, who had signally failed to manipulate Edward, had no doubt of his ability to manipulate Clarence and indeed was already doing so. If a further reason were needed, both men resented Edward for pushing them aside in favour of the Woodvilles. When Edward refused to let his brother marry the Lady Isobel Neville and sent envoys to Rome to argue against the grant of a dispensation, that proved the final straw. From that moment on, Clarence and Warwick were plotting treason. There were still plenty of old Lancastrians about and these, combined with disaffected Nevilles and disappointed Yorkists pushed aside for preferment by the swarming Woodvilles, would provide Warwick with plenty of allies for a rising against the King.

The first stirrings of rebellion began in the north. In the spring of 1469 two groups of rebels went on the rampage in Yorkshire, and though they appear to have had no connection with each other, both chose the name Robin as a pseudonym for their leader. One called himself Robin of Holderness, the other Robin of Redesdale. It is hard to think of a parallel today, but at the time the name Robin carried implications hinting that the leader was a champion of the poor and a righter of wrongs, a successor to Robin Hood, warring against a corrupt system and a usurping prince, in support of the public well-being, common justice and the rightful heir to the throne. In 1469, people had no difficulty fitting current names to those ancient legendary roles.

Warwick's brother, Montagu, now Earl of Northumberland, had no difficulty suppressing Robin of Holderness and applied himself with vigour to the task, since one of the claims in Robin's manifesto was that the Earldom of Northumberland should be returned to its rightful heirs, the attainted Percies. Montagu, therefore, captured Robin of Holderness and cut off his head.

The manifesto produced and circulated by Robin of Redesdale was a much more subtle document. The clauses it contained went right to the heart of Warwick's arguments and plenty of people saw his hand behind it. The King, it stated, had turned his back on his loyal supporters, the old nobility, the long-standing props of the throne and most of the princes of the blood, to listen to the words of his wife's low-bred relatives and their clique. This new group included all the Woodvilles, Lord Herbert, Lord Stafford, recently elevated to the Earldom of Devon, and Lord Audley, son of that notorious Lancastrian who had been killed by Warwick's father at Blore Heath. These were all people for whom Warwick had cultivated a considerable animosity, and it was noticed that while Montagu was quick to suppress Robin of Holderness, the Nevilles somehow seemed unable to stamp out the activities of his namesake of Redesdale.

Robin of Redesdale was soon known to be the pseudonym of either Sir William Conyers or his brother, Sir John, two Yorkshire knights of the Neville affinity. Redesdale's forces were still active in the mid-summer of

1469, and their numbers were growing, so with Warwick proving ineffective, King Edward decided to take matters into his own hands.

He began by moving to his family home at Fotheringhay and sending his supporters out to muster men. The Herberts went into Wales and Humphrey Stafford, the new Earl of Devon, began recruiting in the west, while Edward began a Royal progress towards Walsingham, raising men as he went and taking with him his younger brother, Richard, Duke of Gloucester, now a knight aged 16. Of his other brother, Clarence, and his own friend Warwick, there was no sign at all.

East Anglia was in need of a Royal visit because the region was in turmoil. The cause of this situation is known in great detail to history because it concerned that communicative family, the Pastons, who were involved in a serious dispute with the local magnate, the Duke of Norfolk. Apart from the Duke's general indifference to law and order, the dispute centred on Caister Castle, which the Pastons claimed to own and which the Duke was desperate to possess.

The Pastons were a long-established East Anglian county family, of no particular rank or distinction, though by 1469 they were knights and gentlemen of coat-armour. Their subsequent fame rests on the 1,000-strong collection of letters – the Paston letters – exchanged between members of the family and their friends in the middle decades of the fifteenth century. These have provided posterity with insights of life at the time, within a typical gently bred family and at the courts and castles of the greater men with whom the family were associated.

In the early years of the fifteenth century, Sir William Paston became a Justice of the Peace, and then a judge. The law was even then profitable and his eldest son, John Paston, also became a lawyer, the only money-making profession open to a gentleman of quality. Unfortunately, lawyer Paston was a crook. One of his clients was a venerable knight of the French wars, Sir John Fastolf, a servant of Henry V. Having made his mark and his money in France, where he was the victor of the Battle of the Herrings in 1428, and served in many other campaigns, Fastolf returned to Norfolk, where he invested his money in land and built a beautiful little fortified manor near Yarmouth, called Caister Castle. All his legal affairs, including his will, were handled by lawyer Paston, and when the old knight died in 1459, a will was produced in which Sir John had apparently left Caister Castle and most of his property to his lawyer. The local gentry, and in particular the Duke of Norfolk, were highly suspicious of this testament.

The rest of lawyer Paston's life, until his death in May 1466, was largely occupied with legal wrangles with the Duke over Sir John's estates, interspersed with riots, attacks and attempted assassinations. One of the Paston letters referred to an incident in 1461 or 1462 when 'it is talked how ye and Howard have striven together on the Shire-Day and one of Howard's men had struck at ye twice with a dagger and so ye should have been hurt but for the good doublet ye had on, blest be God ye had it.' Legal arguments can go one way and another as appeal follows appeal. By 1469 the Duke of Norfolk had had enough of all this shilly-shallying, and decided to evict the Pastons from Caister by force of arms.

The King had already instructed the Duke and the Pastons to stop their quarrelling and lay the case before him at the King's Bench in London. The Paston–Norfolk affair was dividing the nobility and was a clear incitement for other litigants to ignore the law and settle disputes by force, a short step on the road to anarchy. The King had enough problems to contend with already, but Norfolk's men continued to ravage Paston lands and were still doing so when the King rode to Walsingham.

After visiting the shrine at Walsingham, Edward led his forces back to his castle at Fotheringhay, where he was joined by the Queen and many of the Woodville affinity. While they were there, they heard that George, Duke of Clarence, had finally obtained a Papal dispensation, crossed the Channel and married Warwick's eldest daughter, Isobel, against the King's express wishes. The marriage took place in Calais on 11 July 1469, with the Archbishop of York, George Neville, officiating and a host of Nevilles in the church stalls. Another guest at the wedding feast was the young John de Vere, Earl of Oxford, who hated Edward IV for executing his father, and would support any attempt to bring him down. Shortly after the ceremony, the Nevilles issued a proclamation calling on the men of Kent to join them and free the people of England from the corrupt persons now ruling the mind and person of the King. This done, they crossed the Channel to Sandwich and marched on London, gathering men as they came.

When the news reached him that Warwick and Clarence had risen and were in the field, Edward was still at Fotheringhay, waiting on reinforcements from the Herberts in the west and Wales, where William, Lord Herbert had become Earl of Pembroke in 1468. To combine his forces before they could be overwhelmed in detail, Edward marched west, hoping to meet the forces of the Earl of Devon and Lord Pembroke, but before he could do so, Robin of Redesdale's army, coming from the north, met Lord Herbert's Welshmen at Edgecote Field on 26 July 1469. Redesdale's men swiftly overcame and slaughtered the Welsh before the Earl of Devon's men could arrive, and although Devon's troops then drove off Redesdale's forces, they were overwhelmed in their turn by the much larger army of the Earl of Warwick, which arrived when the battle was finely balanced. The Nevilles triumphed and held the field, the Welshmen suffered grievous losses and the Yorkist Earl of Pembroke, Lord Herbert, was captured, taken to Northampton and beheaded.

This much achieved, Warwick proceeded to hunt down and execute all the King's men he could find. The Earl of Devon was swiftly caught and as swiftly executed, while a search party along the March of Wales captured and beheaded Earl Rivers, the Queen's father, and her brother, Sir John Woodville. The enmity between the Nevilles and the Woodvilles must have been great indeed to cause such wilful slaughter, but Warwick had gone too far to draw back. His actions were stark treason and his only remedy was to seize the King... and kill him.

At this moment, with his allies defeated and his close relatives and supporters either executed or driven into hiding, King Edward made a shrewd move. He dismissed his forces to avoid further conflict and on 29 July placed himself into the hands of George Neville, Archbishop of York, at Olney, in Buckinghamshire. He had thereby placed himself and his crown under the protection of the Church and the Earl of Warwick was suddenly thwarted. Warwick and Clarence had banked on the King's pugnacity, hoping that he would fall on them with his small army and perish in the resulting defeat. His surrender to the archbishop left them baffled, and uncertain how to proceed.

Edward was still King. Though the King remained a prisoner until October 1469, Warwick and Clarence dare not kill him. Neither did they release Henry of Windsor from the Tower, nor make any approaches to the Lancastrians in France. Warwick was playing another game to advance his own House, but he did not know how to play it, even with two kings in his hands. There then came a Lancastrian rebellion in the north, led by two more Nevilles, Humphrey and Charles, from the Westmorland branch of the family, in support of Henry VI. The Earl of Warwick promptly led the royal army north to subdue his relatives, both of whom were executed, and while he was there, Edward was released from his captivity in Coventry.

The King entered London in triumph in mid-October, restored again to his throne and kingdom, and rode into the City accompanied by

Warwick's brother, Montagu. Edward also had most of his adherents at his side, including his brother Gloucester and the Duke of Norfolk and, or so it was said, 'the King spoke of Clarence, Warwick and the Archbishop as his friends, but his Household men have other language'.

Montagu's presence at the King's side is interesting, for he was Warwick's brother, and he had his own dispute with the King. Montagu was at present Earl of Northumberland, but Edward had come to an arrangement whereby his son and heir, George Neville, would marry Edward's eldest daughter, the Lady Elizabeth. In exchange, Montagu would relinquish his title to the Earldom of Northumberland, which would be handed back to the attainted and imprisoned Henry Percy, a prisoner in the Tower since his father had died at Towton, who would be released and returned to his ancestral estates. The point of all this, from Edward's point of view, was that by putting a Percy back in the north, he would be placing a rival to the Nevilles in their northern heartland. This might give them more to think about than deposing their King in the south. Why Montagu agreed to this is not clear, unless the thought of a Royal connection proved too tempting to resist.

Montagu did insist on the award of an elevation in status from earl to the rank of marquis, with the promise of fresh lands to support his new dignity, so he must have anticipated a rise in status and income. The agreement also stipulated the reward of the Dukedom of Bedford for his son, George. Should anything happen to King Edward – which was highly possible – young George Neville, as husband of the King's eldest daughter, stood as good a chance of the throne as Clarence and Warwick's daughter, Isobel. All these arrangements were effected by the end of January 1470, but none of them held good for long and the marriage never took place.

The King was then able to reward his close supporters because Warwick's unlawful execution of the Woodvilles had left a number of vacant posts. The fearsome Tiptoft was recalled from Ireland and joined the Royal Council, while Sir John Howard became Lord Howard, and the young Duke of Gloucester, now aged 18, was made Constable of England, in succession to the executed Earl Rivers. Meanwhile, Warwick had returned cautiously from the north. With the Duke of Clarence at his side he attended a Great Council in December, in which they and their adherents were pardoned for their recent rebellion, so the year of 1469 ended with an uneasy peace holding in the English kingdom. No one expected it to last.

CHAPTER TEN

WARWICK'S REBELLION (1470–71)

I thinke the Earle of Warwike a glorious man, for if
he had not good virtues the people would not have
loved him like they did. But God be with and send
his soule rest, for sure his body never had any, and
though he dyed, yet the civill warrs ceased not.

A MIRROR FOR MAGISTRATES (1569)

The fragile peace held until the spring of 1470, when the lawless lords of Lincolnshire supplied the spark which ignited the fire. Three knights, Lord Welles, his son Sir Robert Welles, and Sir Thomas Dymoke, the King's champion, attacked and burned property belonging to a local rival, Sir Thomas Burgh, one of King Edward's household. Lord Welles was a partisan of Warwick, but using the excuse that this was a rising on behalf of the Lancastrians, Welles's father having fought and died for the Lancastrians at Towton, Warwick and Clarence began to raise soldiers, ostensibly to aid the King.

Edward countered this move by having Lord Welles and Sir Thomas Dymoke brought to London and imprisoned in the Tower. There they were examined and admitted to knowledge of an intended rising by Warwick. The King would have left at once for Lincolnshire, but Clarence arrived and detained him in London. Edward left London on 6 March and two days later received a friendly letter from Clarence offering to bring forces up in support of the King. Edward was pleased with this and immediately sent commissions, ordering Clarence and Warwick to raise troops.

All this was deception. Clarence and Warwick had been in touch with Welles and Dymoke from the outset, and Clarence was only trying to delay and dupe his brother until the rebel forces could muster. The next news was that the army was assembling in Lincolnshire under Sir Robert Welles with the intention of marching on London to rescue Lord Welles and Dymoke. Edward, therefore, organized a swift trial and cut off their heads. This done, he marched to Fotheringhay, gathering troops on the way, and on 12 March he routed the army of Sir Robert Welles at Empingham, near Stamford. The fight was over in a few minutes and after one salvo from the King's artillery, Welles's men rushed from the battle, throwing off their livery with such alacrity that the 'battle' became known as Losecoat Field.

An interrogation of prisoners now revealed what the King already suspected: that this rebellion had been fostered by his brother, Clarence, and the Earl of Warwick. Sir Robert Welles confirmed as much when he was captured a few days later, though this did not save him from execution. His head was cut off in Doncaster market-place on 19 March 1470, by which time King Edward was fully in the field and in hot pursuit of Warwick and Clarence, who were withdrawing at all speed to the west.

The total failure of this new rebellion seems to have dismayed the rebel lords. Warwick sent messengers to his family, instructing them to gather their valuables with all speed and await him at Exeter. His mother, Clarence's wife, Isobel, and her sister, Anne, were waiting there when Warwick and Clarence rode in on 3 April. They all took ship for Calais, where Warwick was still recognized as captain. The rough seas distressed the ladies, especially the Lady Isobel, who was more than eight months pregnant with her first child. On arrival, they were given a cautious welcome by that slippery lord, Warwick's deputy, Lord Wenlock, who sent supplies to their ships but refused to let even the ladies land or Warwick's ships anchor in the harbour.

Edward and his army arrived at Exeter on 14 April, having issued a proclamation against 'our traitors, the rebels Duke of Clarence and the Earl of Warwick'. The King was entertained by the mayor and corporation to dinner in the guildhall, where on noticing that the roof vault was decorated with the bear and ragged staff badge of Warwick, the King left behind his sword as a reminder of his power. Both mementoes are still preserved by the corporation of Exeter. The point was driven home more brutally by Tiptoft, who took 20 'gentlemen and yeomen' of Warwick's affinity to Southampton, where they were drawn and quartered and their reassembled bodies impaled on stakes, to the great disgust of the citizens.

Across the narrow seas at Calais, Warwick and Clarence were meeting difficulties. Wenlock was reluctant to allow 'our traitors and rebels', within the gates of the town, and although he sent gifts of wine out to their ships, he advised Warwick to seek shelter elsewhere. More terrible still was the situation of the poor Lady Isobel, whose baby was born at sea while the ships tossed in the Channel off Calais harbour, but shortly afterwards, to her great distress, the baby died. The Duke of Burgundy was no friend of Warwick, which barred them from landing at the ports of Flanders, so the party coasted south, out of Picardy into Normandy, and finally came ashore in early May at Honfleur, at the mouth of the Seine. From there they went in easy stages up the river to the court of King Louis in Paris.

Whatever his faults, the Earl of Warwick was never short of ideas. It is from this period of his life, from June 1470 to April 1471, that he gets his enduring nickname of 'the kingmaker'. His power had made a king out of Edward, Earl of March, and his power could drag that king down. What he needed now was another king to put in Edward's place. Henry VI was quite useless and the devious nature of his son-in-law, the Duke of Clarence, was already becoming apparent. Fortunately, Warwick had the means to find another son-in-law.

The young Lancastrian, Prince Edward, son of Margaret of Anjou, was now 16 and just the right age for kingship. It is probable, therefore, that Warwick's plan was to marry his youngest daughter, Anne, to this Prince, raise an army and, on returning to England, release King Henry and defeat King Edward in the field. That done, King Henry could abdicate and the new King Edward would ascend the throne, leaning gratefully on the arm of his father-in-law, Warwick. All that Warwick had to do was make his peace with Margaret of Anjou; that, Warwick admitted, might be a problem.

Margaret of Anjou hated the Earl of Warwick. She had hated the Duke of York too, but in her quieter moments Margaret must have reflected that with all his faults, York was a duke, and a prince of the blood, and that he did have a claim – a small one, of course – but, nevertheless, a valid claim to the throne. If only her husband Henry had been more of a man, none of this might have happened . . . .

For Richard Neville, Earl of Warwick, the Queen could find no such excuses. He was a rebel, a turncoat, a traitor, an upstart, a man who had slandered her, a patronizing war-lord, the sort of subject any sensible monarch would wish to see shortened by a head. Margaret could trace all her problems back to this man. It was pleasant to see him so cast down, even by the usurper Edward of March, but the thought of returning to England in his train and thanking him for his support thereafter almost choked her.

However, needs must. The Lancastrians had now been in exile for nine years. Most of Margaret's followers wanted only to return to their estates in England and see their wives again. Her life had been hard of late and money was short, and she must look to the future, and in the event, forgiving Warwick was not so hard. King Louis pleaded; Sir John Fortescue presented legal arguments; and the Earl of Warwick went on his knees before her, begging for forgiveness in a most pleasing fashion. However bloody her private thoughts, Margaret raised the Earl to his feet and gave her consent to the marriage of Prince Edward and the Lady Anne. King Louis, a man not noted for his generosity, loaned the money for a Papal dispensation and the couple were betrothed in the cathedral at Tours on St James's Day, 25 July 1470.

None of this particularly pleased the Duke of Clarence. All he got out of it, as a sop for his support, was the reversion of the crown to his heirs if Prince Edward's line should fail. Clarence's plan called for the immediate overthrow of his brother and his own ascent to the throne. Now Warwick was proposing to support his lifelong enemies of Lancaster, who were far from friendly to King Edward's brother and seemed to assume Clarence would simply go along with this scheme. By the time of the betrothal, he was already in touch with King Edward. Warwick, meanwhile, had come to an agreement with King Louis whereby, having recaptured England, he would raise and send a force of English archers to France, where they would help King Louis conquer Burgundy.

Plans for an invasion of England were then swiftly put in train. In early September 1470, after the Burgundian fleet blockading Honfleur had been forced away by the autumn gales, the new Lancastrian army began to go ashore in England. It was led by the Duke of Somerset and the Earl of Devon, who landed in the West Country, followed shortly afterwards by Warwick, Clarence, Jasper Tudor, the Lancastrian Earl of Pembroke, and John de Vere, Earl of Oxford. For the moment, Queen Margaret, Prince Edward and the Warwick ladies stayed in France to raise more soldiers. All the Lancastrian contingents were ashore by 13 September and marching hard for the north, gathering forces as they went.

King Edward, usually so astute in military affairs, was taken by surprise. He had been kept informed of Warwick's activities in France through the spies of the Duke of Burgundy, who was openly on his side. However, in

August, assuming that the Burgundian fleet was keeping Warwick's invasion force at Honfleur, he marched north to subdue a rising led by a Neville supporter, Lord Fitzhugh. While he was up there, Warwick's men landed at Dartmouth and Plymouth.

Edward started at once for London, where his Queen, once again pregnant, had taken sanctuary at Westminster with her daughters, leaving Marquis Montagu, Warwick's brother, to follow on behind with his forces, while the Earl of Northumberland was still mustering men. On the following night, Edward was roused from his bed at Doncaster and told that Montagu had gone over to the Lancastrians and was even now marching on him from Pontefract Castle, intent on his capture. Edward was caught between the closing pincers of Warwick and Montagu, and left with no choice but retreat. His forces were not sufficient to fight a battle, and if he fell into Warwick's hands, his head would come off within hours.

Accompanied by the ever-loyal Duke of Gloucester, now aged 18, by Anthony, Earl Rivers, by William, Lord Hastings, and Lord Say, he rode hard for the east coast, to Lynn in Norfolk, where on 29 September they took ship for Bruges and the protection of the Duke of Burgundy. Edward was so short of money he had to pay for their passage with his fur-lined cloak, and they took shelter in Bruges with Edward's old friend, Louis de la Gruthuyse, the Governor of Holland.

In spite of the problems that took him there, King Edward appears to have enjoyed his stay in Bruges, where his visit is still mentioned by the citizens. In the 1470s Bruges was an attractive, prosperous city, the 'Venice of the north' in the opinion of the citizens. With his two capitals, Dijon and Brussels, Bruges was the jewel in the coronet of the Duke of Burgundy. It had, and still has, magnificent buildings, fine cobbled streets, many canals and public gardens and an imposing cathedral among a score of splendid churches. If a king had to go into exile, this was the place where it might be endurable. They had to wait some time to see the Duke, for Duke Charles had plans afoot to conquer Lorraine, and no particular interest in either provoking King Louis or helping his brother-in-law, in spite of the pleading of Edward's sister, his wife, the Duchess Margaret, who was always a splendid advocate of her family's cause.

Edward and Richard, therefore, devoted themselves to cultivating friends among the citizens and merchants, while the Duchess sought an audience for them with Duke Charles. While awaiting a summons, they browsed in the splendid library of their host, Louis de la Gruthuyse, and became very interested in a new-fangled machine for printing books. This had been invented in Germany and one of the machines had been brought to Bruges by a fellow Englishman, William Caxton. Caxton was a financial adviser to Edward's sister, Margaret, and governor of the Bruges office for the London-based Guild of Merchant Adventurers. Caxton had been to Cologne to learn the art of printing from Gutenberg and had now set up his own press in Bruges. For the moment he conferred with Edward on more immediate matters, the raising of loans for arms and the state of affairs in England.

With King Edward gone, England had lapsed into chaos. As the rebel earls approached London, Queen Elizabeth and her children took sanctuary at Westminster and the citizens of London closed the gates and manned the walls against the bands of French mercenaries who came up to loot and burn the outer suburbs. Order was only restored when Warwick and Clarence rode in on 6 October, accompanied by George Neville, the Archbishop of York. Their first act was to fetch King Henry from the Tower, where he was found 'not so worshipfully arrayed nor cleanly kept as should become such a prince', and have him crowned again at St Paul's on 13 October. Henry was King again but several people noticed that all the lords and knights present at this second coronation wore the bear and ragged staff badge of Warwick, who had assumed the role of the King's Lieutenant.

Outward appearances are not everything. Warwick knew that this fresh Lancastrian grasp on the sceptre was not secure. He had made a great gamble and had won the first throw, but the game was not over yet. Edward was in Burgundy but would surely return. Henry VI was a poor substitute, the young Prince Edward was a total stranger in England and still loitering in France, and his various allies at home were notoriously fickle. Aware that his position was delicate, the Earl proceeded to do what he could. He began by replacing the Yorkist councillors with Lancastrians, or to be more exact, by Nevilles, and in keeping with the traditions of this war, he executed those Yorkist supporters who had been unable or unwilling to flee.

His ally, the young John de Vere, thirteenth Earl of Oxford, asked for and obtained the right to execute John Tiptoft, Earl of Worcester, who had brutally executed his father and brother. Oxford was, therefore, appointed Constable of England, and Tiptoft's execution, by the axe, took place on Tower Hill on 18 October before an enthusiastic crowd, the Earl having been captured a week before while hiding in a tree near Huntingdon. Tiptoft had executed many men and he knew how to die, going to his death with considerable panache, dressed in his best clothes. After tipping the executioner, he commanded the headsman to cut off his head in three strokes, 'for the Honour of the Trinity'.

Marquis Montagu paid a small sum in return for King Henry's pardon and was sent to guard the north, while Archbishop Neville regained the Chancellorship and the Great Seal from Bishop Stillington, who was now in sanctuary at Westminster with Queen Elizabeth. The other Lancastrian lords were sent back to their estates to mete out justice, suppress Yorkists and gather men. On returning to his strong castle at Pembroke, Jasper Tudor met his young nephew, Henry Tudor, now 13 and still a ward of Lady Herbert. Jasper Tudor took the boy with him when he returned to London.

On 2 November, news came from the Westminster sanctuary that Edward's Queen, Elizabeth, had finally given birth to a boy who had been christened Edward after his father. England now had two crowned kings, Henry VI and Edward IV, and two heirs-apparent, Edward of Lancaster and Edward of Westminster. Warwick, therefore, lost no time in clarifying the legal position, summoning a Parliament which opened within earshot of the Westminster sanctuary on 26 November 1470.

This Parliament declared that Edward IV had been a bastard and he and all his heirs were therefore disinherited from all rank and title and claims to the throne. This was done by reviving the tale about Duchess Cecily and Blackburn, the archer of Rouen. Parliament also declared that if King Henry's line should fail, then the heir-presumptive should be George, Duke of Clarence, who by that same Act became Richard Plantagenet's eldest *legitimate* son. What the elderly Duchess Cecily thought of all this is not recorded. She was still living quietly in London at Baynards Castle.

The commoners, the country folk of England and the citizens of London, seem to have observed these goings-on without comment. It made no great difference to them who sat on the throne or at the Council table. If the Earl of Warwick had put King Henry back on the throne, well and good, and if King Edward came back and overthrew him, that would be acceptable also. As long as the City merchants were left in peace to make money and the country folk to till their fields in relative tranquillity, the nobles and their soldiers could fight among themselves if they pleased.

Warwick now gave thought to the terms of his arrangement with King Louis, and began to assemble an army which would join Louis for an assault on Burgundy or, if Edward should return, could be deployed against him. This action was to recoil sharply on the Earl of Warwick, for the news that he was keeping his pledge and mustering archers, encouraged King Louis to move. In December 1470 he sent his troops into Flanders, an act which galvanized Duke Charles to offer support to his brother-in-law, King Edward of England.

Edward IV and his brother, Richard, had not had a rapturous welcome in Burgundy. Duke Charles was friendly with Somerset and had even given pensions to the exiled Lancastrians, declaring that any king 'who contented the English, contented him'. It was the New Year of 1471, more than two months after Edward arrived at Bruges, before the Duke even consented to see him, and only then after repeated urging from his wife, Margaret. Even wifely urging might not have been sufficient, but in early December Burgundy's spies at the French court reported that King Louis was only waiting for Warwick's promised force of English archers before he advanced in arms upon the Duchy of Burgundy. When Louis actually began to move, seizing St Quintain on 10 December, the Duke suddenly warmed to the problems of King Edward.

The Duke urged Edward to return at once to his kingdom and put an end to the Earl of Warwick. He refused him soldiers, for he had need of those on his southern border in Artois, but he offered money and gave Edward permission to raise soldiers in Burgundy if he could find them. Edward already had good connections with the merchants of Flanders, where he had already cultivated the support of the merchant classes, and he had sufficient funds for a small force. By 15 February 1471 he had assembled his army at Bruges and was ready to sail.

News of Edward's preparations soon reached England and France; Warwick began to muster men in the Midlands and sent his allies to guard the coasts. Oxford went to East Anglia, Montagu to the north, Jasper Tudor to Wales, while Warwick remained in London to recruit men from Kent and arm them from the military stores in the Tower. Meanwhile, Queen Margaret continued to raise forces in France, but Warwick wanted more than this: what he really needed was Prince Edward, a fresh, attractive figurehead, for the wavering lords to rally round. Sending urgent messages for the Queen and Prince to join him, Warwick mustered his troops and prepared for another campaign in the wars of York and Lancaster.

Edward's invading army was not large; some 1,300 soldiers embarked with him from the quays at the port of Damme, near Bruges, and after coasting up East Anglia to find a safe harbour, they came ashore at Ravenspur, a small port on the Humber, on 14 March 1471. Ravenspur has since vanished but it remains particularly famous as the place where Henry Bolingbroke landed in 1399 on his way to overthrow King Richard II. Edward arrived at the same port 72 years later and offered the same explanation. He had not come, he said, to claim the throne, but simply to regain his ancestral estates as Duke of York. Those who chose to believe this, therefore, had an excuse to let him pass unhindered, and Edward's small army marched on to York. Edward's activities are known in great detail because this campaign was recorded in a contemporary chronicle, *The Arrivall of King Edward*, which continues up to the battle at Tewkesbury.

When Edward's army drew near York, he learned that the Mayor and Council of York were most reluctant to admit him. Edward still carried on and eventually entered the city with his army; after a night's rest there, he turned south, marching at a steady 15 miles a day towards London. The route took them past Pontefract – or as it was then called, Pomfret – Castle, held at the time by Marquis Montagu, but he, like the Earl of Northumberland who still lurked in the north, did nothing to impede King Edward's progress. As more and more Lancastrian garrisons failed to engage his forces, or fled before him, Edward slowly began to gather men, especially at Leicester, where Sir William Stanley, usually a notorious fence-sitter, was waiting with 2,000 soldiers, all bearing the Stanley three-legged badge of Man. Since the Stanleys never supported anyone until they knew who was winning, this was a very good omen.

His army now a substantial 5,000 men strong, Edward marched directly for Warwick's mustering point at Coventry, where the Earl had gathered in 6,000 or 7,000 men. Safe behind the city walls, Warwick refused both Edward's offer of a pardon and his challenges to come out and fight. He was clearly waiting for his ally, the Duke of Clarence, to come up with his army from the south before giving battle, but in this hope of support Warwick was sadly mistaken.

Edward declined to wait. He led his men away to Warwick, where he dropped the pretence of his ducal claim and declared himself King again. He then sent messengers, including his brother, Richard of Gloucester, to parley with Clarence, who was coming up with a force from the Cotswolds. The King and the Duke of Gloucester finally met their brother Clarence on a road near Banbury. Both armies deployed for battle before the meeting, but the confrontation lasted only a few minutes before a reconciliation was reached. Warwick was abandoned and Clarence's 4,000 men were added to those of the King's, raising Edward's force to around 10,000 men – an interesting example of fifteenth-century loyalties.

It is hardly likely that all the 4,000 men at Clarence's back were private soldiers, common bill-men and archers, paid to follow Clarence and obey his orders. Clarence can only have directly commanded a few hundred at the most. The rest must have come from other affinities and been led by their own officers, local knights and squires, gentlemen of coat-armour, even lords, who had come north with Clarence, expecting to fight for the Lancastrian cause he currently espoused.

Then, in the space of half a day or less, the entire contingent had switched sides and gone over to the Yorkist Edward IV. The only explanations are that either those outside the close circle around the crown did not care who they fought for, or that they cared only to be on the winning side. Perhaps the sight of Edward's army, deployed for battle, with his royal banners displayed, plus the clear evidence that Clarence was wavering, was enough to make them change sides. Whatever the reason, it is a clear example of how shallow the loyalties were to either House. The two armies joined together and marched on London, which Edward entered on Tuesday, 11 April 1471, going first to a service in St Paul's and then to Westminster, where the crown was again placed briefly on his head. This done, he returned to the City. Among those waiting to see him at the Tower were the Queen, with his new son, Edward, and their other children, and his cousin, Henry VI, or Henry of Windsor as the Yorkists called him. Henry greeted King Edward with the words, 'Cousin Edward, I am right glad to see you. I hold my life in no danger from your hands.'

Even after 500 years, that trusting sentence evokes a sudden stab of pity for poor King Henry. As he clasped Edward's hands and asked only to return to his prison quarters in the Tower, Henry of Windsor had just six weeks left to live.

CHAPTER ELEVEN

THE END OF LANCASTER (1471)

*Ye shall hear of wars and rumours of war; see that ye
be not troubled, for all these things must come to
pass, but the end is not yet.*

MATTHEW 26:6

King Edward was back in his capital but his troubles were not over.
Warwick and his brother, Montagu, were in the field and marching south
with a large army, while Queen Margaret and Prince Edward were
expected to land at any moment in the south or west, and that persistent
opponent, Jasper Tudor, was still raising men in Wales. It was, therefore,
essential for the King to deal with Warwick before all these forces could
combine into one overwhelming army.

Sir John Paston and his brother, another John, fought at Barnet for the
Lancastrian party, on the orders of his 'good lord', the Earl of Oxford, who
sent him a peremptory summons: Wherefore in the King's name and by
authority aforesaid I straitly charge and command you that all excuses laid
apart ye and each of you defensibly arranged with as many good men as ye
can muster be on Friday next at Lynn and forth to Newark. Summonses
like this were going out to men of the various affinities in every part of
England.

Edward waited two days in London, resting his men and waiting for
news of Warwick and Montagu, who were coming south towards that old
battleground, St Albans. On Easter Saturday, 13 April 1471, King Edward
left London with his army and rode north towards Barnet, leaving his
Queen and her children in the safety of the Tower. He took with him his
cousin, King Henry, who had now been present at a great many battles for
such a peaceable man, and an army of some 10,000 men.

On arriving in Barnet that evening, the Royal vanguard had to expel a number of Lancastrian harbingers seeking lodgings for Warwick's army, and then the two armies, already deployed in battle array, settled down for the night, just north of the town, by Hadley Green, south of the fork where the road north from Barnet divides for St Albans and Hatfield. Warwick's guns fired on the Royal army at intervals throughout the night but did no damage, partly because the King's forces were in a hollow, partly because a thick mist came up to conceal the armies' camp-fires from each other's sight. The battle began soon after dawn on Easter Sunday.

The two armies were deployed in an east-to-west line just south of where the High Stone now stands at the present road junction. The Earl of Oxford commanded Warwick's right, with Montagu commanding in the centre, and the Duke of Exeter on the left. Warwick himself commanded a small reserve behind the centre, from where he could keep an eye on his wayward brother, though since the day was foggy, it is likely that he came forward to join and perhaps command the centre division. There is some doubt about the presence of the Duke of Somerset at Barnet: the first

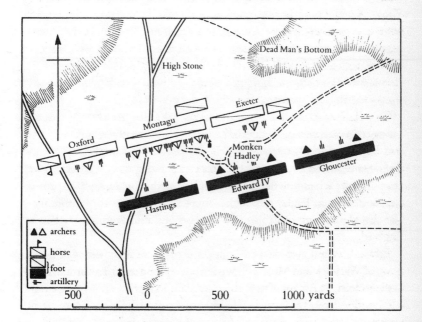

The Battle of Barnet (1471).
Note the overlapping right wing of either army.

person to mention his presence is Edward Hall, writing in the next century; the Pastons, who wrote several letters about the battle and were present in the fight, made no mention of Somerset, so it is unlikely that he was there.

Edward's men were also deployed in the usual three battles, with Hastings on the left, the King in the centre, and Gloucester on the right; but when the King's army had come up from Barnet on the previous evening, it had deployed in the dark and so overlapped Warwick's line on the right, while Oxford's men extended far beyond those of Hastings on the left. This tactical blunder was to have drastic consequences.

The battle began with the usual exchanges of arrows and artillery with some hand-gun fire from Edward's small contingent of hackbut men. All the missiles were shot off into a thick enveloping mist, after which the two armies plunged towards each other and began the deciding-work of hand-strokes with sword, mace, battleaxe and pole-axe, when the right-hand division of both armies discovered that their field was bare.

Oxford's division hooked into Hastings's battle and struck it a solid blow from the left flank, sending some men scurrying to the King's centre battle, but the bulk of those not immediately hacked down in the mud fled back towards Barnet, with Oxford's men hot on their heels. Some of the fugitives picked up horses and rode into London with news of Edward's defeat.

Meanwhile, with the King hotly engaged with Warwick and Montagu in the centre; the young Duke of Gloucester was attacking the Duke of Exeter, taking Exeter's men in the flank, but since his advance was up a slope, Gloucester was unable to make the same headway as Oxford had managed against Hastings. However, he did succeed in pushing Exeter's men back and, to keep its position together in the mist, Warwick's battle steadily gave ground, wheeling until the battle line was roughly north-to-south, almost at right angles to the original line. It was at this time, when the issue hung in the balance, that the Earl of Oxford returned to the fray with about 800 of his men.

The thick fog which enveloped the field now caused even more confusion, for when Warwick's men glimpsed Oxford's banner of the Enrayed Star in the mist, they mistook it for King Edward's banner of the Sun in Splendour, and greeted the returning troops with volleys of arrows. Oxford's men went down in heaps, crying out 'Treason!' as they fell, and those who could, then fled the field, with many of Warwick's men joining them.

The mist was now thinning and, at last, able to see what was happening, the King could bring the bulk of his force to bear on Warwick's line. Gloucester, advancing on the right, had also hit open air, but unlike Oxford had kept his men in hand and could now turn in on the battle commanded by Warwick and Montagu. A great hand-to-hand mêlée now took place in the mist, centring around the church at Hadley Green.

Edward stayed out of this mêlée and called up his mounted reserve, which he now launched into the fray at the point still known as Dead Man's Bottom. Under the impetus of their assault, the Lancastrian front collapsed. Marquis Montagu was killed, Oxford fled and Warwick, who had been fighting on foot, realized the battle was lost, left the fray and began to lumber back towards the horse lines. With his departure, the whole line gave way and the Yorkist soldiers, recognizing his blazoned surcoat, had no difficulty in catching him and cutting him down. No one knows what actually happened to the great Earl of Warwick, except that he got as far as Wrotham Park before Edward's men-at-arms ran him down and killed him.

The Battle of Barnet only lasted about three hours, so it was still early morning when the killing was done. Edward had lost a number of his stoutest supporters, including Lords Say and Cromwell, Sir William Blount and Sir Humphrey Bourchier. Apart from Warwick and Montagu, the Duke of Exeter had been left for dead but was later found naked in the field and taken to the Westminster sanctuary, where he recovered from his wounds and was then sent as a prisoner to the Tower. The death toll on both sides totalled some 1,500 men.

The King, with his chief supporters, including his brother, Gloucester, who had been slightly wounded and the bewildered King Henry, left the battlefield by 9 o'clock and rode directly for London, where they arrived at St Paul's Cathedral in the middle of the morning service. Henry went on to the Tower while the King and Gloucester entered the church, striding up the centre aisle in full armour to lay the torn and muddy banners of Warwick and Montagu on the high altar.

Later that day a cart rumbled up to St Paul's, bearing the hacked-about bodies of Warwick and Montagu, which were then exposed for all to see for three days, 'lest seditious fellows say they yet live', before being taken for burial to the Salisbury mausoleum at Bisham Abbey, near Marlow-on-Thames. So died the mighty Earl of Warwick, York's stout supporter, King Edward's close friend, a man who at one time had the whole kingdom in his gift, a man destroyed by his ambition.

Four days after the battle Sir John Paston wrote to his mother:

> Blessed be God my brother John is alive and fareth well and is in no peril of death tho' hurt with an arrow in his left arm beneath the elbow, and I have sent him a surgeon which has dressed him. I am in good care and in no jeopardy of my life for I am at my liberty as needs be. There were killed upon the field half a mile from Barnet the Earl of Warwick, Marquis Montagu, Sir William Tyrell and divers other esquires of our country. On the King's party Lord Cromwell, Lord Say and Sir Humphrey Bourchier of our county, which is a sore missed man here and of all other people on both sides to the number of one thousand. It is understood here that Queen Margaret has landed with her son in the West Country and King Edward will depart from hence to drive her out again.

On Saturday, 13 April, the day Edward rode out to meet Warwick at Barnet Field, Queen Margaret returned to England. With her was her only child, Prince Edward, now aged 17, and his new bride, Anne Neville, who was just 14. Soldiers in the party included Lord Wenlock, who had changed sides yet again, Sir John Langstrother, Prior of the Knights of St John, John Beaufort, brother of the Duke of Somerset, and a small force of French mercenaries. Others in the party included that wily prelate, Dr John Morton, and by some accounts, Sir John Fortescue, the eminent jurist and tutor to Prince Edward. The Queen and her party rode from Weymouth to Cerne Abbey, in Dorset, where they met Somerset with the news of the disaster at Barnet.

The Queen's first, and most understandable reaction, was to abandon her expedition and return at once to France. The others present, but particularly the Prince, encouraged her to wait. All was not yet lost. On the following day, the Earl of Devon arrived with a strong contingent, and as more supporters and the undaunted survivors of Barnet Field trickled in, still full of fight, her hopes began to revive. The decision was made to avoid battle with Edward until the Queen's army had gained more strength and joined with that of Jasper Tudor, who was still mustering men in Wales.

The command of the army was given to Somerset, and he ordered his forces to march west to Exeter and then turn north to Bristol, where they could collect artillery before crossing the Severn into Wales and making a junction with Jasper Tudor. This seemed a wise course of action and the army set out at once for the Severn valley. More troops, under Sir Hugh

Courtenay and Sir John Arundel, joined at Exeter, while at Bristol on 30 April, the Lancastrian army was able to collect a useful supply of field artillery. So the Lancastrian prospects continued to brighten.

Edward had received the news of Margaret's landing on 16 April, two days after Barnet Field. The bulk of the army that had won that victory had already dispersed, so a fresh muster was ordered for Windsor, where the King arrived on 19 April, staying on for the Garter Service on St George's Day, 23 April.

The King left Windsor on 24 April and on Sunday, 28 April, he arrived at Abingdon-on-Thames, marching on the next day to Cirencester. On 30 April, the day the Lancastrians arrived at Bristol, King Edward's army entered Malmesbury and was now in position, given some hard marching to the west, to cut the Lancastrians off before they could reach Gloucester, where there was a bridge across the Severn into Wales. The race to intercept Somerset's army before it could escape to join Jasper Tudor was now on.

Somerset then struck on a ruse. He sent his vanguard east as though to offer Edward battle on Sodbury Hill, while the rest of the army, with all the baggage and the artillery, marched hard for Gloucester, by the vale of Berkeley. This feint gained the Lancastrians a full day, though the hard march in the heat of an unusually hot May day took a severe toll of the soldiers' strength, and in the event their efforts proved fruitless. Edward had sent messengers spurring to Gloucester and ordered the Constable of Gloucester Castle, Sir Richard Beauchamp, to hold the town and the vital bridge at all costs, until Edward could come up with his army.

This Sir Richard did, leaving the weary Lancastrian army with no option but to march on to Tewkesbury, where there was another crossing. The Lancastrian army arrived at Tewkesbury early on Friday evening, having marched all the previous night and day from Bristol and covered some 45 miles in one stretch, 'in foul country all in lanes and stony ways, without any good refreshing'. There was still no rest, for defences had to be prepared. They took up position 'in a field at the towne's end, the abbey and towne at their baks, with lanes and dikes on either hand, as vile a place as could well be devised.' Their exact position is still doubtful, though Edward's chronicle, *The Arrivall*, states that the Lancastrians had 'the town and abbey at their baks'.

Edward's army had followed, making an equally arduous march along the Cotswold encampment. Edward reached Tewkesbury early on the morning of Saturday, 4 May 1461, and found the Lancastrians already drawn up for battle. The best estimates give the King some 5,000 men, of whom 3,500 were archers; while Somerset probably had slightly more, say 6,000, most of them archers. Somerset had put the veteran 70-year-old Lord Wenlock in command of the centre battle, while the Earl of Devon commanded on the left. Somerset, with Prince Edward at his side, took up his position on the right flank, facing the Duke of Gloucester's battle. The King, with Clarence at his side, and under his eye, commanded the centre battle of the Yorkist army, and Lord Hastings, who clearly had not suffered in reputation following his unfortunate time at Barnet, commanded the right. According to one account, Queen Margaret watched the battle from the tower of the abbey church.

One of the marks of a good commander is the ability to keep some force in reserve, to exploit an advantage or provide support in a crisis. Edward always kept something in reserve, and here, to flush out any ambush or act against Somerset's flank at some stage, the King sent 200 armoured horsemen out to his left flank, where they were to wait and take advantage of any opportunity for a flanking attack somewhere in Tewkesbury Park. This done, he opened the battle with an arrow and artillery bombardment of the Lancastrian line, concentrating in particular on Somerset's division. Thus galled, Somerset promptly advanced his banner against the Duke of Gloucester who, once Somerset was fully engaged, was swiftly supported by the 200 horsemen charging in with couched lances from the left. The pressure on Somerset's battle would have been greatly eased had Wenlock or Devon also advanced to the attack, but neither did so.

After 30 minutes of bitter fighting, Somerset's division gave way, many being cut down in the field in a hollow by the River Avon, still known as Bloody Meadow. Others fled for the elusive safety of Tewkesbury Abbey, while those still willing to fight went to join Lord Wenlock in the centre. Among these was the Duke of Somerset who, having raged at Wenlock for his lack of support, is said by Hall to have concluded the heated debate by dashing out Wenlock's brains with his battleaxe.

At this critical moment, the King and Lord Hastings threw their divisions hard against the Lancastrian line. There were a few moments of hacking and stabbing and then the entire Lancastrian front gave way, heavily armoured men lumbering from the fray, pushed aside by sprinting archers, cut down by the Yorkists harrying at their backs. Edward's reserve of mounted knights and men-at-arms then got among the fugitives with sword and battleaxe. The rout continued into the town and the abbey precincts and more Lancastrians perished in the trap of Bloody Meadow, while others were drowned in the Tirle brook or in the Avon. The young Prince Edward, easily recognized in his bright surcoat blazoned with the arms of England, was cut down and trampled in the dusty ground, 'fleeing to the town and slayne in the field', though according to the *Warwick Chronicle* he died calling on his brother-in-law, Clarence, for help. There is no evidence at all that he was taken prisoner and then murdered by the King and his brothers. The Earl of Devon was killed in the fray, as was John Beaufort, Somerset's younger brother, and a score of Lancastrian knights, among 2,000 other men; a few took shelter in the abbey church, begging the abbot to give them sanctuary.

Hot on their heels came the King with his brothers, Gloucester and Clarence, and Lord Hastings, pressing into the abbey precincts with drawn swords, until the abbot and his monks made them leave again. The King and the abbot then had a heated debate in the church porch: the abbot ordering the King to refrain from polluting holy ground; the King pointing out that the abbey was not an official sanctuary and demanding the expulsion of the traitors now sheltering under its roof. It was soon very clear that the King would take these men out, sanctuary or not, and on the promise of safe conduct and a fair trial, the abbot gave up his wards into the King's hands. The common soldiers, men-at-arms and archers, were made to surrender their arms and then dismissed, and the monks later gathered discarded armour from the field and nailed it to the doors of the abbey sacristy. The noble prisoners included the Duke of Somerset, Sir John Langstrother and 15 others. Next day they were given a brief trial by Richard, Duke of Gloucester, now the Constable of England, and the Duke of Norfolk, the Earl Marshal, and then beheaded in the market-place at Tewkesbury.

Three days later, Queen Margaret and the Princess Anne were captured in 'a poor religious place,' probably the priory at Malvern, and taken to meet the King who was marching hard back to London, where Warwick's nephew, the Bastard of Fauconberg, had sailed up the Thames with a fleet of ships and was laying siege to the City, aided by a large force of rebels from Kent. Fauconberg still had the City under siege and the Tower under cannon fire when Edward came in from the Midlands to drive them away. King Edward and his brothers re-entered the City in triumph on 21 May, with the captive Queen Margaret in their train. That night King Henry VI was done to death in the Tower.

With the demise of his heir, Prince Edward, there was no longer any need to keep the 50-year-old King Henry alive, and while *The Arrivall* states that Henry died 'of pure displeasure and melancholy', as well he might have done, there can be little doubt that he was put to death and that the King ordered his execution.

There is no direct evidence that Richard of Gloucester murdered King Henry, as Shakespeare maintains, though he was certainly in the Tower that night – so were the King and the Duke of Clarence, and a score of other men who would have been willing, if not eager, to carry out the King's slightest wish. How King Henry died is not known, but when his body was placed on view in St Paul's, it was kept closely guarded by day and night, with only the face exposed. The remains were then taken by barge to Chertsey Abbey, where they rested for many years until Richard III had them transferred to St George's Chapel, at Windsor, where they still lie, just across the nave from those of Edward IV and his Queen.

So died Henry of Windsor, a prince born at a most fortunate hour, son of a famous father and heir to two rich kingdoms. Much of the blame that has since attached to King Henry cannot really be substantiated. The gift of kingship is not hereditary and Henry of Windsor never demonstrated the stuff of which great kings are made. Even so, many of the disasters which littered his reign were not his fault. The war in France was lost long before he took the reins of power into his hands, from the time when Joan of Arc entered Orléans – when Henry was only 9 – and certainly after the Duke of Burgundy threw off his allegiance in 1435.

Henry's reign provides the perfect example of a good man making a bad king; weakness can be as fatal as wickedness and it takes a strong man to rule turbulent men in difficult times. Henry was kind, generous and pious, but his natural virtues could not compensate for his lack of kingly qualities. That he made so little of his inheritance and brought decades of death and strife to England was his own fault, but only in so far as a man's nature is his fault. Poor judgement of his fellow men and weakness in the face of their demands were the underlying causes of his failure. Now the King was dead and with him died all the hopes of Lancaster, though far away in Wales, Jasper Tudor was still at large. What he thought when he heard of King Henry's death can only be wondered at, but we know what he did: he fled away to Brittany, taking with him his nephew, Henry Tudor, Earl of Richmond.

CHAPTER TWELVE

THE END OF CLARENCE (1471–78)

Once more we sit on England's Royal Throne,
Repurchas'd with the blood of enemies.
What valiant foemen, like to autumn's corn
Have we mowed down in tops of all their pride.

EDWARD IV IN *HENRY VI*

King Edward IV reigned in England from 1461 until 1483, but his rule only really began after the final defeat of the Lancastrians at Tewkesbury. The death of Henry VI and his son, Prince Edward, did not mean that there were no contenders for his throne. There were still plenty of would-be pretenders available if the time was right or the chance arose. Some, like Clarence and Gloucester and the Duke of Buckingham, were at the King's court, and the Duke of Exeter had replaced King Henry in the Tower. Others, like Charles of Burgundy, the King's brother-in-law, were otherwise engaged and Henry Tudor, the Beaufort candidate, was virtually a prisoner in Brittany. The future can never be certain, but as Edward returned to London in May 1471, he could at last feel secure and devote himself to the welfare of his House and kingdom.

He was aided in this pleasant task by a steady stream of supplicants who had previously been steadfast to the House of Lancaster. Among them were Judge Fortescue, a noted advocate, a former tutor to Prince Edward and author of *The Governance of England*, a major work of fifteenth-century jurisprudence. Another new-found friend was Dr John Morton. Morton was suspect, but clever, and the King could use clever men. Within two years Morton was Master of the Rolls, and by the end of the decade, Bishop of Ely. Other posts would follow. Among the ranks of the nobility, so thinned in the wars, new men were making their way forward. Among them John, Lord Howard, and Thomas, Lord Stanley. The Stanleys were a careful family, experts in staying neutral in these wars, who among various possessions owned the Isle of Man. Thomas Stanley had been married to Warwick's sister, Lady Eleanor, but she had died and he had now become the fourth husband of a Beaufort lady, Margaret Beaufort, Countess of Richmond, who had stamped out any thoughts of romance by declaring on her wedding day that from now on she would be celibate. Margaret's son by her first husband, Edmund Tudor, was the exiled Earl of Richmond, Henry Tudor, another candidate for England's throne. Keeping Stanley and his lady close to the court could only be prudent.

Some men, on the other hand, were on their way down. George Neville, Archbishop of York, had played his hand well over the years, but he was at best an unrepentant Neville, and the King did not trust him. Only the Pope could remove a bishop from his see, but in 1472 George was arrested, sent to Calais and imprisoned in the castle of Hammes, accused of conspiring with the unreconciled John de Vere, Earl of Oxford, who was still raiding the English coast. Oxford later took St Michael's Mount, in Cornwall, where he was closely besieged. He finally surrendered in 1474 and joined the archbishop in Hammes Castle, where the archbishop remained in comfortable restraint for some years. He was released in 1476 and died in Canterbury two years later, without making any further contribution to public affairs.

In 1471, the post of Chancellor went to another interesting figure, Bishop Robert Stillington of Bath and Wells. Stillington was in poor health and far from competent, and two years later he was suddenly dismissed from all Royal appointments. Shortly afterwards he was summoned to Rome and there questioned closely by the Pope himself on matters still undisclosed 500 years later. Much chastened by these rebukes, Stillington returned to his See of Bath and Wells and nothing more was heard of him for the next decade.

Among the King's friends, William, Lord Hastings, remained at Court and became the King's Chamberlain, a powerful position, for the Chamberlain controlled access to the King. This soon brought him into conflict with the Woodvilles and in particular with Queen Elizabeth's son by her first marriage, Thomas Grey, now Marquis Dorset, apparently because they stole each other's mistresses. Anthony, formerly Lord Scales, the famous jouster, was now Earl Rivers and, with the Queen, the leader of the Woodville faction at court. In 1473 King Edward appointed him both tutor to the young Prince of Wales and Constable of Ludlow Castle, the old Yorkist stronghold on the March of Wales, where the Prince and Earl Rivers spent most of the next ten years.

If the realm itself was peaceful, the Court had leisure to bicker, and before long there were quarrels enough to go round. Faction can rear its head in the most surprising places, and a serious quarrel soon broke out between the King's brothers, Clarence and Gloucester.

There is something immensely irritating about Clarence. He seems to have had no sense of shame or remorse, no sense of duty or loyalty. He was factious, vain, self-centred and demanding. His turncoat behaviour, changing sides between the King and Warwick, which would have made most men ashamed and silent, seemed to bother Clarence not at all. How his brothers put up with him for so long is hard to understand.

The fact that he had betrayed his brother, the King, assisted in the judicial murder of the Queen's father and fought for Warwick at Edgecote and then betrayed Warwick in his turn, left Clarence not a whit abashed. He had come out on the winning side at Tewkesbury and, therefore, looked for rewards. To ensure that he got them, he remained at Court, and began to filch lands and titles wherever he could find them.

His principal target seems to have been his brother, Gloucester. Once restored to his estates in 1471, Clarence was allowed to take all the Beauchamp–Despenser lands in right of his wife, Isobel. He then persuaded the King to grant him the post of Grand Chamberlain of England, which currently belonged to Gloucester. This was given to him in April 1472. Long wrangles followed when Clarence discovered that Richard wished to marry Anne Neville, Prince Edward's widow and Isobel's sister. It is even possible that Anne and Richard were in love, or had been childhood sweethearts, but fanciful romances apart, with her hand Gloucester should acquire half of the wealthy Warwick lands. The other half would stay with her sister, Isobel, the wife of Clarence, although as the widowed Countess of Warwick pointed out, until her death *all* the great Earl's possessions and her own family lands legally belonged to her.

Warwick had never been attainted, and even if he had, the Countess was still entitled to the lands of her Beauchamp ancestors. It is worth pointing out that over the matter of the Warwick lands, the Duke of Gloucester showed himself to be every bit as grasping as his brother, Clarence, and the marriage with the Lady Anne was largely a step towards acquiring her inheritance. It is not likely that personal feelings ever came into it.

In any event, Clarence decided to prevent the match. He spirited Anne away to London, but Gloucester followed and found the lady hidden in Clarence's house, some say disguised as a kitchen maid. Gloucester rescued her and placed her in sanctuary at the Convent of St Martin-le-Grand, while he disputed with his brother over the Warwick lands. This argument, which sorely tried the King's patience, lasted on and off for three whole years. In February 1472, Clarence and Gloucester debated their respective rights to the Beauchamp–Neville lands before the King and the Council, but this debate, though reflecting credit on the arguments of both parties, brought no resolution to the dispute. In April 1472, Gloucester made the next move by marrying the Lady Anne, who was now 15. This was within a year of her husband Edward's death and without the necessary Papal dispensation, for they were cousins within the bounds of consanguinity. The marriage infuriated the volatile Clarence, who said openly that Gloucester might have the lady but he would not have her lands.

By the autumn of 1473 it looked likely that their private quarrel would lead to open war. Armed conflict was only averted in 1474 by a special Act of Parliament, where the King displayed the hand of firm government and used it to administer a slap. The brothers each wished to obtain the Warwick lands by inheritance, as land obtained by Royal grant could be repossessed at any time by an Act of Resumption. Such an Act was introduced in Parliament in November 1473 and aimed directly at Clarence, depriving him of all the lands he then held by Royal grant with no exemptions. Clarence was naturally horrified.

This was then followed by another Act which declared that Gloucester and Clarence should share the Warwick estates equally and at once, 'in like manner and form as if the Countess of Warwick was now dead,' which, to say the least, was grossly unfair to Warwick's widow. The Beauchamp–Despenser lands, therefore, went with Isobel to Clarence, the Salisbury–Neville estates went with Anne to Gloucester and the Countess was left with nothing. The penniless Countess was offered a home with Richard and Anne at Middleham Castle, in Wensleydale, and escorted to the north by one of Richard's adherents, Sir James Tyrell, brother of the Walter Tyrell killed at Barnet.

Any thoughts of a childhood romance between Anne and Richard may be dispelled by a clause added to the Act, stating that whatever happened to the Countess or her daughters, even in the event of Richard's marriage to Anne being judged invalid, since they were within the limits of consanguinity and had not obtained a Papal dispensation, her husband Richard should continue to enjoy her estates, even if they were divorced or the marriage annulled, unless he should marry again. Unfair as it was, the Countess had no choice but to live on her daughter's bounty, and the dispute, though not forgotten, eventually subsided. This achieved in 1475, Edward turned his attention to Burgundy and France.

It has to be remembered that, in spite of all the internal broils affecting England, her explusion from France was still of recent date, and, therefore, still a matter of concern. The Kings of England still called themselves Kings of France, unless they were petitioning the French king for aid and shelter, and they still quartered the lilies with the leopards on their coat of arms. If he could secure the help of Burgundy, Edward might be able to reassert the claim of his House to the throne of France. Duke Charles, who was always willing to attack his cousin, King Louis, undertook to provide support, and Edward thereupon agreed to invade France in July 1475 with an army of 10,000 men, joining with Duke Charles, who would bring a similar force, and together they would march on Paris.

Treaties towards this end were duly drawn up, Duke Charles promising to aid Edward in recovering Normandy and Guyenne, 'and also the kingdom of France', while Edward agreed to cede vast tracts of land to Duke Charles, including the counties of Champagne and Nevers, and the Duchy of Bar, in full sovereignty and without homage, though the Duke would permit Edward to be crowned King of France in Reims Cathedral.

The King of France does not seem to have been unduly bothered by news of these warlike preparations. He probably knew Duke Charles too well, and when the English heralds came to deliver Edward's formal defiance, he sent them back with three gifts – a donkey to symbolize the Duke of Brittany, another party to the alliance, a wolf for the King of England, and for the Duke of Burgundy, a boar.

Whether Edward himself really believed in the reopening of this old wound is doubtful, but his lords, and in particular his brother, Gloucester, were certain that the time was ripe to try again. The Parliament of 1472 had voted Edward funds sufficient for 12,000 archers, and there had been further grants for his expedition from the merchants and the clergy, though most of these monies went straight into the King's coffers.

Apart from the quarrels between Clarence and Gloucester, Edward probably thought it unwise to leave his kingdom so soon after Tewkesbury. The economic affairs of the kingdom were in a mess and trade with the continent virtually at a standstill, apart from the regular shipment of wool to Flanders. Since France was hostile, efforts had to be made elsewhere and a long-standing dispute with the Hanse towns was settled in September 1473, when depots, or steelyards, were opened in London, Boston and Hull.

The King spent the summer of 1474 in the Midlands, supporting the justices and attempting to restore respect for law and order in the hearts and minds of his people. He also used these progresses to gather money, for on his return to London 1471, he had found his treasury empty.

Edward was always happy to improve the Royal finances and was to die a very rich man, free from all debt and with a cellarful of treasure. He now found an excellent way of increasing the flow of funds into his coffers by introducing the idea of 'benevolences', or willing loans. These loans were not repaid but extracted more or less willingly from all with an income of more than £40 a year. The King's method was to greet some substantial person jovially, and after a little talk, ask how much this person would contribute to the French war. If the King thought the offer too small, he would point out, regretfully, that some mutual acquaintance, though poorer, had contributed more... and the amount was inevitably increased. The usual benevolence covered the wages of an archer for six months, about £4.50, but some people gave much more. In addition to these benevolences, more funds were voted in subsequent Parliaments, and in June 1475 the English army – marvellously well equipped – began to flow across the Channel to Calais.

According to reports reaching Paris and faithfully recorded by Philip de Comines, Edward's army included 15,000 archers, all mounted, and 1,200 men-at-arms, as well as knights and squires, a large artillery train and the even longer tail of miners, armourers, ostlers, and even surgeons. It was probably somewhat smaller. Ramsey gives a total figure of 13,000 men, which includes 2,000 archers sent to Brittany under Lord Audley; while Thomas Basin, the Bishop of Lisieux, suggests the huge figure of 36,000 men, though this may be an estimate of the total Anglo–Burgundian force. The largest contingents from England were led by the Dukes of Clarence and Gloucester, with 1,000 archers and 120 men-at-arms each. Other lords in the field included the Dukes of Buckingham, Norfolk and Suffolk, the Marquis of Dorset, and the Stanleys, as well as the Duke of Exeter, released under guard from the Tower and taken along in the king's train. This force began crossing to Calais on 20 June 1475.

Edward opened his campaign by sending Louis his formal challenge and defiance, restating his claim to be the lawful King of France and demanding that the throne be handed over to him. After this public declaration, the English herald intimated to the King in private that Edward had no real wish to wage war and would make more reasonable proposals later. This was necessary because the Duke of Burgundy had not appeared as promised. He was, in fact, currently besieging Neuss, a city on the Rhine, which he had been attacking for a year. The siege of Neuss was a military and political event of epic proportions which dazzled Europe at the time. Duke Charles was, therefore, unlikely to have been able to give Edward serious help, which all goes to deepen the mystery of Edward's French adventure. Perhaps the King, like Henry V before him, wished to 'busy idle minds with foreign quarrels' and unite his people in battle with the old enemy, France. This may be the reason why that normally combative and skilled soldier, Edward IV, appears to have had little or no intention of actually campaigning in France.

The tactics of Duke Charles, on the other hand, were now becoming very evident. Far from him assisting Edward to regain the throne of France, he merely wanted to set the French and English at each other's throats and to secure his rear while he marched east to conquer and create a kingdom of Burgundy in Lorraine. Edward learned of this intention from his sister, Duchess Margaret, when he landed at Calais in July. The King could hardly go straight home again, so sending messengers galloping to Neuss to remind Duke Charles of his previous pledges, the King marched out of the Calais pale on 18 July and began to plod across the downlands of Picardy and Artois.

Then followed a month of great political manoeuvrings and a handful of small skirmishes. Few lives were lost on either side for no one wished to engage, and by the end of August both armies had settled down amicably around the city of Amiens. The French were inside and the English were outside, but the gates were open for people to pass to and fro. There was jousting for the knights and archery competitions for the common soldiers, and a great deal of drinking, but no signs of hostility. While the vulgar soldiery were thus at play, preparations were put in hand for a peace conference. Edward's terms for peace began with the usual demand for the return of all the old Plantagenet lands in France, a seven-year truce, a mutual defence pact – aimed at Burgundy – and the marriage of the Dauphin Charles to his eldest daughter, the Lady Elizabeth.

These demands soon moderated to a lump sum of 75,000 crowns to defray the current costs of the English army and a yearly tribute – or bribe, as the French preferred to call it – of 50,000 crowns. Louis also agreed to ransom Margaret of Anjou for a further 50,000 crowns and to provide for her from the lands of her old father, good King René. These terms, especially the one concerning mutual defence, enraged Duke Charles, who had made no effort to help Edward but was still insistent that Edward should keep his side of the bargain, and war with King Louis to the death.

The meeting between the Kings took place at the town of Picquigny, on the River Somme, on 29 August 1475. To guard against treachery, a bridge was built across the river with a stout palisade in the middle, through which the Kings could converse without the risk of sudden assassination, such as had occurred on the bridge at Montereau in 1419, when a French knight killed the then Duke of Burgundy, John the Fearless, with a battleaxe.

In spite of the barrier, the Kings got on well, rather to their mutual surprise, and the campaign ended with a most satisfactory agreement, the Treaty of Picquigny, which finally ended the Hundred Years War. King Louis, in particular, was very pleased with the outcome. 'I have chased the English out of France more easily than my father did,' he remarked to his court at the celebration banquet, 'for he had to drive them out with armies, while I have seen them off with venison and good French wine.'

The English army withdrew to Calais and by the end of September the King was home again, never having drawn his sword. The citizens of London, who were in any case more interested in trade than war, gave him a rapturous welcome. The only notable casualty in the campaign was the prisoner, Henry Holland, Duke of Exeter, whom Edward had taken along on the expedition. On the voyage home, the Duke of Exeter fell, or was pushed, overboard. His body was found floating in the Channel, and yet another threat to Edward's throne had been removed from the scene.

Duke Charles, passionate, excitable and never totally stable, was so furious at the news of the Treaty of Picquigny that he ate his ribbon of the Garter. He was even less fortunate in his continuing wars in Lorraine and along the Rhône. Having captured Nancy in November 1475, in 1476 he attacked Lorraine and so drew on to himself the enmity of the hardy citizens and peasant pikemen of Switzerland. The Duke fought the Swiss three times in the space of a year: at Grandson in March 1476, at Morat in June 1476, and again at Nancy in January 1477. In the first battle he lost his treasure, in the second his army, in the third his life. His death ended the glittering line of the Valois Dukes of Burgundy, and his vast estates went either to the King of France or to his daughter Mary, wife of Maximilian of Habsburg, a marriage which eventually brought the Spanish and a century of misery to the Low Countries.

* * *

Edward added most of his field artillery and siege artillery to the defences of Calais and returned from his expedition to France to find fresh problems at home, and problems coming from a now all-too-familiar source. The King had restored the Royal fortunes and settled the old dispute with France. The nation's trade was increasing and the realm was becoming prosperous. The Scottish border was troublesome, as usual, but taken as a whole, all was right with his world. The one exception, inevitably, was the Duke of Clarence.

Clarence was incorrigible. It was not so much a question of giving him what he wanted (though he always wanted something), as in finding out what he wanted and why. He was a constant source of trouble and the King's patience was already thin when, in the spring of 1477, an extraordinary affair took place at Warwick. Clarence, now Earl of Warwick, had been living in the old Earl's great castle since 1473.

It appears that in October 1476, Isobel Neville, Clarence's wife, gave birth to a child in the abbey infirmary at Tewkesbury. Two months later, the Lady Isobel died, and the baby, a boy, died a few days later, on 1 January 1477. So far, so tragic, but three months later a party of Clarence's men suddenly rode into Somerset and descended on the home of a worthy widow, Ankarette Twynho of Frome, and carried her off by force, first to Bath and then back to Warwick Castle. There she was met by a furious Clarence. Ankarette was abused, interrogated, stripped of all her possessions and finally brought before the justices, where she was accused of sorcery and of poisoning the Lady Isobel to whom Ankarette had been lady-in-waiting.

A verdict of guilty was swiftly brought and an hour later the unfortunate lady was taken to the town gallows and hanged. The whole process, from accusation to execution, took three hours. A citizen of Warwick, John Thirsby, was also hanged for murdering Isobel's baby, and a local knight, Sir Roger Tucotes, was accused of involvement but escaped to report these events to the Royal Council. The account he gave was not published, but before the echoes of this affair had died away, another scandal broke, again concerning the Duke of Clarence.

In May 1477, three men, Thomas Blake, Thomas Burdett and John Stacey, were arrested and tried in London for plotting to use sorcery against the King's welfare. A confession was tortured out of Stacey but the evidence was slight, though Burdett and Stacey were then hanged and Blake imprisoned. Thomas Burdett was a member of Clarence's household and while this fact was being digested, there was a small rising against the King in Cambridgeshire, which Clarence was alleged to have inspired.

Edward finally decided that Clarence had to be stopped. He rode from Windsor to London, summoned Clarence to a meeting and after a furious row before the mayor and the council, where the King accused Clarence of discrediting the King's law over Ankarette Twynho, he sent him to the Tower. Clarence was then brought before the Privy Council and accused of placing himself above the law by taking and hanging Ankarette Twynho. The Duke was sent back to the Tower, where he remained with the King ignoring all appeals for his release. Six months later, on 16 January 1478, Parliament met again at Westminster, when the main subject for discussion was the attainting for treason of the King's brother, the Duke of Clarence.

The indictment listed all Clarence's misdemeanours of recent years, including the judicial murder of Ankarette Twynho and claimed that Clarence had put it about that Burdett and Stacey had been unlawfully put to death for accusing the King of employing magical acts. The Bill of Attainder first covered the period before Tewkesbury Field and then the period after it, but the King's evident disapproval of Clarence appears in every line of the indictment: 'Of tender youth until the time [the King] had ever loved and cheryssed hym [Clarence] as kindly as any man might his natural brother even to persuading the Yorkist Lords to swear allegiance to Clarence as next in succession.' The King's reward for this had been Clarence's conspiracy with Warwick.

The second part of the bill was concerned with more recent matters. The Duke had taken the law into his own hands and then attempted to discredit the King over Burdett. He had suggested that the King used 'necromancy and craft to poison his subjects' and alleged that the King was a bastard. The King concluded by stating that his brother was 'incorrigible'.

The charges were vague, as was often the way with attainders, where the will or intention of treason was judged as treacherous as the deed, but the sum total was that Clarence had to die. Parliament deliberated for two weeks until 26 February, when the Bill of Attainder was duly passed, and Clarence was sentenced to lose all his estates and titles. The responsibility for the execution of a death sentence now rested on a Court of Chivalry called under the Constable of England, the Duke of Buckingham who, not unnaturally, was reluctant to act, though the patent for his appointment says he was to arrange 'the execution of the Duke of Clarence' – *pro executione ducis Clarence*. The bill was passed on 7 February 1478, but when Clarence was still alive ten days later, a deputation from the Commons went to see Buckingham and demanded execution of the sentence.

Buckingham's hesitation is not surprising. It was no light matter to execute the King's brother and he had only been made Constable in place of Gloucester to prevent Gloucester committing the sin of fratricide. The King had used Parliament to rubber-stamp his desire for the Duke's execution for the same reason, but the final responsibility for the actual deed now rested on the shoulders of the Duke of Buckingham.

The blame for 'urging the Duke of Clarence's death' has been laid at the door of the Woodvilles, who certainly made no efforts to dissuade the King from his chosen course of action, but the real responsibility rests with the King himself, though there is very little evidence that Gloucester raised any strong objections. The 'incorrigible' Duke of Clarence had finally gone too far and death came for him on the night of 18 February 1478, though how the Duke died is uncertain.

He may have been drowned in a barrel of malmsey wine. So legend has it, based on stories then current, which often have a strong element of truth in them. At the time, wine casks were also used as baths, so he may have been taken unawares in his bath and held under until he drowned. Either way, Clarence was gone and few people mourned him. His body was coffined in the Tower and taken to the abbey at Tewkesbury. There he still lies, close to his wife Isobel and the headless bodies of those Lancastrian lords whom Clarence had been so eager to execute just seven years before.

CHAPTER THIRTEEN

EDWARD AND RICHARD (1478–83)

No simple man sees
This jarring discord of nobility,
This shouldering of each other in the Court,
This factious bandying of their favourites,
But that it doth pressage some ill event.

Henry VI

With Clarence dead and foreign affairs settled, the last five years of Edward IV's reign were relatively peaceful. The King gave himself over to the duties of kingship and, with rather more enthusiasm, to the pleasures of debauchery. The smack of firm government was supplied from time to time by his younger brother, Richard of Gloucester, who now began to make his way to the forefront of public affairs.

When Clarence died in 1478, Richard of Gloucester was 26 and, unlike his brother Clarence and most of the other lords about the court, he had been his brother's stout partisan, in victory and defeat, since the age of 15, certainly from the time the King fell out with Warwick. After Tewkesbury, and particularly after the death of Clarence, he began to get his just rewards.

In July 1471, soon after the battles at Barnet and Tewkesbury, he became Steward of the Duchy of Lancaster. A week or so later, he received the grant of all the Neville lands north of the Trent, including the Neville castle at Middleham, which was to become his favourite home. He was also made Constable and Admiral of England and Warden of the West March. In December 1471 he received the lands of the Earl of Oxford, who was still in arms against the King, and some time after Easter 1472, he married Warwick's younger daughter, Anne Neville, and eventually acquired the greater part of the Warwick inheritance.

The quarrels with Clarence over Anne's estates have already been described, but over the next few years the King continued to add to his brother Gloucester's inheritance, and it is noticeable how much of Richard's power and possessions were in the north. He made little effort to increase his standing in the south. In February 1475, for example, Gloucester received all the northern lands of the Marquis Montagu, Warwick's brother. Like Warwick, Montagu had never been attainted, so this Act was actually illegal. It also stripped Montagu's son, George, now Duke of Bedford, of all his possessions. To add insult to injury, a few weeks later George Neville was stripped of his dukedom on the grounds that he now lacked the wealth to support it. This Act had a curious clause whereby if George died without a male heir, Richard would only have life tenure of the Neville lands, which on his death would revert to the Latimer line of the Nevilles. By the grant of Warwick and Montagu lands, he became heir to the great Neville affinity and, as the years passed, the leading magnate beyond the Trent. Richard seemed to prefer the north and seldom came to Court. He stayed on his estates, conducted the King's business as directed and became very popular with the northern people.

The King still ruled and ruled well, but as the decade closed his health was beginning to fail. He was growing fat, ate hugely, drank, and indeed 'overmuch consumed his Royal person.' Though the King now had two sturdy sons, Edward, Prince of Wales, born in November 1470, and Richard, Duke of York, born in August 1473, they were still children and the coming man for the next few years was their uncle, the powerful Duke of Gloucester. This, inevitably, put Gloucester at odds with the Woodvilles, and the tensions may have increased when Richard's son, another Edward, was born in 1473. Richard now had an heir to look out for, though whatever his admirers and defenders claim, he was never slow to snap up any post or position or vacant preferment.

Any discussion of the Duke of Gloucester is at once confronted with the picture of him created by the Tudor writers. Richard's murderous image has been woven into the nation's historical conscience by the skilful pen of William Shakespeare too firmly for anyone to ignore, but though Shakespeare's Richard III bears little relation to reality, Shakespeare, or his Tudor sources, did not invent all the evil tales they helped to spread about him. As we shall see, there were plenty of contemporary chroniclers who were by no means enamoured of the Duke of Gloucester.

Richard is a man who always appears in primary colours. Even after 500 years, no one who knew him or now knows about him is indifferent to him. He is either loved or hated, praised or execrated. Much of the original comment on Richard comes not from playwrights or political trimmers, but from people who are well able to obtain all the known facts and come to an objective judgement. Few people seem able to do this. His partisans, and they are many and still growing, will not hear a word said against him. His enemies will believe any tale or slander, however unlikely or previously disproved. In such a situation it is as well to begin with a few facts.

Richard, Duke of Gloucester, was born on 2 October 1452, at the family castle of Fotheringhay. Apart from the fact that the elder members of his family were constantly in conflict with their Lancastrian relatives from the time he was 3, his childhood was unremarkable, but not entirely undisturbed. In 1459 he and his brother George were hustled out of Ludlow and sent to live with their mother in the care of the Duchess of Bedford, and a year later, after the death of his father at Wakefield, the two brothers were sent to Burgundy and lived with Duke Philip until brother Edward took the throne.

From the age of 10 he was 'nourished' in the Neville castle at Middleham in Yorkshire by the family of his cousin, the Earl of Warwick, and there he learned the knightly arts in company with his lifelong friends, Lord Lovell of Minster Lovell in Oxfordshire, who had wide estates in the north, and Richard Ratcliff, the son of local gentry in Derwentwater. In his off-duty moments, he would have played with Warwick's daughters, the Lady Isobel and the Lady Anne. While he was growing up, the hard times began, but he was not even present at, let alone a ferocious participant in, all the early battles of the wars, as Shakespeare avers in *Henry VI*. He was, however, clearly devoted to his older brother, Edward, and Edward to him. Edward was a good brother, protective of his sibling. One of the Paston letters for 12 October 1460 records: 'The Tuesday next after My Lord [the Duke of York] sent for her [the Duchess] that she should come to Hereford...leaving behind the Lord George and the Lord Richard...and the Earl of March comes every day to see them.' This was an affection which by all accounts never wavered.

In 1468, when he was 16, Richard had been appointed Lord High Admiral, Constable of England, and Chief Justice for the Marches of Wales. Two years later, in 1470, his brother, Edward the King, and his cousin of Warwick, took up arms against each other. Clarence sided with Warwick but Richard stayed loyal to the King and followed Edward into exile at Bruges. He supported his brother in exile and returned to fight at his side at Barnet and Tewkesbury. Some accounts record that it was Richard who rode into Clarence's camp near Banbury and made peace between his two older brothers. He then commanded the right wing of Edward's army at Barnet, where he was wounded, and fought at Tewkesbury, where he again commanded a division of the King's army. There is no evidence that he killed the young Prince Edward after the battle. Although he was certainly present in the Tower on the night King Henry VI was murdered, so was every other Yorkist of note. There is no evidence whatsoever that Richard gave the order for King Henry's death, let alone that he carried out the execution with his own hands. He certainly fell out with his brother, Clarence, over the matter of Anne Neville and the Beauchamp–Despenser estates, but it was Edward and the Parliament who agreed to Clarence's well-merited death in 1478, and the Duke of Buckingham who arranged the actual details. Most of the crimes later laid at his door were not of his doing.

From 1472 Richard was usually in the north, at Middleham Castle in Wensleydale, which had been his childhood home for some years. He lived there with Anne, his wife, who had a wasting sickness, probably tuberculosis, and their son Edward, who was born some time in 1473 and was never strong, and with his mother-in-law, the old Countess of Warwick. Richard was entrusted with the Lordship of the North, which meant that he was responsible to the King for law, order and public affairs in all England north of the River Trent. These responsibilities included the defence of the Scottish border, where he found himself obliged to keep a close eye on those shifty lords, the Percies and the Stanleys, and the surviving Nevilles of the Westmorland affinity.

In spite of Shakespeare's text and Tudor distortion, all the available hard evidence confirms that Richard Gloucester, by his honesty and fair dealing, by his firmness and good judgement, made a great success of this position, though he was quick to take advantage of any land or titles that came his way. On the whole though, he was popular and this cannot have been easy, for the north-east was the country of the Nevilles and the Percies and their various long-standing affinities, and the country west of the Pennines had long been a Lancastrian stronghold, and was a base for the large Stanley affinity, a family which had proved adept at sitting on the fence during the wars of York and Lancaster.

It seems that Richard eventually won everyone round and did all the better for avoiding the inevitable gossip and in-fighting that took place at Court. He still came south at regular intervals to attend Royal Councils, and was careful to see that his voice was heard and his opinions considered when any matters of importance were under discussion. He had many friends at Court and was particularly close to William, Lord Hastings, the King's Chamberlain, who no doubt kept him well informed on all the Court's intrigues. No one ever said that Richard was a fool and he was certainly well aware of how much he would lose if the Woodvilles ever came to power.

It should be remembered that the Woodville family position in the Court and kingdom depended entirely on the King. Their rise had begun when Edward married Elizabeth Woodville, and their decline might follow when the King died. The old nobility certainly did not welcome the Woodvilles at Court and there is no evidence that their popularity increased in any way as time went by; if anything, they continued to make enemies and they must have been well aware that if anything happened to the King, who was no longer well, their fragile power base would surely crumble.

Richard came south with 1,000 soldiers in 1475 to join Edward's expedition to France. It is said that he returned disgusted with the result of the Treaty of Picquigny, considering the terms dishonourable, and he certainly declined to take part in discussing the terms it contained. This is hardly to be wondered at, for even if Edward were not hot for war, the terms of the treaty, which involved Edward accepting a bribe – or a 'tribute' as Edward preferred to call it – from King Louis to go away and bother him no more, were clearly insulting.

In 1478 Gloucester was in London again for the marriage of his nephew, the King's younger son, Richard, Duke of York, to Anne Mowbray, the Norfolk heiress, at which he escorted the bride to the altar. This marriage was a jolly affair, not least because the groom was 4 and the bride 5. Gloucester stayed on at Court for the less happy discussions and secret dealings which culminated in the judicial murder of the Duke of Clarence a few weeks later.

According to the Italian diplomat, Mancini, Gloucester blamed the King for conspiring with the Woodvilles to cause Clarence's death. Gloucester may well have disapproved of Clarence's execution, though it is unlikely that he said anything against it, and if he could have used that event to blacken the name of the Woodvilles, he would surely have done so. Gloucester was probably more concerned with the health of his brother, the King, for a periodic visitor will see changes in a man which those in daily contact tend to overlook.

The King was beginning to show the effects of hard living. He drank heavily, ate huge meals, kept several mistresses and took little exercise outside the bedchamber. His companions on these revels were Hastings and various Woodvilles, especially the Marquis of Dorset. Edward was growing unpleasantly fat and was altogether a different person from the tall, golden knight of Richard's youth, and Philip de Comines, for one, was shocked at the sight of Edward's physical decline in 1475.

It is unlikely that Gloucester was happy at Court. He was never a courtier, but it is not a wise thing for a man who depends on power to stay away from power's centre. Richard's role in the north was important, even vital, but up there, many days ride from London, he was out of the mainstream of events. His voice was not heard in Council and his Court affinity, if he ever had one, gradually drifted away to other men. His power and position, and in those reeling times perhaps even his life, depended on the continued support of his brother the King. The fate of Clarence had pointed out with particular clarity that the King's affection could not keep a man from the block if the need arose. While the King lived, that support, the mutual love of one for the other, brother for brother, went unquestioned. When the King died, it would be another matter, and given the way the King was now living, his death was a distinct possibility.

Edward was a sensual man who had always kept several mistresses, and consumed a great many other women as well, as they came to court or were encountered on his progresses. By 1478 he had three known mistresses, of whom the chief was Elizabeth (or Jane) Shore, the wife of a city merchant. Edward claimed that she was 'the merriest mistress in the realm', and in this fact lay her attraction to him: she made the King laugh, and being intelligent and kindly, had many close friends among the King's circle. Her complacent husband, William Shore, was a well-known figure in City circles, as was her father, but her marriage to William Shore ran into difficulties in 1476, when three bishops sat to consider her petition for divorce on the grounds that William was 'frigides et impotens' and had denied her children. Her petition must have been granted because her liaison with the King was soon an open secret, and the King flaunted her about the court 'for many he had but her he loved'. This affection was not shared in any way by the King's brother, Gloucester, who blamed her for the rapid and obvious decline in the King's health.

Mistresses and revelling apart, the King was busy with public affairs. He took a great interest in trade and with his 'benevolences' and sensible investments, notably in the wool trade, gradually restored the Royal fortunes. During his exile in Bruges, he had been impressed by the library of Louis de Gruthuyse, and had assembled a great quantity of manuscripts. He was also a patron of Master William Caxton, who with the assistance of the Woodville lord, Earl Rivers, had set up shop in Westminster with one of those new-fangled German printing presses, a device which looked like putting the clerical scribes out of business.

Edward had little need to call on Parliament, but a stream of laws poured from the Royal Councils. Young men must be encouraged to practice archery, so laws were passed to restrict the spread of sports like football and quoits. Trade was increasing, so the regulations governing markets – the pie-powder courts – had to be overhauled. Extravagances must be curtailed, so new sumptuary laws went through regulating what each class might wear and what materials they might choose for their clothes. In the 1470s a new and growing vice was card playing. Cards had just been invented in France (the modern court cards still show kings and queens in fifteenth-century dress) and the game was already bringing ruin to the Court gamblers.

Edward had always been interested in trade and one of his intentions was to widen both the range of goods for export and the market for English goods abroad. The wool trade was still important, but other goods, tin, fish and grain were soon bringing in worthwhile returns, while English ships were taking grain, wool and cloth to the Mediterranean ports.

Edward also maintained firm but friendly relations with the Holy See, and with the many monastic foundations at home, not least because they were providing the teachers for the growing literacy of the King's subjects. This is the time when the grammar schools were founded, but though the scholars were destined for trade, the instruction came from clerics. There were more than 800 monasteries in England, and as farmers, teachers and spiritual leaders, their power and influence was worth cultivating and applying to the King's ends.

Edward also devoted considerable sums to maintaining Henry VI's foundations of Eton College and King's College, Cambridge, as well as rebuilding the Chapel of St George, at Windsor, for the Knights of the Garter; while his Queen took over responsibility for Margaret of Anjou's foundation, Queens' College in Cambridge. The work on St George's was not fully completed until 1528, but Edward was able to attend Garter services in the chapel shortly before he died. Further sums were spent in

1476 moving the bodies of his father, York, and his brother, Rutland, from their graves in York to the family chapel at Fotheringhay Castle. These worthwhile tasks were interrupted in 1480 by more trouble in the north and in Calais.

In 1479 Louis XI fell ill and, fearing that his end was coming, he resolved to complete his father's work and expel the English from Calais. With the death of Charles the Rash in 1477, King Louis, openly delighted, lost no time in reoccupying that part of his cousin's lands that were the French apanage of the Valois Dukes of Burgundy. This done, he was free to turn his attention to that other minor irritation, the continual English occupation of the Calais pale. The English had done wonders with Calais – it may be imagined as a medieval Hong-Kong – now a thriving centre for trade and industry, but such a jewel would have fitted nicely into the crown of France.

Louis saw no reason not to grab Calais, for whatever his domestic successes Edward IV had no great skill at foreign policy. He had forged few political alliances with the great powers of continental Europe – with Spain or France or the rich city-states of Italy. If his actions at Picquigny are any yardstick, it seems probable that he simply was not interested in foreign affairs, which cost money and could lead to risks, though this was not for want of trying. Edward was constantly trying to forge alliances through marriage, and his Queen gave him ten children to treat with. He proposed Mary for the King of Denmark, Cicely for the Protector for Scotland, Anne for the heir of Burgundy, Elizabeth for the Dauphin of France, Catherine for the Prince of Spain. None of these marriages took place. The result wat that when Burgundy fell, Edward found himself with enemies on every hand, and few cards to play when the Scottish border burst into flames and Louis' professional army moved towards Calais across Picardy. He was, however, the man who had emerged victorious from every field and his combativeness was soon again apparent.

Word of Louis' interests soon reached England and strong reinforcements were rushed across the Channel to William, Lord Hastings, now the Lieutenant of Calais. The walls were manned in 1481 when Louis came marching across France with a large army, though he advised Hastings by letter that this was purely a training exercise and no offensive action was intended. King Louis's *chevauchée* in Picardy was only a diversion, but he had successfully stirred up his allies, the Scots, who burned Bamburgh in September 1480 and were in the field again in the spring of 1481. As Gloucester was in the north and supported by the Nevilles and Percies, the border was secure – or fairly secure – but the King decided to invade Scotland with the particular aim of retaking Berwick.

Men and supplies were sent north in the winter of 1481–82 and in the spring of 1482 the King ordered Gloucester to muster men in the north for an invasion of Scotland, which the King would lead in person. Loyal as ever, Gloucester began to assemble forces in front of Berwick in early April, but by then King Edward was very ill, possibly having suffered a heart attack. Command of the expedition was, therefore, given to Gloucester, who was ordered to invade Scotland, overthrow the King, James III, and replace him with his exiled brother, Alexander, Duke of Albany, who had newly arrived in England from France. The scheme then was for him to marry one of Edward's daughters, the Lady Cicely, and so confirm a lasting peace between the two kingdoms. The fact that Albany had recently married Anne de la Tour, daughter of the Count of Boulogne, was seen as no impediment to the scheme, and the terms of this agreement were drawn up at Fotheringhay Castle in June 1482.

Albany and Gloucester duly marched north to meet with Lord Stanley and the Earl of Northumberland, their combined forces amounting to some 20,000 men. Stanley took over the siege of Berwick, while the others crossed the Tweed with the field army and advanced on Edinburgh, which fell without opposition, the Scots garrison having withdrawn into the castle. From that moment on, Gloucester and Albany's invasion fell apart.

The Scots lords greatly preferred their weak King James III to the usurping Albany and any English bride. Besides, it was King James's courtiers they took exception to, and having hanged many of them off the bridge at Lauder, the Scots were prepared to buckle on their armour and fight for the King. Albany, on the other hand, was happy to settle for the restoration of his Scottish lands. After a fruitless week or two in Scotland, Gloucester ordered a withdrawal, only pausing on his way south to recapture the castle and town of Berwick-on-Tweed, which had been in Scots' hands since Queen Margaret had surrendered it before the campaign leading to the second Battle of St Albans, in 1455. By August 1482, the invasion force had dispersed to their homes and Richard was back again with his wife, Anne, at Middleham Castle.

While Gloucester had been occupied in Scotland, problems had arisen at Court. Tensions there had already been exacerbated by worries over the failing health of King Edward, but this new quarrel seemed to be an extension of the former dispute between the 'old' nobility, and in particular Lord Hastings, and the 'new' nobility, represented by the King's relatives, the Woodvilles and Greys. In fact, the 'nobility' of Hastings and Buckingham was no older than that of the Woodvilles. Buckingham became a Duke only in 1448, though the Stafford Earldom dated back to the 14th century. The difference was that the Woodvilles were isolated and seen as favourites of the King, by virtue of their relative, the Queen. The leaders in this particular outburst were Hastings and the King's stepson, George, Marquis of Dorset, and before long the sick King's court had split into factions: on the one hand the Woodvilles and the Queen; on the other the 'old' nobility, Hastings, the Duke of Buckingham, Lord Howard, Lord Stanley, and his brother, Sir William Stanley. The exact causes for this particular quarrel are not known, but without the King to keep the peace, there was little difficulty in finding reasons to argue.

The last Parliament of King Edward's reign opened in January 1483. The main matter before the Commons was to vote fresh funds for another assault on Scotland, to be led by the Duke of Gloucester. The King was present at the opening of Parliament, but long before it ended he was forced to withdraw and retired to his castle at Windsor, where some time towards the end of March he again became seriously ill. He was carried back to his palace at Westminster in a litter and there, on 9 April 1483, he died, aged 41.

Edward had been King of England for over 21 years, and had he lived another five years, until his eldest son was old enough to take over, the history of England might have been very different. On the whole he had been very successful. He had fought and won all his battles and restored the Royal finances. Edward was a successful monarch – affable, sensible, resolute in war. He was the first king for generations to die solvent, and under his benign rule, trade and the trading classes flourished. He had ended the war with France and extracted tribute for doing so, though the payments ended in 1482. He had picked up the sword of his ancestors from his dead father's hand and overthrown the mighty House of Lancaster. He had slaughtered the nobility of England if they came in arms against him, and destroyed the great Earl of Warwick. All this done, he had given his people peace, and taken all in all, his reign had been successful.

In his youth he was the most handsome prince in Europe, brave and intelligent and not noticeably bloodthirsty. It would, however, be a mistake to see Edward as totally benevolent: a saintly man could not be a good king. Henry VI was a good example of that sad fact and Edward could be ruthless when he had to be. When Henry VI or Clarence got in his way, he dealt with them, and if heads had to come off, the King neither hesitated to act nor lost a night's sleep over it. Now he was gone, but he had left his affairs in order and the new reign could be anticipated with a degree of optimism. King Edward had done all that a king could do to ensure the success of his line after his death, and the throne would surely pass to his eldest son, Edward V, now Prince of Wales and living with his tutors at Ludlow.

Edward V was only 12, but that hardly mattered. In the fifteenth century a king could start to rule as well as reign at 15 or 16, so it would not be long before this new Edward came into his full inheritance. In the meantime, he was a king's son, he had loyal relatives and a full treasury, and during his brief three- or four-year minority, the welfare of the realm would be in the safe and capable hands of his powerful uncle, the late King's loyal brother, Richard, Duke of Gloucester.

CHAPTER FOURTEEN

LONG LIVE RICHARD III (1483)

*Most reverend Father in God, you have oft
besought me to put in writing by what machinations
Richard the Third, now reigning in England,
attained the degree of Kingship.*

DOMINIC MANCINI TO ANGELO CATO, BISHOP OF

VIENNE, IN 1483

King Edward IV's body was exposed in Westminster Hall, while the lords, prelates and the aldermen of London came to view it. It was then embalmed and lay in state for eight days, so it was not until 17 April that the funeral service took place in Westminster Abbey. The body was taken to Windsor on the 18th, resting overnight at Syon Abbey, and buried in Edward's Chapel of St George at Windsor Castle on the following day. When the King died, only the Queen and the Marquis of Dorset were at Court, together with the young Duke of York, who was 10. Very few peers were able to attend his burial at Windsor, though Lord Howard arrived from Norfolk in time to carry the Royal banner at the funeral. The Lords Stanley and Hastings were also present, but of the other great lords, Richard of Gloucester was at Middleham in Yorkshire, the Duke of Buckingham at his castle in Brecon, and the Prince of Wales and his tutor, Anthony, Lord Rivers, were at Ludlow. Given the nine days that had elapsed since the King's death, it is more than curious that none of these people was able to attend the funeral. Even in early spring and on the poor English roads, one would have thought that every peer able to attend would hasten to pay his respects. The conclusion has to be that not all of them were told, or that the news had been kept from them while certain preparations were put in train.

Given the tensions at Court, it is not surprising that everyone who could sought positions of personal advantage as soon as the King was dead.

Dorset hurried at once to the Tower and dipped his hands into the late King's coffers, for ready money was always useful at such a time, and he and the Queen soon had charge of most of Edward's money. Sir Edward Woodville swiftly took command of the Royal ships on the Thames and made them ready; while a detachment of 500 archers went to reinforce the garrison of Calais in case the French should lunge at the town during the interregnum.

These moves took place while the question of government was still open. The late King had clearly intended that Gloucester should be Protector, but as soon as the King died, his Queen put forward a claim for the Regency. The lords in the Council, on the other hand, led by Hastings and the Duke of Buckingham, preferred the idea of a Royal Council, with Richard of Gloucester as Protector, as in the early days of Henry VI.

The normal ceremonies surrounding the death of one English king and the accession of another then took place. On 11 April, two days after the King's death, Garter King of Arms, principal herald of the realm, pronounced the rule of Edward V at Westminster and on the steps of St Paul's, and by then the coronation had already been fixed by the Royal Council for 4 May. The young King was now 12 and since majority came early in the Middle Ages, he might expect to rule as well as reign in three or four years, certainly by the age of 16. The question at the moment was what would happen in the meantime. For an answer they had the late King's will and wishes.

There seems to have been a general acceptance that King Edward IV wished his brother, Gloucester, to be Protector of the Realm during his son's minority, or at least until the coronation, a matter of days. After that he would advise the King with the help and consent of the Royal Council. This would have been the obvious and wisest choice, and the actions taken in the days after Edward's death seem to confirm that this course of action was generally acknowledged. Strange, therefore, that the Woodvilles in London, who had sent messengers to Ludlow, where the sad news arrived around 14 April, did not see fit to advise and summon the Duke of Gloucester from Yorkshire.

On the rough roads of fifteenth-century England, a horseman might normally expect to cover 40 miles in a day, perhaps 50 miles if riding hard and changing mounts, so, given the urgency of the time, the news should have reached Richard in four or five days at the most. This failure to inform the Duke of Gloucester is the first indication that the Woodvilles were plotting against him.

There were already two parties in London jostling for influence over the young King. On the one side were the 'new' nobility, the Queen and her family, the Greys and Woodvilles and their adherents. On the other stood the 'old' nobility, which contained the Dukes of Gloucester, Buckingham and Norfolk, as well as powerful lords like Lord Stanley and the dead King's great friend, William, Lord Hastings. Of the 'old' nobility only Hastings was at court.

Gloucester did not officially learn of his brother's death until 20 April, and then in a letter from Lord Hastings. By that time, the Woodvilles had seized the King's treasure in the Tower, put the fleet at readiness and arranged for the coronation. They had already quarrelled with Lord Hastings over the size of the force which would convey the Prince of Wales to London. The Woodvilles intended to raise all the men they could and pack London with troops, but Hastings insisted on a limit of 2,000 men, threatening to withdraw to the safety of Calais if his wishes were ignored. As Hastings was Lieutenant of Calais, and Calais contained a large garrison of professional soldiers, this was no light threat. Hastings also knew that Gloucester and Buckingham could match a Woodville force of 2,000 men from their own retainers, without causing further alarm by raising troops from their affinities. On being assured that Rivers and Grey would not arrive in London with an army, Hastings stayed in London, but put all this information in a letter to the Duke of Gloucester.

There can be little doubt that the Woodvilles intended to get the young King to London and the crown on his head as quickly as possible, while moving into positions about his Court from which they could not easily be dislodged. Once the King was crowned, the Protector's room to manoeuvre could be limited by the Royal Council, which, with the assistance of the King and the Queen-dowager, the Woodvilles might hope to influence. The trick was to do this before Richard of Gloucester could arrive and seize the slack reins of government.

Once informed that he was to be named Protector of the Realm, Gloucester began to act, but as the King's nearest relative, not as Protector. His first move was to send a letter of sympathy to the Queen and order Requiem Masses throughout the north. He then led the Mayor and citizens of York in taking an oath of allegiance to the young King Edward in York Minster. Nothing could have been more normal or more correct.

This much done, he then set out for London, taking with him 'six hundred gentlemen of the North', his 'mourning train'. Richard's defenders make considerable play with this small company, comparing

Richard's 600 mourners with the 2,000 armed men coming with Earl Rivers and the young Prince of Wales from Ludlow, but this argument will not stand up to close inspection. To begin with, the Prince of Wales was riding to his coronation, and a large escort would be normal. Many of his friends from Ludlow would also want to be at the ceremony to support him and, no doubt, receive some reward for past services, for any coronation was accompanied by knighthoods for the King's friends and the redistribution of honours. Neither is it surprising that the King's party was armed and had brought its armour. They were Marchmen from the Welsh border, where all men went about armed, and the coronation would probably be followed by a tournament and other celebrations.

Richard's 600 gentlemen of the north, if they were gentlemen of coat-armour or knights and squires, would certainly not have travelled unescorted. If each gentlemen had only three retainers, and most would have had more, then Richard was coming south with at least 2,000 men. The disparity, if any, is certainly not as wide as his supporters claim. A little thought reveals that it is Gloucester's force which might require some explanation, and the reason for it rests in the contents of Hastings's letter which must have told Gloucester about events in London.

The intention of the Council, now dominated by the Woodville clique, including Thomas Grey, Marquis Dorset, and John Morton, now Bishop of Ely, was to get the young Prince to London and set the crown on his head as soon as possible. They also hoped either to prevent Richard becoming Protector or to limit his powers in office. The Protectorship would, in any event, have to be confirmed by the Royal Council. The matter was one of timing, and speed was of the essence.

Richard had already received more news of the various Woodville moves in London, as well as a letter of support and condolence from his cousin, the Duke of Buckingham. Richard replied to this, asking the Duke to meet him at Northampton, where he hoped to meet the Royal party riding in from Ludlow. Henry Stafford, Shakespeare's 'princely Buckingham', was another descendant of Edward III and had resented his marriage, as a Royal ward, to Catherine Woodville, one of the Queen's numerous sisters.

The Queen had, meanwhile, demanded that she should be Regent, and though Hastings and Buckingham demurred, as Regent she could have appointed a Protector from her own affinity. Both parties were now bringing their forces to London and were set on a collision course. The collision came at Northampton.

Richard arrived at Northampton on the evening of 29 April 1483 to find that Anthony Woodville, Earl Rivers, was waiting for him with the news that the Prince and his party had ridden on to Stony Stratford, 15 miles closer to London, say half a day's journey further on. Gloucester seems to have said nothing to this news. While Richard and Rivers were dining, the Duke of Buckingham came riding in with 300 armed men, who were quartered about the town, and Buckingham joined them at table. Earl Rivers then went to bed, while the two Dukes stayed on over their wine, discussing affairs of state. As one of the 'old' nobility, Buckingham had no love of the Woodvilles and had been at Court more often, and more recently, than Gloucester. Whatever news he brought with him, or whatever suspicions he managed to plant in Gloucester's mind, cannot now be known, but early next morning the first crack appeared in the fragile alliance around the Prince.

Earl Rivers was arrested in his bed and detained while the two Dukes hustled out their men and galloped down to Stony Stratford, where they placed Sir Richard Grey and Sir Thomas Vaughan under arrest. These knights were sent back to join Rivers at Northampton, after which all four were taken under guard to Pontefract Castle. The 2,000 fighting men from Wales were ordered home, while the two Dukes rode on with the Prince of Wales in easy stages towards London.

The thoughts of the young Prince of Wales at this time are on record, and the arrests of his Woodville guardians and companions clearly upset him. He could not accept the allegation by Gloucester and Buckingham that they were dangerous. The young Prince of Wales was mature beyond his years – he was now 12 – and he told the Dukes bluntly that he saw no harm or malice in his Woodville friends, either towards himself or Gloucester, pointing out that they had been appointed by the King, his father, and that 'he had seen no evil in them.' This provoked an outburst from Buckingham, who said that he 'loathed the Queen and her race and if the Prince cherished any confidence in the Queen his mother, he had better relinquish it now.'

Why Richard did this, and so suddenly, remains a mystery. His many supporters, notably Mrs V. B. Lamb, claim that these men were arrested to avert 'considerable bloodshed', but she produces no evidence that Rivers, Grey and Vaughan were doing more than escorting the Prince to London. It could well be that Richard was simply making a pre-emptive strike against the ambitious Woodvilles, removing them from the scene and disbanding their forces before they could combine with the Queen's force in London. Whatever his intentions, the news of his actions against Lord Rivers and the others swiftly reached London and threw the Woodvilles into panic.

The Marquis of Dorset fled at once to France while the Queen took her daughters, the young Duke of York and all her valuables into sanctuary at Westminster Abbey. She was still there when Gloucester arrived with the Prince of Wales and Buckingham on 4 May, the day fixed for the coronation. Gloucester went to stay with his mother, Duchess Cecily, at Baynards Castle, near Ludgate, while the Prince went to stay at the Palace of the Bishop of London. Apart from the arrests of the Woodvilles and the flight of the Queen, all was quite normal.

For the next few days Gloucester went about his affairs as anyone in his position might do, consulting his friends and advisers, keeping clear of the Westminster sanctuary. The Privy Council met on 7 May and removed the Great Seal from the Chancellor, Archbishop Rotherham, a partisan of the Queen. This meeting was attended by Richard's supporters, Hastings, Stanley, Buckingham and the Earl of Arundel, and held at Baynards Castle, the home of Duke Richard's mother.

On 10 May, the Privy Council confirmed Richard's appointment as Protector. Bishop Russell became Chancellor and Sir John Wade, the Speaker of the Commons, became treasurer. The coronation was rescheduled for 22 June and all proclamations were made in the name of Edward V 'by the advice of our dear uncle, the Duke of Gloucester, Protector during our young age.' When the Prince went to the Tower on 19 May, he was simply following custom, for the Tower was much more than a prison; it was the most secure fortress in the country, a Royal palace, an arsenal and a garrison. From here the King would progress through the City to his coronation at Westminster, 3 miles away down the river, cheered on by the citizens and loyal people already flocking in from the surrounding counties. Other lords were arriving in London for the coronation and the only embarrassment was the Queen and her family sheltering in Westminster, and the four prisoners at Pontefract, who were in deadly peril.

Gloucester was now demanding that Rivers, Vaughan and the rest should be condemned and executed as traitors, but traitors to whom? When he arrested them, Gloucester was not Protector of the Realm and the Woodville lords were clearly bringing the King to London for his coronation. Where in this was treason?

Apart from moving against the Woodvilles, Gloucester was rewarding his own supporters. Buckingham became Justice of North and South Wales and Constable of all the Royal castles along the Welsh Marches, charged with the duty of issuing Commissions of Array to raise soldiers. Lord Howard was appointed Steward of the Duchy of Lancaster, south of the Trent. Northumberland had recently become Warden of the East and Middle Marches in the north and was reappointed to these positions. Francis Lovell became Constable of Wallingford Castle and the post of Chief Butler was taken from the imprisoned Rivers and given to him. Stanley became Chamberlain of the Chester Palatinate and Hastings, apart from being reconfirmed as the King's chamberlain, became Master of the Royal Mint. All these posts were made in the King's name, but they all went either to Richard's friends or to people he needed to influence.

The great change in Gloucester's behaviour came on 9 June, just two weeks before the coronation. The Royal Council was now meeting daily, for there was much to arrange and discuss, but what happened when the Council met at Westminster on 9 June has never been recorded. Next day, Gloucester wrote urgently to York, requesting reinforcements against 'the Queen, her blood, and their affinity which have intended and daily doth intend to murder us and Our Cousin the Duke of Buckingham and the Old Royal Blood of this Realm.'

This letter is interesting. For example, the request for 'reinforcements' implies that Richard's original 'mourning train' had not been an inadequately armed collection of sorrowing gentry, but an armed band. Once again, one senses the hand of the princely Duke of Buckingham, 'Our Cousin', who had sparked off this train of events at Northampton and whose antipathy to the Woodvilles was well known. This letter was carried north by Sir Richard Ratcliffe, who carried a similar request for help to Ralph Neville, Earl of Westmorland. Ratcliffe also took orders to the Duke of Northumberland at Pontefract, that Rivers, Grey, Haute and Vaughan should be tried immediately for high treason. Matters had suddenly taken an ugly turn – but what had provoked it?

Three days later, on 13 June 1483, came the next and fatal Council meeting. Council meetings were now being held in the greater security of the Tower, and on the morning of 13 June, Duke Richard arrived after the rest were seated. Hardly had the meeting begun than the Duke suddenly accused King Edward's old friend, William, Lord Hastings, of treason and ordered his immediate execution. This is the scene dramatically and accurately portrayed by Shakespeare. The accusation was followed by Richard's men, previously concealed, bursting into the Council chamber.

After a brief scuffle, in which Lord Stanley was slightly wounded, they hustled Hastings out on to Tower Green and struck his head off over a log. Lord Stanley, Archbishop Rotherham and Bishop Morton were arrested, but Stanley was freed next day, while Morton was committed into the custody of the Duke of Buckingham, who sent him under guard to his castle at Brecon on the Welsh border. Gloucester also ordered the arrest, on charges of sorcery, of the late King's mistress, the 'harlot', Jane Shore', who was put in the prison of the Bishop of London, accused of conspiracy with Hastings against the welfare of the Lord Protector.

To kill the King's oldest friend without trial, and to imprison the King's favourite mistress, were bold moves indeed. The whole city was soon buzzing with anger, for Hastings had been popular and was known to have been King Edward's oldest and most loyal companion, a fervent supporter of the Prince of Wales. Why then, when Hastings's murder can only have caused her further alarm and had already led to riots in the City, did Queen Elizabeth allow her youngest son, the Duke of York, to leave their sanctuary on 16 June to join the Prince, his brother, in the Tower? She may have had no choice, or she may have been persuaded that only by surrendering the young Duke could she prevent worse happening to her other children. Archbishop Bourchier and Bishop Russell went into the sanctuary and brought out the Duke, who was presented first to Buckingham, and then, at the door of the Star Chamber, to his uncle, Gloucester, who had him conveyed under escort to the Tower.

Richard continued to act swiftly, ruthlessly and illegally. Orders now went to Pontefract for the immediate execution of Rivers, Grey, Vaughan and Haute. The coronation arranged for 22 June was cancelled, as was the calling of Parliament for 25 June. What we have now is not a man securing his own political position but a *coup d'état*.

Hastings had clearly been willing to support Gloucester against the Woodvilles, but at the meeting on 9 June either Hastings had realized that Gloucester was planning to take the crown or he had made it very clear that *if* Gloucester had any such intention, Hastings would not support him. Hence the call for assistance to the north on 10 June, and hence the ambush of Hastings at the meeting on 13 June. That may account for Richard's actions, but why, after years of loyal service and his actions since the King's death, had Richard suddenly lunged towards the throne?

Like the Woodvilles, Richard's position was largely dependent on his brother, the King, and it must surely have occurred to Richard on his journey south, if not before, that with the King dead, he was now surrounded by enemies. If the new King followed the wishes of the Woodville faction, Richard could expect to see his powers and his position steadily eroded. He also had his own son, the fruit of his marriage with an heiress of the mighty Warwick, who might make a better king in time than any scion of the Woodvilles. Whatever his thoughts about the future, unless Richard took some pre-emptive action now, it could only be a matter of time before the Woodvilles engineered his downfall.

Another possible reason for Richard's *coup* came a week after Hastings's death, on 22 June 1483, when a preacher, Dr Shaw, brother of the Mayor of London, delivered a sermon at St Paul's Cross. In this, Dr Shaw claimed that the Princes – indeed all the children of the late King by Elizabeth Woodville – were illegitimate because at the time of his marriage to Elizabeth, the King was already betrothed, if not actually married, to Lady Eleanor Butler, daughter of the Earl of Wiltshire. If the King had been married, or betrothed to the Lady Eleanor, who was more likely to know about it than his old friend and companion in debauchery, Lord Hastings, and his merry mistress, Jane Shore? If this is the information that came out at the meeting on 9 June, it must have given Gloucester a great shock, for this disastrous news threw open the whole question of the title to the throne.

Bastards were very common in the families of great men. Most of the lords mentioned in this book had sired illegitimate children. As a rule, bastards were accepted, educated and found suitable marriages, much as the legitimate children were, but in one respect at least they were very different: bastards had no rights to succession or inheritance. A title and all that went with it would go to the most remote cousin rather than to a deceased lord's eldest but illegitimate son. There had been tales that Edward IV had himself been the bastard son of an archer, and this tale, too, was soon going the rounds, but that Edward IV's children were born out of wedlock was more than just a shock. If true, it was a disaster. If the late King's heirs were bastards, all manner of people might put in a bid for the throne, not least his brother, Richard, or his cousin, princely Buckingham.

The simplest and most likely explanation for Hastings's execution is that Hastings was killed not because he had covered up his king's indiscretions but because he would not support Gloucester in a bid for the throne. Even so, this returns us to the question of Richard's character, for Gloucester had been his brother's loyal supporter for over 20 years. Now, within weeks of his death, we have him slandering the late King's memory and planning to usurp the throne. It is all too much. A compromise solution might be that whether the story was true or not, Gloucester believed it.

The question is – was it true? Historians have tended to dismiss the story of the pre-contract with Eleanor Butler as a fabrication put up to justify Gloucester's seizure of the throne, but given Edward's character, a pre-contract is not necessarily unlikely. The late King had, after all, married his Queen in secret, and kept that secret from the whole country for several months. So where did this story come from? Ralph Shaw claimed that the story came from Robert Stillington, now Bishop of Bath and Wells. Stillington claimed to have actually married Edward to Lady Eleanor, and the story may, therefore, well be true, for Stillington produced proofs. Although they have since disappeared, these proofs were available at the time and later embodied in an Act of Parliament legitimizing Gloucester's claim to the throne. Stillington must have had some proofs. No one would simply have taken his word for it over such a serious matter, and those who state, with good reason, that Stillington was untrustworthy, simply strengthen the case for some supporting evidence.

Stillington had certainly enjoyed great fortune with the late King Edward, at least early in the reign, rising from obscurity to become Chancellor of England, though Stillington had no recorded talent for finance or administration. Then, in 1473, it will be recalled, he was suddenly stripped of his offices, sent to the Tower by the King, and in 1475 he was summoned to Rome and closely examined by a Papal commission at the Vatican. What they wanted to know is still a secret in the Vatican archives, but being threatened by the King and then censured by the Pope following his involvement in an act of bigamy might account for his sudden fall. Everything is speculation, but everyone can speculate.

The matter again hinges on character. Was Edward the sort of man to have married Elizabeth Woodville if he had previously contracted to marry or had actually married Lady Eleanor Butler? The answer to that question is – probably. The Lady Eleanor was now dead and could not be questioned, but his marriage to Elizabeth had also been hasty, ill-advised and secret. He had kept that marriage secret from his council and kingdom for four months after the ceremony, even knowing that everyone, especially the Earl of Warwick, expected him to marry Bona of Savoy. What had been done once could have been done before. Sir Thomas More, though an otherwise untrustworthy source on the Yorkists, also recounts that at about the time of his marriage to Elizabeth Woodville, the King's mother, the Duchess of York, had written to Edward begging him 'not to commit bigamy'. If this is true, then perhaps his mother knew of Edward's pre-contract with Lady Eleanor Butler. This is all plausible, but this is not proof, because there is no proof, and there are several snags with it anyway.

Lady Eleanor Butler died in 1468, so the King and his Queen could then have married – or remarried – privately. This would have legitimized the princes, for Edward, Prince of Wales, was not born until 1471 and his brother, Richard of York, arrived in 1473. It is also worth mentioning that very few people believed Stillington's tale other than those, like Richard and Buckingham, who had personal reasons for doing so.

The whole story, a rather elaborate one, was probably engineered simply to clear the path to the throne for Richard by declaring the late King's marriage unlawful and his heirs therefore illegitimate. Since this step was necessary to give Gloucester good title to the throne, it may be the most likely explanation, but again it flies in the face of all we know about Gloucester's background, character and actions up to the middle of 1483, for he had always been his brother's most loyal and faithful supporter.

On the other hand, power changes people. It is possible, that faced with the thought of more rebellions and the possibility of war with the Woodville affinity over the conduct of affairs, he decided to cut through all the opposition and take the throne for himself. The snag here is that declaring Edward's children bastards would not in itself achieve this end, for if they were bastards, what about Edward, Earl of Warwick, son of the late Duke of Clarence? Although Edward of Warwick was the son of an attainted traitor, attainders could be and usually were reversed sooner or later. Young Warwick was next in line to the throne after Edward's children, and therefore a threat to Richard, so Gloucester had him brought to London and lodged under heavy guard in the Tower, where he spent the rest of his life.

On the other hand, if the story of the pre-contract was true, it is reasonable to assume that if the fact of the children's illegitimacy was now known to Richard it was also known to the Woodvilles. Their reaction on the King's death would be to get the young King crowned as soon as possible, corner the Protectorship and so stifle everyone who might make the tale public, which is exactly what they tried to do.

The Woodvilles produced no evidence to disprove the allegations about the Royal marriage, but then they had already made many enemies who would believe any story, however far fetched, if it destroyed all Woodville pretensions.

Whatever the truth of the matter, the tale was believed, or at least generally accepted by Richard's council and the court. Two days after Dr Shaw spoke out at St Paul's, Buckingham led the Mayor of London and a delegation from the peers and the Commons to see Richard at Crosby Place, where they begged him to take the crown. On the next day, 25 June, a strong contingent from the Lords and Commons assembled, and Parliament again asked Richard to take the crown, and they did so again on the next day, 26 June, after which Richard went to Westminster and sat for the first time on the King's Bench.

Other petitions were then presented to Richard by the Duke of Buckingham, who also declared that the country dare not face another dispute over the title to the throne, coupled with minority rule. He added that if Gloucester would not take the crown, it would not go to the sons of King Edward, for they would choose someone else, which was interesting because apart from Henry Tudor, Earl of Richmond, still lingering in Brittany, another in line to the throne was the Duke of Buckingham himself. Richard consented to accept the crown, though apparently with great reluctance.

Richard took the Coronation Oath on 26 June and was then proclaimed by the heralds as Richard III and crowned with his Queen, Anne Neville, on Sunday 6 July 1483, both of them being 29 years old. The Duke of Buckingham carried the King's train, Northumberland bore Curtana, the Sword of Mercy, and the Earl of Surrey the Sword of State. Close by were the new King's childhood companions, William Catesby and Viscount Lovell, and at the coronation banquet men shouted for Richard when the King's Champion, Sir Robert Dymoke, rode into the hall in full armour and threw down the gauntlet to any man who doubted that this was the lawful king.

Out on the river, on the island of the Westminster sanctuary, the sound of these revels must have reached the ears of Queen Elizabeth and her daughters, taking their thoughts upriver to the Tower, where her sons were now in jeopardy. The ranks of the Woodvilles had already been thinned. On 25 June, the day Richard accepted the crown, his friend, Richard Ratcliffe, led Earl Rivers, Sir Richard Grey, Sir Thomas Vaughan and Sir Richard Haute to their execution at Pontefract Castle.

CHAPTER FIFTEEN

THE PRINCES IN THE TOWER

*I have heard reports that after this deed was done, he
never went easy of his mind but was troubled with
fearsome dreams, starting up to run about his
chamber, in stopping remembrance of his abominable
deed.*

SIR THOMAS MORE, *HISTORY OF KING RICHARD III*

If it were not for the matter of the Princes in the Tower, the reputation of
Richard of Gloucester would be no worse than those of other great
magnates. His high-handed actions over Hastings, Rivers and the rest
were on a par with other men's actions, but in the matter of the Princes
and his culpability in their deaths, rests the main case against him and his
reputation. Even after 500 years, when the life and character of Richard
III comes to be discussed, one question, and one question alone,
dominates the argument: did he do it?

The Tudor historians, notably Sir Thomas More, have portrayed
Richard III as a villain of the deepest dye and the world at large has been
overwhelmed and influenced by the portrait presented by Shakespeare in
which Richard of Gloucester is guilty of every crime in the wars of York
and Lancaster, no matter who really committed it. In recent years, on the
other hand, the balance has swung the other way. Josephine Tey wrote a
spirited and persuasive defence in *The Daughter of Time*, which has
influenced many people in Richard's favour, and when a television
company presented a documentary film, *The Trial of Richard III*, in 1984,
with lawyers stating the known facts of the case and the defence and the
prosecution calling experts on the period before a jury, that jury brought
in a verdict of 'not guilty'. A better verdict might have been the Scots'
option of 'not proven'.

Richard's defenders in the matter of the Princes base their case on the admitted fact that, by all the previous evidence, he was not murderously inclined. They also claim that he was not present at the scene but on a progress through the west when the Princes died. The latter point is weak, because he could have given the orders to his henchmen, and so still be guilty of the crime: no one actually suggests that Richard murdered his nephews with his own hands. The only fact we can be sure of is that the two young Princes, Edward, Prince of Wales, and his brother, Richard, Duke of York, were both in the Tower by Monday, 16 June 1483 and, as far as is known, never came out alive. The events surrounding that fact have intrigued the world for centuries, and are so complex that they must be taken step by step, for the events must be known and their purpose understood before they can be explained or accounted for. The facts that are known are as follows.

Immediately after his coronation on 6 July 1483, King Richard III took his place on the King's Bench in Westminster Hall and called on the judges and lords there assembled to administer the law fairly and give justice to all. Two weeks later, on 23 July, he left London on a Royal progress through the kingdom, taking with him his Queen and his loyal ally, the Duke of Buckingham. Buckingham left the Royal party at Gloucester and rode off to Brecon Castle, where he had the company of the new King's prisoner, John Morton, Bishop of Ely.

Richard's progress was a great success. He refused all grants of money offered by his new subjects, though much of the Royal treasure accumulated by his brother, Edward IV, had been stolen by the Woodvilles since the King's death. Passing through Reading, Oxford, Gloucester, Tewkesbury – where he showed his Queen the battlefield of 1471 – Warwick and Leicester, Richard arrived in York in early September, where on the 8th he knighted his heir, the 10-year-old Edward of Middleham. Then, after a few days at Middleham Castle, his favourite home, he turned again towards the cares of his capital. He had ridden as far as Lincoln when, on 11 October, he heard the news that a rebellion had broken out in the west, led by his princely cousin, the Duke of Buckingham, the man who had officiated at Richard's coronation only six weeks before.

This rebellion of 1483 broke out in three places: in Kent, where a group of King Edward's old servants were in arms; in Berkshire and Wiltshire; and in the West Country and Wales, where Buckingham took the field. The rebellions seem to have been co-ordinated, but the co-ordination broke down. Had all these rebellions occurred simultaneously, Richard might have been overwhelmed, but he had the support of his Neville affinity in the north and the new Duke of Norfolk in East Anglia, and the rebellion, or rebellions, were quickly suppressed.

As to the cause of all this, the *Chronicle of London* declares that: 'the said King Richard has put to death the Lord Chamberlain [Hastings] and other gentlemen, as before it is said he put to death the two children of King Edward, for which cause he lost the hearts of the people. And thereupon many gentlemen intended his destruction.'

Shakespeare, following Hall, puts the split down to Richard's refusal to grant Buckingham the Earldom of Hereford, but this title was, in fact, granted to Buckingham on 13 July, and the duke was already enjoying the revenues. Thomas More believes that the cause was because Richard refused to let Buckingham's daughter marry Edward of Middleham, his son, which he would certainly have forbidden. There are, however, two other reasons for the breach.

It seems to have been widely overlooked that Buckingham himself was a candidate for the throne. Since 1399 it had been clear that the throne of England belonged to the person who could get and keep it. Buckingham was the great-grandson of Thomas of Woodstock, youngest son of Edward III, so with the direct Lancastrian line dead and the direct Yorkist line disinherited, he stood a good chance of the throne if Richard could be dislodged. As long ago as 1454, Buckingham had obtained a grant to the arms of Thomas of Woodstock 'indifferenced by any mark of cadency and near to the coat of the blode royall'. It is also worth noting that his family had always been staunch Lancastrians. His father and grandfather had both died fighting for the Lancastrian side, so Buckingham's rebellion might almost have been expected.

The simplest explanation for the rebellion is that a number of Edward IV's old followers decided to rebel, rescue Prince Edward from the Tower, kill Richard and put the young Prince on the throne. In this aim, they were joined by the Duke of Buckingham. It then became known that the young Princes were dead and the aims of the rebellions now changed to those of deposing the murderous Richard and replacing him with the Lancastrian contender, Henry Tudor, Earl of Richmond.

Plans were already afoot among the old Woodville and Lancastrian cliques to bring Henry Tudor over from Brittany and marry him to Elizabeth Woodville, the late king's daughter, putting him on the throne and so uniting the Houses of York and Lancaster. This story was around by the end of September 1483, two months after Richard's coronation, and swiftly attached itself to the causes of rebellion even before it was known or accepted that the Princes in the Tower were dead. Few people would have wished to replace Richard with Buckingham and various reasons have been advanced for Buckingham's action, including the ones offered by Shakespeare, that he was horrified at the death of the Princes and feared a similar fate for himself.

Buckingham's main allies at this time were Lady Stanley, the mother of Henry Tudor by her first husband, Edmund, Earl of Richmond, and John Morton, Bishop of Ely, who had been Buckingham's prisoner at Brecon and may have thought up the whole idea. Richard III disliked Morton, so he had no hope of advancement while Richard was on the throne. Other conspirators were former followers of Edward IV who wished to support the direct Yorkist line, and the Woodvilles, including Sir Richard Woodville and Lionel Woodville, the Bishop of Salisbury. The Courtenay brothers, from that loyal Lancastrian family, were at large in Devon, and others included Sir Richard Haute and others from Edward IV's household. Most of these people wanted the restoration of Edward V, which may have been the cause of the Princes' murder. By murdering them, Richard removed the reason for rebellion, though this act paved the way for the weak claim of the Earl of Richmond.

The revolt began almost simultaneously in counties from Kent to Wales on 18 October, but the weather was terrible. Heavy rain and flooding soon made the roads impassable, so the rebel forces were unable to unite. Buckingham's rebellion soon collapsed, and by the end of the month he was a prisoner. On 1 November, he was taken to Salisbury, where he was refused a hearing before the King, who had arrived the previous day, given a brief trial and beheaded in the market square.

The second strand of the rebellion, a landing by Henry Tudor with forces from Brittany, had also unravelled. The storms that swamped the western roads had raged as gales in the English Channel, scattering Richmond's small fleet. After attempting a landing at Poole and again, on 12 November, at Plymouth, he gave up for the winter and returned to Brittany.

The rebellions of 1483, therefore, had two aims: firstly to restore Edward V to the throne of his father, and then, following the Prince's death, to marry the pretender, the Earl of Richmond, Henry Tudor, to Edward IV's eldest daughter, Elizabeth, and put him on the throne. The latter objective would only make sense if both the Princes in the Tower were known to be dead by the end of October 1483.

Bishop Morton now fled across the Channel to join Henry Tudor, while Lady Stanley was given into the care of her husband, who was made responsible for her actions and specifically ordered to prevent any communication between the lady and her son, Henry Tudor. Although the rebellions were quickly suppressed, they unsettled the kingdom. They also established Richmond as a candidate for the throne and made him a source of disaffection. Those who escaped King Richard's spreading vengeance followed Morton to Richmond's court in Brittany, where he soon had a considerable following, all awaiting the campaigning season of 1484.

In January 1484 Richard held a Parliament at Westminster, the only one of his brief reign. Acts passed included an extension of the right to bail, and tackled abuses over land tenure. There was also yet another attempt to limit or suppress the raising of private armies and the practice of livery and maintenance. The King agreed, without argument, to abandon the practice of seeking 'benevolences', so useful to his predecessor, Edward IV, so detested by those who had to prove themselves benevolent. One of Richard's more enduring acts was to establish a College of Arms to regulate and approve the grant of heraldic arms. The most important act of this Parliament, however, was the one known as *Titulus Regius*, which set out in detail the events which brought King Richard to the throne and confirmed his title to it.

Buckingham's rebellion had delayed the start of this Parliament, called originally for November 1483, and only 37 lords answered the summons, with William Catesby being elected Speaker of the House of Commons. The matter of the King's title and how he came by it were covered in considerable detail, and the details are known because although Richard's successor ordered the repeal 'unread' of *Titulus Regius* and had all available copies destroyed, a copy turned up centuries later in the Tower archives.

Parliament then moved on to attainting those lords who had taken part in the recent rebellion, including Buckingham and 'Henry Tydder, calling himsylf Earle of Richemound', and nearly a hundred others now dead or fled to Brittany.

This Act of *Titulus Regius* and these attainders are both important because rumours were spreading, at home and abroad, concerning the fate of the two Princes in the Tower, Edward and Richard. They seemed to have vanished from human ken and the belief was that they were dead. Very little hard evidence exists about their true fate. All that can be known is known, and there is very little more evidence available, even under the heading of intelligent guesses or informed opinion.

The story spread by the Tudor propagandists and immortalized by Shakespeare is great drama, but very poor history: full of incident, short on facts. However, since this is the received and popular version of the story of the Princes, it has a place here and it should be made clear that neither Shakespeare nor his Tudor sources invented the story of the Princes in the Tower. There is plenty of contemporary evidence that they were somehow done to death in 1483.

According to Shakespeare's story, drawing on Hall and others, Richard had always hated his brothers and the world in general because of his physical deformities, his humped back and withered arm, but all this could be forgotten if he could only get the crown. To this end, he killed Edward of Lancaster at Tewkesbury, murdered King Henry in the Tower, conspired to murder Clarence, poisoned his wife, executed Rivers, Grey and the rest, and finally cleared his path to the throne by murdering his two young nephews, after declaring them bastards.

Over the matter of the Princes, the story becomes quite detailed. Apparently, when Richard III left London on his Royal progress in August 1483, he had already decided that they must die. After bidding goodbye to Buckingham at Gloucester, he sent a messenger, John Green, to Sir Robert Brackenbury, Constable of the Tower, ordering him to put the children to death. Horrified, Brackenbury declined to do this. The messenger returned to inform Richard who, casting about for a murderer, chanced on James Tyrell, a man 'apt for any villainy'.

Equipped with the king's signet, and accompanied by his groom, John Deighton, Tyrell was sent to London with instructions which enabled him to take over the Tower for one night. On seeing Tyrell's commission, Brackenbury handed over the keys. The Princes were duly smothered in their beds by Deighton, assisted by Miles Forrest, a hired killer, and another man, Will Slaughter. Having murdered the Princes, their bodies were hurriedly interred under a stairwell, 'metely depe under a great heape of stones', and Tyrell rode back to Richard to receive his reward and a knighthood. All this is said to have taken place towards the end of August 1483.

Before we go any further, parts of this story should be ventilated. To begin with, Richard was not physically deformed. He did not have a withered arm. He was not a hunchback. If one shoulder was a trifle higher than the other, then any tailor can confirm that this small defect is quite common. Neither was Richard ill-favoured. The Countess of Desmond, who lived to a great age, recalled dancing with Richard in her youth and claims that he was, 'the handsomest man in Court after the King, and very well made'. Prince Edward was killed in the rout at Tewkesbury, not at the hands of the three brothers. Sir James Tyrell was knighted for his services at Tewkesbury in 1471, not for murdering the Princes in 1483. He had been in Richard's service for many years and is recorded as escorting the elderly Countess of Warwick, Richard's mother-in-law, up to Middleham Castle in 1472.

It is because none of the above is true that Richard's defenders have a platform. When a few facts are cloaked in a tissue of lies, the facts themselves become suspect. His defenders claim that since Richard did not have a withered arm or a hunchback, all the rest of this tale is lies, so the obvious conclusion is that neither did he murder his nephews, which would be a despicable act whatever the circumstances.

On the other hand, Richard was a man of his time. He had ordered and attended executions and was not sentimental over the fate of his enemies. To make him out to be too decent for the deed is to go too far, but there are so many holes in this story that it is no wonder many people doubt it.

The story of how this famous tale of the two Princes arose is curious. Sir James Tyrell had been a faithful servant to Edward IV and Richard when the latter was Duke of Gloucester, and at the time of Bosworth in 1485, Tyrell was the Constable of Guines Castle in the Calais pale. Though deprived of his estates in Wales, he then received a full pardon from Henry VII and was reinstated in his post at Guines, receiving grants of lands in France to compensate for the loss of his Welsh possessions.

Tyrell remained in Henry VII's service for another 16 years. Then, in 1502, he was accused of treasonable correspondence with the Earl of Suffolk, a nephew of Richard III and a contender for the throne. Before he could defend himself, Tyrell was taken on board a ship in Calais harbour, conveyed to the Tower, tried for 'matters of treason' and executed on Tower Hill in May 1502. Only when he was dead was the story of how the Princes in the Tower were murdered related to the public as Tyrell's 'confession'. Why he was not obliged to make this 'confession' personally and to a large audience before his execution can only be wondered at. Forrest and Slaughter were dead by 1502 and Brackenbury had died at Bosworth, fighting for Richard III, but John Deighton was still alive and he remained at liberty in Calais. He even received a state pension on the condition that he stayed away from

England. If this fanciful tale were all there is to go on, the murder of the Princes could not have been laid at King Richard's door. There are, however, other more persuasive details.

First, it is necessary to establish a few dates. The Princes were certainly alive in June 1483, but shortly after this they disappeared from view. Richard was killed at Bosworth in August 1485, so if the Princes died between these dates, whoever did the actual deed, Richard III was clearly responsible.

Various early writers have left works on the wars of York and Lancaster, the probable fate of the Princes, and the reign of Richard III. William Shakespeare drew most of his background from a lawyer, Edward Hall, who produced a book in 1548 entitled *Union of the Two Illustrious Families of York and Lancaster*, largely to praise Henry VIII and recall the triumph of the Tudors. Hall drew much of his information from Sir Thomas More's *History of Richard III*. Sir Thomas More, a lawyer, a councillor of state, a martyr and a saint, is a hard man to argue with, but his tale is basically Tyrell's 'confession' of 1502, with dramatic embellishments and certain links to Polydore Vergil's *History of England*, and More's tale ends abruptly with Morton's flight to join Richmond in 1483.

Polydore Vergil is a more serious contender than Sir Thomas More, whom he almost certainly knew. Vergil came to England in 1501 as a collector of Peter's Pence for the Borgia Pope, Alexander VI. In 1507, Henry VII asked him to write a history of England, and the work was completed by 1517, at least up to the end of Richard's reign, though Henry VII died in 1509. Vergil clearly attempted to get at the truth of all the matters surrounding the reign of Richard III and the accession of Henry VII, and states that to do so he talked to 'men of age formerly occupied with important public affairs'. Going to the horse's mouth for your facts is a course all true historians must recommend, but there were precious few people around in 1507 who spoke in favour of Richard III. Since his book was commissioned by the King, Vergil had access to all the King's ministers and long-term supporters, but not to Cardinal John Morton, that slippery prelate who died in 1500, having risen to become both Archbishop of Canterbury and Chancellor. Vergil did meet and discuss matters, including the late Chancellor's varied career, with Morton's protégé, Sir Thomas More.

From those who were obliged to get their information second-hand, let us move back to other contemporary sources, written by reputable men living around 1483–84. For this period, three main sources are available, excluding the suspect work of John Rous. Rous produced two versions of his history, one praising Richard III and an amended version written after Richard's death at Bosworth, which utterly damns the late King and is clearly designed to ingratiate Rous with the new King Henry VII.

The first worthwhile account of events in London in 1483–84 is found in the *Chronicles of London*, one of a series of medieval accounts which record current events, and especially events in the City of London. The *Chronicle* covering 1483 is now known as the *Great Chronicle of London*, and was written by Robert Fabyan, Alderman and Sheriff of the City, who died in 1513. His account plainly states that the Princes were murdered by their uncle, but adds that in 1483 this was only a belief, 'a whispering among the people'. This belief must have been common before Bosworth, since the reference concludes with the news of Richard's death.

The second source is one of the accounts written in the Fenland abbey of Croyland. Known as *The Second Continuation of the Croyland Chronicle*, this was written in April 1486, probably by John Russell, Bishop of Lincoln, or perhaps by Henry Sharpe, another cleric. Russell had been Chancellor to Richard III, and was therefore in a position to know what went on at his Court. Where his account can be checked, he is accurate, and his work is very hostile to King Richard. He records Richard's devious behaviour over Rivers and Grey, and Richard's vehement denial of any intention to marry his niece, the Lady Elizabeth, when he actually intended to do so. The *Chronicle* records the author's belief in Richard's crimes, but stops short of saying in so many words that he murdered the Princes.

The story that Richard poisoned his wife in order to marry his niece is a good example of how Richard was traduced, but that there was such a story in circulation about the end of 1484 is certain because Richard had to issue a statement denying it. Richard's Queen, Anne, had died on 16 March 1485, most probably of tuberculosis.

According to the *Croyland Chronicle*, at the Christmas festivities of 1484 the 'Eldest daughter of the late King Edward danced at her uncle's Court, arrayed like a second Queen', and 'men asked if Richard meant to make her a Queen indeed'. There are stories that the Lady Elizabeth was eager for the match and that Richard was her 'only joy', and that her mother, Elizabeth Woodville, approved of the match. The mind reels. That a lady should want her daughter to marry the man who has just murdered her sons is stretching credibility to the limits. This report was current early in 1485, when the Princes had not been seen by anyone for over a year.

However, to get back to the facts, why should King Richard want to marry the Lady Elizabeth? She had been declared illegitimate and was therefore no asset to his position. If she was not illegitimate, then Richard III had no right to the throne.

The final contemporary chronicler, and one well worth considering, is Dominic Mancini, author of a book entitled *The Usurpation of Richard III.* Mancini was an Italian diplomat who came to England in 1482, on the instructions of his patron, Angelo Cato, Archbishop of Vienna and councillor to Louis XI of France. From this, and from a lack of any other reason for his visit, some people have concluded that Mancini was a spy. Be that as it may, Mancini stayed in England until July 1483, and on returning to France had completed his book by December of that year. Mancini seems to have drifted about the periphery of the English Court and made a confidant of Dr John Argentine, an English physician who had studied in Italy and spoke fluent Italian. More to the point, Argentine was physician to the young Edward, Prince of Wales, now detained in the Tower.

Mancini's account makes it clear that he believed Richard always intended to seize the crown and he makes it plain that many other people in London during June 1483 shared his belief. Dr Argentine told him that the young Prince of Wales was in daily fear of death, and that after the Princes were taken into the Tower, they were gradually seen less and less and their former household attendants, including Dr Argentine, were dismissed. Mancini goes on to state his belief that the Princes were dead by the time he left England in July 1483, 'where already there is a suspicion that they have been done away with, but by what manner of death so far I have not at all discovered.'

So, putting aside tainted evidence from sources such as Rous, More, Hall and Polydore Vergil, here are three contemporary accounts which state a clear and general belief that the Princes were dead by the end of 1483, done to death by the order of their uncle, Richard III. There is no proof, no eyewitness, no record, no letters of commission, simply hearsay, but coupled with the fact that once the Princes went into the Tower they never came out again to any man's knowledge, this common view by three people in positions of authority is damning.

There is one final thread of evidence. In January 1484, the Chancellor of France, Guillaume de Rochfort, speaking to the Estates-General in

Tours, called their attention to the events that had happened recently in England: 'Think of those children, grown and brave, now massacred and the crown transferred to the murderer by the will of the people.' This information probably came from Mancini, who was working on the last draft of his book in the town of Beaugency, further up the River Loire. So, in answer to the question, 'Did he do it?', one can say that by the end of 1483 many reputable people, at home and abroad, were convinced that he had, and damned him for it.

There is an extension to this story. In 1674, during the reign of Charles II, workmen demolishing a staircase at the White Tower, found a wooden chest containing the bones of two children. These, it was concluded, were the bones of the two Princes. The scientific skills of the day could not establish the exact ages of the skeletons or the date of death. The bones were placed in an urn in Westminster Abbey, where they still remain. Then, in 1933, when a degree of forensic skill was available, the urn was opened. The pathologist's conclusion was that they were the bones of two children, one aged about 10, the other about 12, which corresponds well enough with the ages of the Princes in 1483. As with all other aspects of this affair, there are plenty of people to throw doubt on this conclusion, but these bones are *probably* those of the Princes, and perhaps one day a more detailed forensic examination using modern dating methods can establish the facts about these bones beyond any shadow of doubt.

The story now returns to Richard's first Parliament, which met in January 1484, and that act of *Titulus Regius*, or the King's Title. *Titulus Regius* set out in considerable detail all the circumstances surrounding the offer of the crown to Richard in the previous year, and confirmed all the terms it contained. It also went into the question of the late King's association with Eleanor Butler, and confirmed the bastardy of Edward's children, placing the succession on Richard's son, Edward of Middleham.

Ten days after *Titulus Regius* was promulgated, Elizabeth Woodville, lately Queen of England, left the sanctuary at Westminster and placed herself and her daughters under Richard's protection. Here again, the mind reels. Here is a man who has executed her kin, seized her son's throne, and declared her children bastards, and yet here is this lady placing herself in his hands and accepting his word. All this in March 1484, when tales of the death – or murder – of her two boys were already current as far away as France. She then went even further: she wrote to the Marquis of Dorset in France, telling him to return to England where 'the King would treat him well'. It is said by Polydore Vergil and others that Dorset attempted to return but was recaptured and brought back to join Henry Tudor.

Richard's apologists make a great deal of Elizabeth's capitulation, claiming that it demonstrates her final acceptance of Richard's goodwill and that Richard cannot, therefore, have murdered the Princes. Elizabeth Woodville was not that gullible. She came out of sanctuary only under strict and detailed terms. To get her out, King Richard had to swear an oath before a public assembly of lords and bishops and the Aldermen of London: 'I, Richard, promise and swear that if the daughters of Elizabeth, lately called Queen of England, do come to me out of Sanctuary and be guided and ruled by me, I shall give them surety of their lives and they shall not suffer any hurt...'

There are only two logical explanations for Elizabeth's act. Either Elizabeth Woodville was scared out of her wits and would do anything the King wanted for fear of what he might do to her or her daughters, or she trusted in the assurances he gave her once they had been confirmed by public oath. Nothing else makes sense. Although the people of the late Middle Ages were in many ways different from people today, there is no reason to suppose that they were stupid. Elizabeth Woodville had been too long at Court to act hastily. Like many others in the realm of England during 1484, she prayed for the death of Richard III and waited for Henry Tudor.

If there is any truth in the belief that evil will be punished, King Richard's fate in 1484 gives evidence to support it. On 9 April 1484 his only son and heir, Prince Edward, died at Middleham Castle. This left two Yorkist contenders for the throne: Clarence's son, the Earl of Warwick, who was now a prisoner in the Tower, and the Earl of Lincoln, son of the Duke of Suffolk and Richard's sister, Anne. Richard then appointed Lincoln as his heir-apparent.

In November 1484 there was an unpleasant incident when William Collingbourne, a servant of Edward IV, was tried and condemned for 'devising and setting up bills and rhymes to set people against the King'. This rhyme was the famous couplet:

> The Catte, the Ratte, and Lovell our dogg,
> Ruleth all England under an Hogge,

which referred to William Catesby, Richard Ratcliffe and Francis, Viscount Lovell, all close friends of the King, and Richard's device of the white boar, or hog. Collingbourne had been Sheriff of Somerset and

Wiltshire until he was dismissed by Richard in June 1484 and replaced by Viscount Lovell. The indictment also referred to Collingbourne's 'treasonable correspondence' with the Earl of Richmond, which may have been the real reason for Collingbourne's death. The lampoon alone hardly merited the sentence of hanging, drawing and quartering, by which means Collingbourne died in December 1484.

The New Year brought little relief for King Richard, beginning with tales that he intended to kill his wife and then marry King Edward's daughter, his niece Elizabeth; stories which grew when, in March 1485, Richard's Queen Anne died.

The reason behind the constant and increasing rumours and schemes against King Richard were probably that, with the death of his heir, Edward, and then his wife, the question of Richard's ability to rule and establish his line became open. He was now alone and almost without family. All his close relatives and friends, his brothers, Edward and Clarence, his old companions, Hastings and Buckingham, were dead – some of them at Richard's own hands – and his new friends were constantly proving false. There was a steady trickle across the sea to Richmond. The struggle for the throne was clearly not over and must be between King Richard and the young Edward V, if he still lived, or in the event that he was indeed dead, Henry Tudor, Earl of Richmond, for the Earls of Lincoln and Warwick were too young and lacked supporters. Richmond was the main threat as spring arrived in 1485 and in mid-June 1485 Richard withdrew to Nottingham, in the centre of the kingdom, and began to muster men for the struggle that was coming. This proved a wise precaution. On 7 August 1485, Henry Tudor, Earl of Richmond, came ashore with a small army at Milford Haven in the south of Wales.

CHAPTER SIXTEEN

THE END OF KING RICHARD

Accursed and unquiet wrangling days,
How many of you have mine eyes beheld!
My husband lost his life to get the crown;
And often up and down my sons were toss'd,
For me to joy and weep their gain and loss:
And being seated, and domestic broils
Clean over-blown, themselves, the conquerors,
Make war upon themselves; brother to brother,
Blood to blood, self against self: – O, preposterous
And frantic outrage, end thy damned spleen;
Or let me die, to look on death no more!

DUCHESS OF YORK, *KING RICHARD III*

Henry Tudor, Earl of Richmond, arrived on the throne of England by a process of elimination. His was by far the weakest claim to the English crown, but by 1485 everyone else was either dead, discredited, disinherited, or under lock and key. That apart, his claim, though slight, was not without merit.

Henry's father, Edmund Tudor, Earl of Richmond, was the son of Owen Tudor, a body squire of Henry V who claimed to be descended from the legendary Cadwallader, and Henry V's widow, Queen Catherine of Valois. This gave Henry Tudor a connection with the throne of France, though the Salic Law barred him from any advantage. His claim to the English throne, through his mother's line, was rather more persuasive. Margaret Beaufort was the daughter of John Beaufort, first Duke of Somerset, and great-granddaughter of John of Gaunt through Gaunt's marriage to Katherine Swynford.

The initial bastardy of the Beaufort line had never stopped the Earls and Dukes of Somerset playing their full part in England's affairs. Their line had been legitimized by Richard II and again by Henry IV, though Henry IV had put a limit on their pretensions, so that the Beauforts could aspire to any dignity except 'the Royal dignity'. This latter point proved no obstacle to Henry Tudor, Earl of Richmond, who pressed his claim seriously from the time his uncle, Jasper Tudor, Earl of Pembroke, took him to France after Tewkesbury.

Richmond's early years had been troublesome. His grandmother, Queen Catherine of Valois, died in 1437, at a time when his grandfather, Owen, was in Newgate prison. Henry VI, however, was glad to have stepbrothers and Richmond's father, Edmund, was knighted in 1453 and created Earl of Richmond in the same year, at the age of 23. He married the Lady Margaret Beaufort, daughter of John Beaufort, second Duke of Somerset, and therefore a direct descendant of John of Gaunt, but Edmund died in 1456 when Margaret was six months pregnant. The baby was born on St Agnes Day, 28 January 1457, in what is now called Henry VII's Tower in Pembroke Castle, then the home of Henry's uncle, Jasper Tudor, Earl of Pembroke and a stout-hearted Lancastrian.

Four years later, in February 1460, came the battle at Mortimer's Cross and the defeat of Jasper Tudor by Edmund, Earl of March, followed by the execution of grandfather Owen. Jasper fled into Wales and in 1468 Richmond was sheltering in Harlech Castle when William, Lord Herbert, took it by storm. Henry Tudor was now 12 and Edward IV granted his wardship to William Herbert, later the *Yorkist* Earl of Pembroke and his wife, Lady Anne Devereux – Henry's Uncle Jasper being the *Lancastrian* Earl.

The Herberts treated Henry Tudor as their own son, and fully intended to marry him to their daughter Maud, a course of action that would have suited King Edward very well, for it would have reduced any Tudor pretensions to the throne. Then came the rebellions of 1470, the death of William Herbert at Edgecote, and the brief return to power of Henry VI. Jasper Tudor reclaimed his title and his nephew, but then Edward IV returned in 1471, killed Warwick at Barnet, and slaughtered the last of the Lancastrians at Tewkesbury. The murder of Henry VI in the Tower, a few days later, left Henry Tudor as the sole heir of Lancaster, through his links to John of Gaunt. Jasper Tudor and his nephew Henry, both now attainted traitors, fled to Brittany, where Henry spent the next 12 years sheltering in the great castle of Largoet, near Elven. Over the years, a small body of dispossessed Lancastrians gathered about him and kept his slender claim alive, a claim strong enough to worry Edward IV, who made several attempts to lure him to England or to persuade Duke Francis of Brittany to hand him over. All attempts at extradition or kidnap failed, and only served to underline Richmond's claim.

While Henry was abroad, his interests at home were protected and advanced by his formidable mother, Margaret Beaufort, married to Henry Stafford, younger son of the second Duke of Buckingham. In 1482 Stafford died and Margaret promptly married Thomas, Lord Stanley, her third husband, on the clear understanding that he respected her chastity, which seems unusual. Stanley was Edward IV's steward, and after Edward died, Lady Margaret carried the Queen's train at Richard III's coronation. Margaret's influence was soon brought to bear on the Stanleys, whom she urged to support her son, Henry Tudor.

Then came the Duke of Buckingham's rebellion of October 1483. As already related, this broke out in several parts of England, having the initial aim of restoring Edward V to the throne. When it was realized, or rumoured, that the Princes were already dead, this motive changed. The rebels then proposed to bring over Henry Tudor, and having defeated and killed King Richard, marry him to the Lady Elizabeth, daughter of Edward IV, and so finally unite the Houses of York and Lancaster. This scheme had the support of the Queen-dowager, Elizabeth Woodville, and the proposal was taken to Brittany by Buckingham's erstwhile prisoner, John Morton, Bishop of Ely.

Richmond rapidly raised an army of mercenaries, estimated at some 3,000 men, though it was probably smaller, which sailed from St Malo on 12 October 1483 in a fleet of 15 ships. The little fleet was scattered by the autumn gales, Buckingham's army dispersed, and after making a brief landfall at either Poole or Plymouth, Richmond returned to Brittany. Henry was at Paimpol when, in mid-November, the news arrived of Buckingham's execution.

This sad news was soon followed by a stream of supporters, and a useful gift of fresh funds from Duke François. Richmond withdrew to Vannes, where his following now included Jasper Tudor, Thomas Grey, the Marquis of Dorset, Lord Welles, the Courtenay brothers from Devon, Sir Thomas Arundel, that huge and formidable knight, Sir John Cheney, and as his chief councillor, the astute John Morton. These men advised Richmond that all was not lost. They would gather forces and in due course try again, and to seal the pact, on Christmas Day 1483, they swore an oath in the Cathedral of Vannes, greeting Henry Tudor, Earl of Richmond, as King of England, begging him to marry Elizabeth of York.

Richard III was well aware of events in Brittany. He wrote letters to Duke François complaining that the duke was giving aid and shelter to attainted rebels and traitors. This accusation soon took effect. In June 1484 King Richard and Duke François signed an accord, and the Bretons prepared to seize Richmond and his court and send them in chains to England. Richmond and his friends at once fled across the Loire to the castle of Angers, where the new King of France, Charles VIII, gave them aid and protection.

Throughout 1484, Richmond proceeded to muster men and ships, and Charles VIII allowed the fleet to assemble in the Norman port of Honfleur. Meanwhile, other fugitives continued to arrive. Chief of these was John de Vere, Earl of Oxford, a prisoner in Hammes for many years, who arrived in Vannes in early August 1484 accompanied by his gaoler, Sir John Blount, the Yorkist Lieutenant of Calais.

This was a significant defection, which must have increased King Richard's sense of unease, but he was now particularly concerned about the Stanleys, whom he believed, correctly, to be conspiring with Richmond and secretly raising forces in Wales and the north-east, where they had a powerful affinity. Even so, an open breach with such a leading family might only spur others into rebellion, so Richard held his hand. On 22 May 1485, King Richard issued a strong proclamation damning the traitorous activities of 'Henry, calling himself Earle of Richmond, a man of bastard blood,' and calling on the Commissioners of Array throughout the kingdom to muster men and prepare to defend the kingdom. This proclamation was issued to counter one circulated by Richmond – or more likely by the Stanleys on his behalf – which refers to Richard as 'a homicide and unabated tyrant' and assures the English that he will 'cross the sea upon the instant of their sure advertising what power, what captains and what leaders they can muster'. The Earl of Richmond was clearly a cautious man, and would not strike until all was ready.

Lacking a standing army, and fearing to call out the majority of the magnates, King Richard had to rely on his own affinity and on that of three great lords, the new Duke of Norfolk, the Earl of Northumberland, and the Lord Stanley. Two of these were uncertain allies. Norfolk would certainly stand by him, Northumberland would sit on the fence as long as possible, and the Stanleys, who knew all about fence-sitting, would probably stab him in the back. Richard knew all this, but he could not admit it publicly, or Stanley and Northumberland would flee at once to the side of Richmond.

Lord Stanley had to be kept under the King's eye and when, in August 1485, he requested leave to return to his estates and muster men, the King said that Stanley could leave only when his son, George Stanley, Lord Lestrange, came to take his place. Young George arrived at Nottingham on 1 August and Lord Stanley went to round up his followers.

On that same day, the Earl of Richmond sailed from Harfleur with a small force of 2,000 men. All his chief supporters came with him, except the Marquis of Dorset, who had attempted to return to England at the instigation of his mother, Elizabeth Woodville, and was now left behind as security for the French King's loans. The winds were fair, and with his ships crammed with anxious men, Henry Tudor unfurled his banners and set sail for the coast of Wales.

Henry's force came ashore at Milford Haven on 7 August 1485, and swiftly occupied the town of Haverfordwest. From there messengers rode out into the valleys to raise the country and muster men. Richmond based his appeal to the Welsh on his claim of descent from Cadwallader, the ancient King of the Welsh, and the Red Dragon banner of Cadwallader was carried at the head of his army as they set out across Wales for the Middle March.

Richmond also sent secret letters to the Stanleys and the Talbots, stating that he would march across Wales and enter England at Shrewsbury, where he hoped to meet them with their forces. However, when he arrived at Shrewsbury on 14 August, he found the gates shut. After a parley with the sheriff, John Mytton, he was allowed to enter, and he was still there on 16 August when Sir Gilbert Talbot arrived with a force of 500 men, his first recruits from England. Richmond's army now probably mustered some 4,000 men.

Richard was still at Nottingham when the news of Richmond's landing arrived on or around 11 August. Reports continued to arrive from then on, each charting Richmond's gradual progress through Wales, with no reports of any action against him by the Stanleys. This, though no surprise, made the King highly suspicious and his concern mounted when Lord Stanley refused to return to court, claiming illness, and his son, George Stanley, was caught attempting to leave. Questioned by the King, George Stanley said that his uncle, Sir William Stanley, would probably side with Richmond, but that his father certainly would be loyal. This seemed to be confirmed by a report stating that Sir William Stanley had come up with Richmond at Stafford, but neither joined nor attacked him. Richmond then marched on to Litchfield, where Lord Stanley was camped with his considerable affinity. Stanley could have held the town or joined Richmond. Instead, like his brother, he withdrew to Atherstone, followed at a gentle pace by Richmond's swelling army. The Stanleys were again playing a waiting-game and effectively masking the advance of Richmond's army into the Midlands.

The King was mustering men but, with the Stanleys failing to join him, he could not summon an overwhelming force to Nottingham in the time left. There was too much disaffection in the land for all the men of his affinity to leave their estates, but the whole country was put under arms and various supporters were bidden to join him at all speed. He sent to London for Sir Robert Brackenbury and the Tower artillery. Francis, Viscount Lovell, was summoned from the Cotswolds, Norfolk from East Anglia with all his power, Northumberland from the north with his hardy Border soldiers. All these Lords found it difficult to muster men and Brackenbury lost several knights, including Sir Thomas Bourchier and Sir Walter Hungerford, who chose to leave the King's party at Stony Stratford and rode to join with Richmond. Richard's army was, therefore, well below its anticipated strength when he entered Leicester on 19 August 1485.

On 20 August, Richmond met and conferred with the Stanleys in the countryside somewhere west of Leicester, near the village of Market Bosworth. The Stanleys were urged to join Richmond's forces at once but, ever cautious, they declined, saying only that they would not oppose him, and would join him at some suitable juncture as his campaign continued. Richmond took this to mean that they would join when he was winning. He had come too far to draw back, so on the 21st he continued to advance and camped that night on a small ridge, known as the White Moors, a little south of the village of Shenton. Over to the west lay another, higher rise, flanked by a small wood. This rise was known as Ambion Hill, and somewhere beyond that, Richmond's 'scurryers' reported, lay the great power of the King.

King Richard left Leicester early on the 21st, marching south and west to a campsite by the village of Stapleton, where he also spent the night in sight of Ambion Hill. Here his scouts brought in the news that Richmond's army was camped just 3 miles away. The battle that would settle the wars of Lancaster and York would take place the next day, Monday, 22 August 1485.

Although the Battle of Bosworth Field is one of the most important that ever took place on English soil, there are no accurate eyewitness accounts of the fight. The only chronicler present, on Richmond's side, was Bernard André, but he was blind and his account is, therefore, both sketchy and partial. There is also some disagreement about where the battle actually took place, with some people claiming that it was fought not on the slope of Ambion Hill but on the flat plain near Dadlington, just to the south. Local accounts, handed down from the time, plus a certain amount of physical evidence in the form of cannon balls excavated on Ambion Hill, and some of the practical requirements of command, would seem to confirm that Ambion Hill was the site of the battle.

Medieval warriors were not usually masters of either strategy or tactics. Poor communications and the unwillingness of their noble subordinates to accept orders naturally limited their ability to control events, and a medieval lord's main tactic for victory was to turn up for the battle and hit his nearest opponent over the head with an axe. In any age, however, a commander wants to view the field and see what is going on, and there is no reason to believe that, in this respect at least, medieval kings were any different.

To view the fight the war-lord needed to be in the front rank, to sit his horse behind the battle or to occupy some commanding feature. Edward III's windmill at Crécy is a good example of the latter position. The front rank imposes obvious risks and limitations, and since Ambion Hill, though no great height, still commands the immediate countryside, King Richard marched his army there and viewed the surrounding countryside from horseback.

Richard spent the night before the battle in going about his army, in conferring with his commanders, and according to various sources, was plagued in his sleep with terrible dreams. He also sent a peremptory order to Lord Stanley, commanding him to bring up his troops by dawn or his son's head would be in jeopardy. When Stanley failed to appear at daybreak, Richard ordered George Stanley's immediate execution, but the other lords, now in full armour, persuaded him to delay it until after the battle. George Stanley was, therefore, left under guard as the army marched at dawn on the 22nd to take up its positions on Ambion Hill. The army marched in the usual three battle, or divisional, formations: the vanguard led by the Duke of Norfolk, the centre-guard by the King and the rearguard by the Earl of Northumberland. The full muster of the Royal army was about 8,000 men, and the bulk of them were archers, most of them mounted.

Richard's army was in position on Ambion Hill by about eight in the morning, and according to most authorities, including Colonel Alfred Burne, was deployed not in line, as was customary, but in columns of battle, with Norfolk's men in the van, the King's battle following up Norfolk's and Northumberland's division hovering at the rear. This seems a most unusual formation. There are two possible explanations: either the terrain did not permit a full deployment in line, or the King preferred to keep his force in hand, without dismounting or deploying until he could see what the Stanleys would do. It is equally possible that the received wisdom is wrong, and that the King deployed his forces conventionally, in line of battles. Once in position on Ambion Hill, they awaited the arrival of Richmond, and the King had time to review the field, noting the displayed banners of the two Stanley battalions to the north and south of his position.

Ambion Hill rises to a height of just 417 feet and is about 700 yards across, on a line roughly north-west to south-east. The King's army had marched up to it from the north-west, from near Sutton Cheney, and could now see the power of Lord Stanley about half a mile away to the south, and that of Sir William Stanley about the same distance away to the north. This may have been another reason for the curious column deployment for the King's forces. Though on the commanding height, they were also in the jaws of a trap, for although numbers can never be certain, the Stanleys would probably have mustered some 3,000 men, whose intervention would be decisive. On the other hand, if the fight between the King and Richmond went well, the Stanleys would stay neutral. Whatever the outcome, the decision could not be long delayed for the rising sun was now glinting on the armour and lance tips of Richmond's army, marching towards Ambion Hill from the south-west.

Richmond's army, some 5,000 men strong, was up before dawn and marching towards Shenton as the sun rose. As it wheeled right to skirt Ambion Wood and the marsh to the north, beyond which lay the camp of Sir William Stanley, it is recorded that the rising sun struck fully in their eyes. Once clear of the marsh, Richmond's army began to wheel right, in column of battles, with the Earl of Oxford in the van and Richmond's force close behind, marching across the front of King Richard's army, and then wheeling, or turning, into line to face Norfolk's battle. This is a difficult manoeuvre, even on a flat parade ground in peacetime and it has the effect of making the forward elements march much further round the outer rim of the 'wheel' than those at the rear, near the 'hub'.

There is considerable confusion among the authorities as to who was in

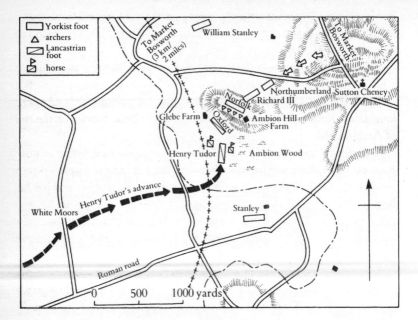

The Battle of Bosworth Field (1485).

command of each battle in Richmond's army, but all agree that the Earl of Oxford's battle engaged first, advancing up the lower slopes of Ambion Hill to open the battle with an exchange of artillery and arrow fire with the Duke of Norfolk. It is, therefore, realistic to assume, having turned uphill, that Oxford was on Richmond's left and so leading the advance. There was no third battle to form on the left, for Richmond had either insufficient men or hoped that Sir William Stanley or his brother would join him before Richmond attacked the King's position.

Oxford was by far the most experienced commander in the field, and he kept his force well in hand, forbidding his men to advance more than ten paces beyond the line of banners. By so doing, his cohesive force soon began to press Norfolk's men back up the slope. Ambion Hill is not large and the slope is gradual, so within minutes the front battles closed and came to handstrokes around the site of the farm – Ambion Farm – which now occupies the south-east slope of the hill.

The fighting here was particularly fierce. Perhaps half an hour after the battle started, the Duke of Norfolk, who was in the front line, was cut down and killed and the King's battle began to go forward in support. The

Stanleys were now on the move, edging cautiously forward to view the fighting and, with the crux of the battle in hand, King Richard decided to strike.

By now, say one hour after the start of the fighting, the bulk of Richard's battle had been sucked down the slope in support of Norfolk's division, but the King still had his own guard of perhaps 200 armoured knights and horsemen mustered about the 'White Boar' banner on the top of Ambion Hill.

If Oxford's and Norfolk's battles were engaged near what is now Ambion Farm, there was no room between the hill and the marsh – now a wood – on Oxford's right. It is likely, therefore, that Richmond led his battle behind Oxford's line, ready to come up on Oxford's left, which also put it on course for a junction with Sir William Stanley. If that junction could be achieved, a general advance on Richard's army could prove decisive.

To prevent that happening, either to settle the outcome with one blow or because he could contain himself no longer, King Richard led his guard down the slope of Ambion Hill, spurring his horse, White Surrey, directly at Richmond's standard.

We know that he got there. Richard is credited with killing Richmond's standard-bearer, Sir William Brandon, and unhorsing the giant knight, Sir John Cheney. Richard and Richmond may even have exchanged handstrokes; who can tell? From the moment the charge began down Ambion Hill, we lose all sight of Richard. Horses do not last long among archers and White Surrey was soon brought down, perhaps in the muddy ground of what is now called 'Richard's Field'. His friends were falling all around him: Lord Ferrers, Walter Devereux died there, and Robert Brackenbury and Sir Richard Ratcliffe and a score besides were brought down by arrows or hauled off their horses and hacked to death, and somewhere in that fatal press, his bodyguard dead and his army scattered, 'King Richard was killed alone, fighting manfully in the press of his enemies.'

The Battle of Bosworth can have lasted no more than two hours. Richmond's army pursued the King's fleeing troops for a few kilometres, then returned to the battlefield, to strip the bodies and loot the dead. Richard's crown was found lying in a thornbush on the battlefield and brought to Richmond by Lord Stanley, who hailed the Earl of Richmond, Henry Tudor, as the new King, Henry VII.

Most of Henry's losses were among Oxford's division, 200 or 300 at the most, while about 1,000 of Richard's men were killed in the battle or the rout. The dead included most of Richard's chief supporters: the Duke of Norfolk, Walter Devereux, Sir Robert Brackenbury, Constable of the Tower, Richard Ratcliffe ('The Rat'), Sir Robert Percy, and a dozen more. Sir William Catesby ('The Cat') was taken and beheaded next day. Viscount Lovell made his escape to fight another day. Norfolk's son, the Earl of Surrey, went briefly to the Tower; the hesitant Earl of Northumberland soon received a full pardon; and the Stanleys swiftly profited from their outright treachery. Lord Stanley became Earl of Derby and carried the Sword of State at Henry's coronation, and Sir William Stanley was rewarded with rich lands in Wales.

Richard's body was stripped naked and slung on the back of a horse led by his herald, Blanc Sangleur, and taken to the city of Leicester, where it was exposed for two days and then buried at the Church of the Greyfriars. He was not, however, to pass from history entirely unrecorded. Whatever Richard's faults, there were still those in England who loved him and were prepared to say so, even in the hour of his death.

On 23 August, the day after the battle, the Recorder of York wrote a minute in the city records: 'This day was it known that King Richard, late mercifully ruling over us was pitiously slain and murdered, to the great heviness of this citie'.

There have been worse epitaphs.

THE EXTIRPATION OF THE PLANTAGENETS (1485)

There must be a period and a stop to all temporal things, an end to names and titles and whatsoever is terrain. Where now is Bohun? Where is Mortimer? Where is Mowbray? Nay, last and most of all, where is Plantagenet? They are immured in the tombs and sepulchres of brief mortality.

LORD JUSTICE CREWE IN A SEVENTEENTH-
CENTURY JUDGMENT ON THE DEFUNCT
EARLDOM OF OXFORD

Henry VII was crowned King of England on 30 October 1485, and called his first Parliament a week later. One of his first acts was to overturn *Titulus Regius*, which detailed King Richard's claim to the throne, and by dating the start of his reign from the day *before* the Battle of Bosworth Field, have King Richard and all his supporters declared attainted traitors. This Parliament declared Henry's title to the throne was due to the fact that he had killed the late King and was sitting on his throne, for Henry wanted his title to be by descent and right of conquest, not by his marriage to Elizabeth of York. It was not until six months after Bosworth, on 8 January 1486, and only then after some pressure from his lords, that Henry married the Lady Elizabeth. The Act of 1484, *Titulus Regius*, which stated the bastardy of Edward IV's children, was deleted from the statute book and all copies destroyed, and our present knowledge of what it contained is due to the fact that the original draft appeared in a set of documents discovered in the Tower some time in the seventeenth century.

Two months later, Henry VII faced his first rebellion. This was led by Viscount Lovell and the Staffords, proclaiming as heir the Earl of Lincoln, son of the Duke of Suffolk and King Richard's sister, Anne. This rebellion failed and the Staffords were taken and executed, though Francis Lovell again made good his escape.

From Richard III's sister, Anne, wife of John de la Pole, Duke of Suffolk, came that John, Earl of Lincoln, who died at Stoke in 1487, and his brother, Edmund, the last Earl of Suffolk, was executed by Henry VIII in 1513. Suffolk's brother, Richard de la Pole, was 'White Rose', who declared himself the heir of York, fled abroad and was killed at the Battle of Pavia in Italy in 1525. Another descendant of Edward IV, Henry, Marquis of Exeter, son of Edward's daughter, Catherine, was executed in 1538, and Henry, Lord Stafford, third and last Duke of Buckingham, was executed in 1521. Richard III left one illegitimate heir, his son, who lived in obscurity as a bricklayer and died in Kent in 1550 under the name of Richard Plantagenet.

Henry's valiant uncle, Jasper Tudor, died in 1495, and John Morton died a Cardinal in 1500. In 1487, Edward IV's Queen-dowager, Elizabeth Woodville, Henry VII's mother-in-law, was sent to the abbey at Bermondsey and remained there in straitened circumstances until her death in 1492, while all her lands and revenues were transferred to her daughter, the Queen. Henry's Queen, Elizabeth of York, died in 1503 aged 35, and Henry VII, that fortunate prince, died in 1509.

In the early summer of 1487 there was another rising, again led by Lovell, who pledged his support to an impostor named Lambert Simnel, who claimed to be Warwick's son, Edward, then a prisoner in the Tower. Lovell and Simnel were again joined in this enterprise by the Earl of Lincoln, whom Richard III had once named as his successor. The Irish supported Simnel, but his forces were no match for those of the King and the Earl of Oxford, who totally defeated them at the Battle of Stoke, where Lincoln was killed. The pretender, Simnel, was set to turning a spit in the King's kitchen and lived until 1534. Lovell disappeared and his skeleton was found two centuries later, walled up in the cellar of his house at Minster Lovell in the Cotswolds.

The Battle of Stoke on 16 June, effectively ended the Plantagenet claims to the throne of England, but the Tudors sat on it uneasily, and hunted the Plantagenets relentlessly for the next 50 years, until all the Plantagenets were dead.

In 1491 a new pretender appeared, Perkin Warbeck. Warbeck's claim was backed by Margaret of York, Richard III's sister, the Dowager Duchess of Burgundy, who had also backed Simnel with 2,000 mercenary soldiers. Warbeck claimed to be Richard of York, one of the Princes in the

Tower, and he stayed at large for five years. In January 1495, that shifty lord, Sir William Stanley, was tried and executed for conspiring with Warbeck against the King. Warbeck was finally captured in 1497 and executed on Tyburn in November 1499. A few days later, Clarence's son, the Earl of Warwick, a captive in the Tower since 1483, was beheaded on Tower Hill. Warwick's sister Margaret, Countess of Salisbury, married Sir Richard Pole and survived until 1541, when Henry VIII finally ordered her execution on the grounds that her son, Henry, had led a rebellion in the west. Henry de la Pole was executed in 1538.

Margaret was 68 years old when she was led out for execution, and the circumstances of her death were particularly horrible. The old lady lost her nerve at the sight of the block and broke from her guards to run screaming about Tower Green, the headsman striking at her as she struggled to escape, the guards playing a deadly game of hide-and-seek until she was caught and pulled down and her head hacked off.

The Tudors, who had risen from obscurity to the throne of England, could not match their Plantagenet predecessors in longevity. The Plantagenets ruled all England and much of France from 1137 to 1485, but the Tudors died out when Elizabeth I died childless in 1601, just 116 years after Bosworth Field.

BIBLIOGRAPHY

Battlefields of Britain, Colonel A. H. Burne. Methuen (1950).

Battles in Britain, William Seymour. Sidgwick & Jackson (1989).

The Battle of Tewkesbury, Hammond, Shearing & Wheeler. Tewkesbury Festival Committee (1971).

The Betrayal of Richard III, V. B. Lamb. Coram (1959).

The Book of the Medieval Knight, Stephen Turnbull. Arms & Armour Press (1985).

The Chronicles of the Wars of the Roses, edited by Elizabeth Hallam. Guild (1988).

The Complete Works of Shakespeare, Odhams & Blackwell (1958).

Edward IV, Charles Ross. Eyre-Methuen (1974).

The End of Lancaster, R. L. Storey. Barrie & Rockcliffe (1966).

England in the Late Middle Ages (1307–1536), A. R. Myers. Penguin (1936).

England in the Later Middle Ages, K. H. Vickers. Methuen (1937).

Exploring Tudor England, P. J. Helm. Robert Hale (1981).

Henry VI, Bertram Wolffe. Eyre Methuen (1981).

Henry VII, Eric N. Simons. Muller (1968).

A History of England, G. M. Trevelyan. Longman (1926).

A History of Everyday Things 1066–1499, M. & C. H. B. Quennell. Batsford (1979).

Holinshed's Chronicles, edited by Allardyce & Josephine Nicoll. Everyman's Library (1963).

The Hundred Years War, Robin Neillands. Routledge (1991).

Lancaster & York, (2 vols), Sir James Ramsey (1892).

Ludford Bridge & Mortimer's Cross, Geoffrey Hodges. Logaston Press (1989).

On Some Bones in Westminster Abbey, Philip Lindsay. Cedric Chivers (1969).

The Paston Letters (2 vols). Everyman's Library (1924).

The Plantagenets, John Harvey. Fontana Books (1967).

The Reign of Edward IV, Eric N. Simons. Muller (1966).

Richard II and the English Nobility, J. A. Tuck. Edward Arnold (1973).

Richard III, Charles Ross. Eyre-Methuen (1981).

Richard the Third, P. M. Kendall. Allen & Unwin (1955).

Richard III & The Princes in the Tower, A. J. Pollard. Alan Sutton (1991).

Richard III: The Road to Bosworth Field, P. W. Hammond & A. F. Sutton. Constable (1985).

Shakespeare's History Plays, E. M. W. Tillyard. Penguin (1962).

This Sun of York, Mary Clive. Macmillan (1973).

The Wars of the Roses, Charles Ross. Thames & Hudson (1976).

Index